P9-CBX-220

Oh My Goddess!

あぁっ女神さまっ 27

STORY AND ART BY
Kosuke Fujishima

TRANSLATION BY
Dana Lewis AND
Christopher Lewis

LETTERING AND TOUCH-UP BY
Susie Lee AND **Betty Dong**
WITH **Tom2K**

DARK HORSE MANGA™

City of Orange
Public Library

APR 14 2008

Orange, CA

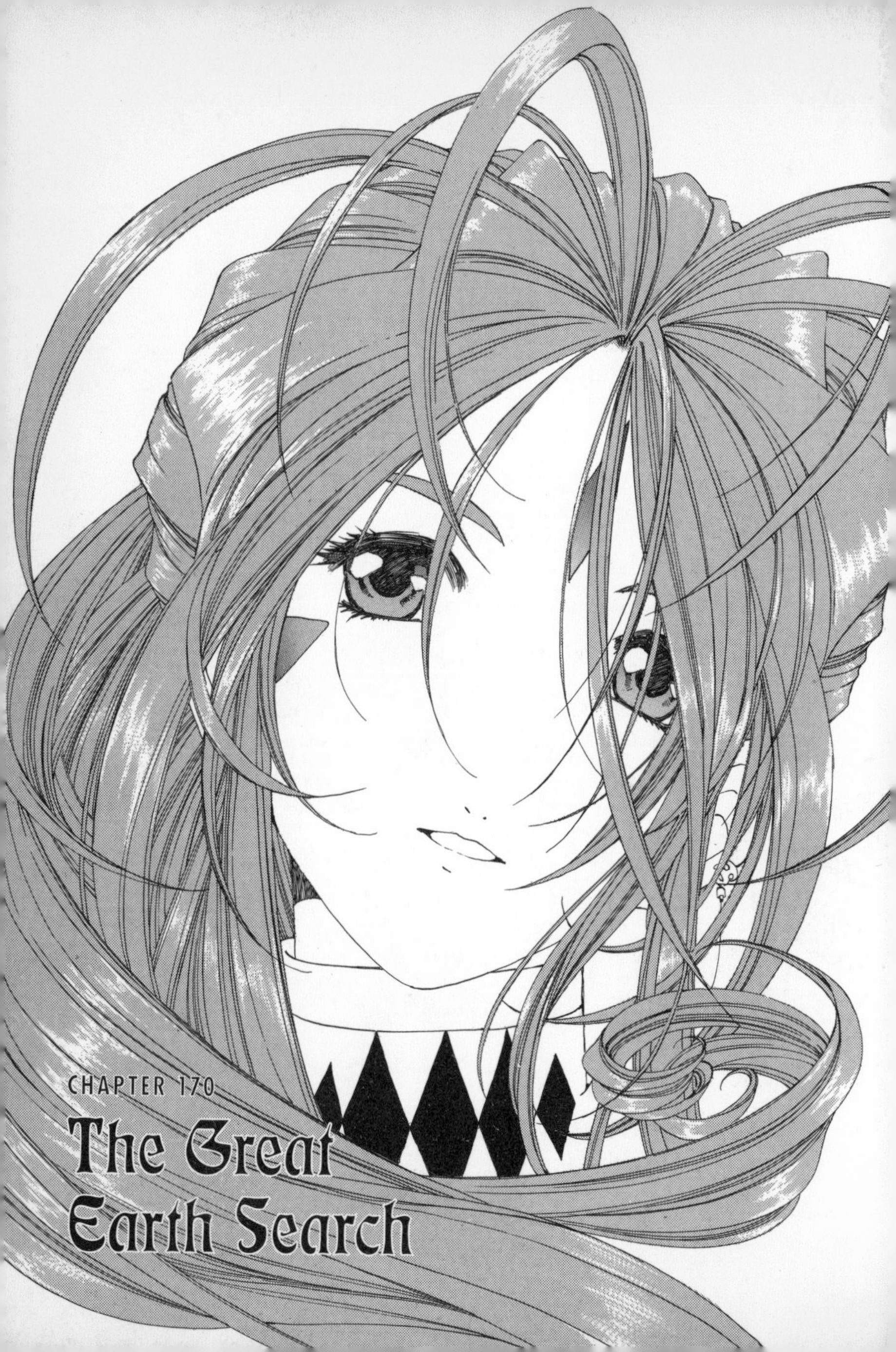

CHAPTER 170

The Great Earth Search

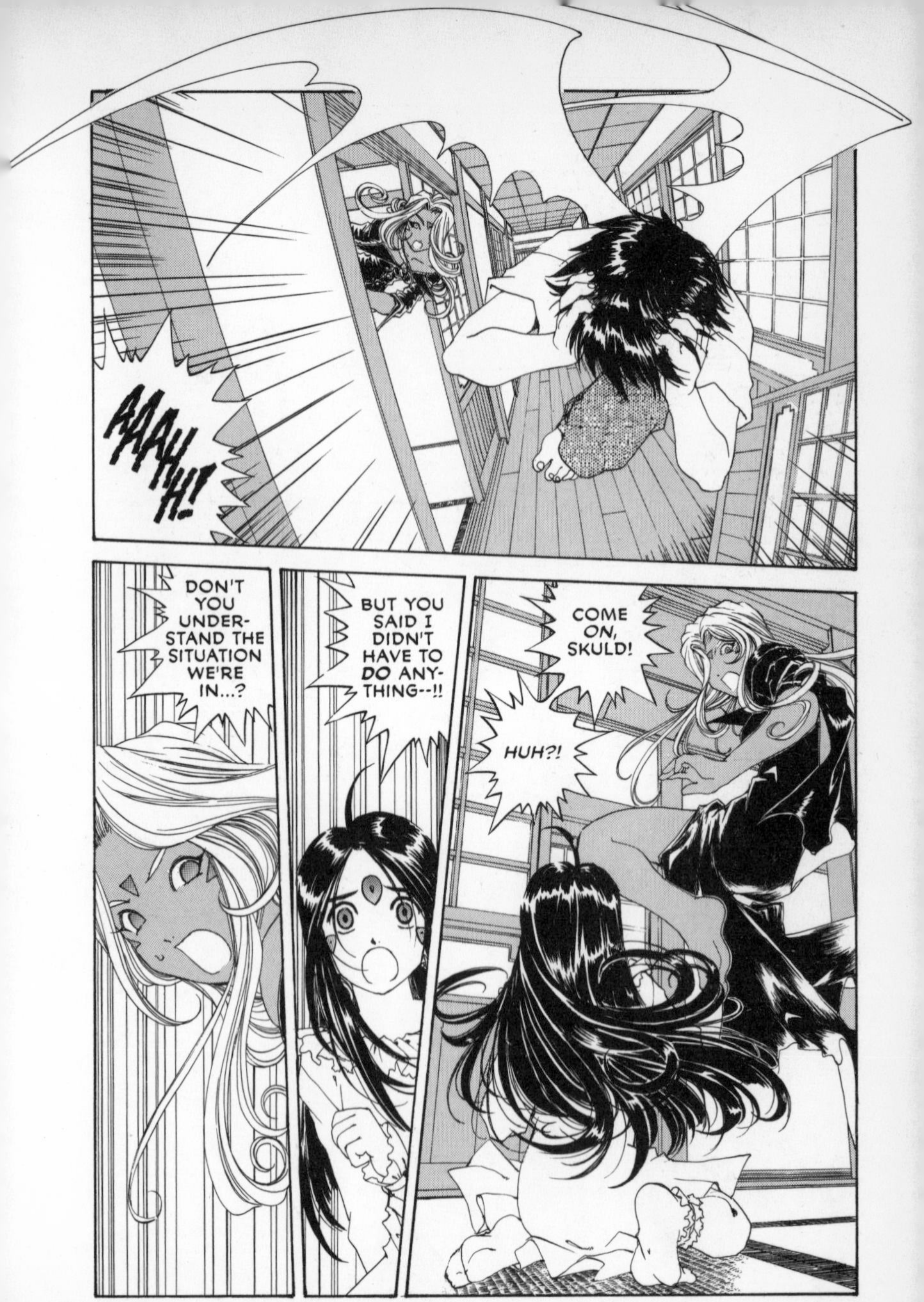
AAAAHH!
COME ON, SKULD!
HUH?!
BUT YOU SAID I DIDN'T HAVE TO DO ANYTHING--!!
DON'T YOU UNDERSTAND THE SITUATION WE'RE IN...?

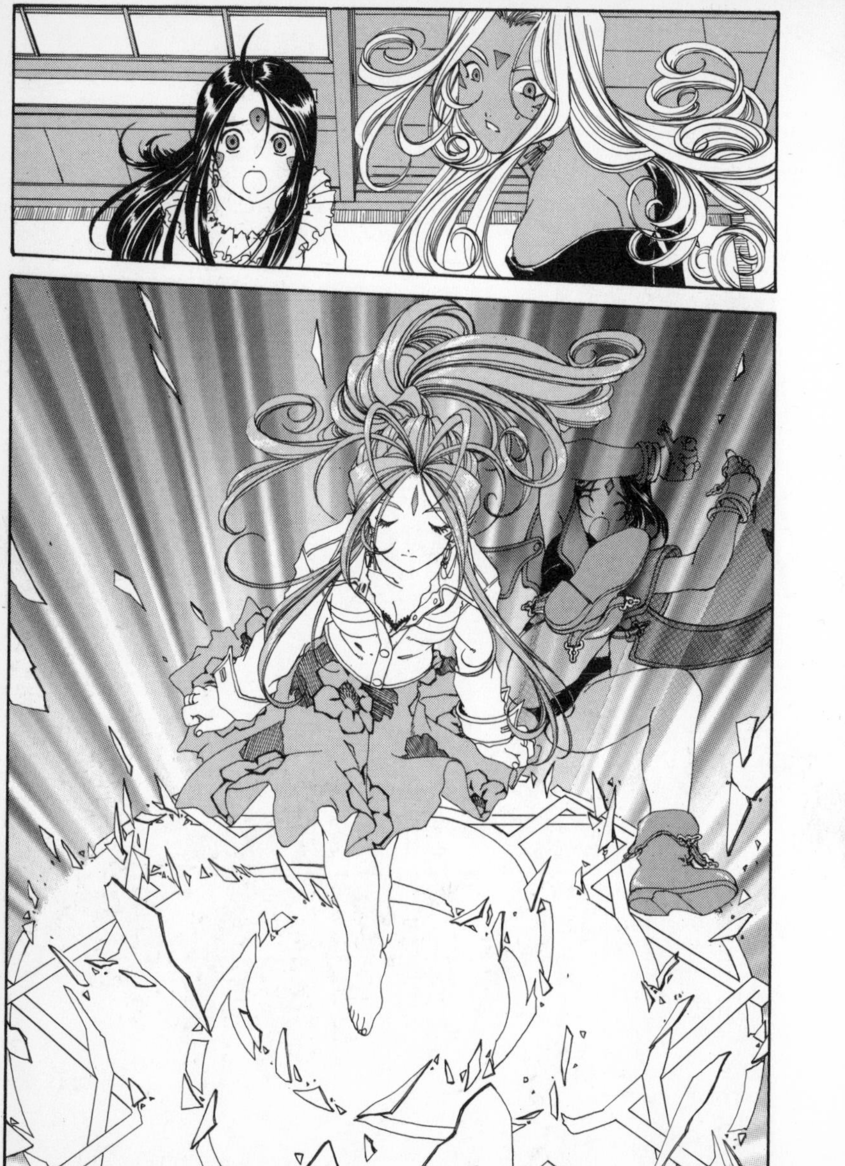

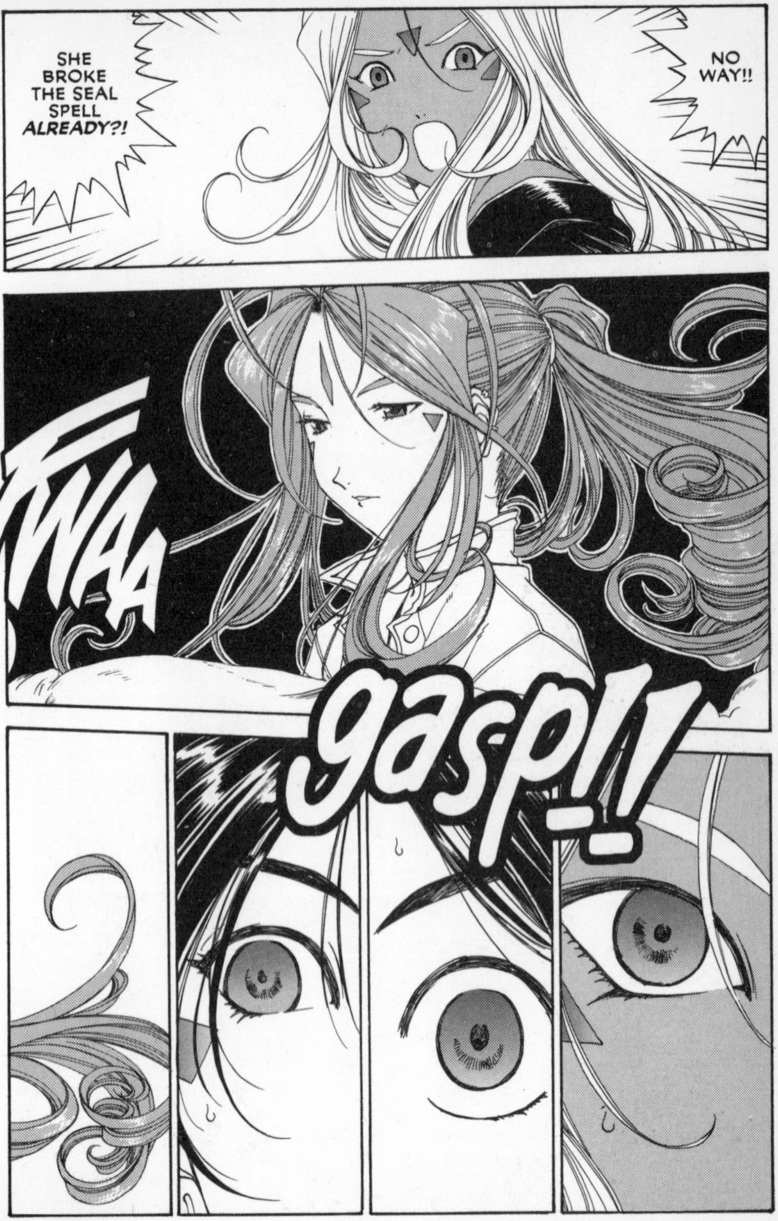
NO WAY!!
SHE BROKE THE SEAL SPELL ALREADY?!
FWAA
gasp!!

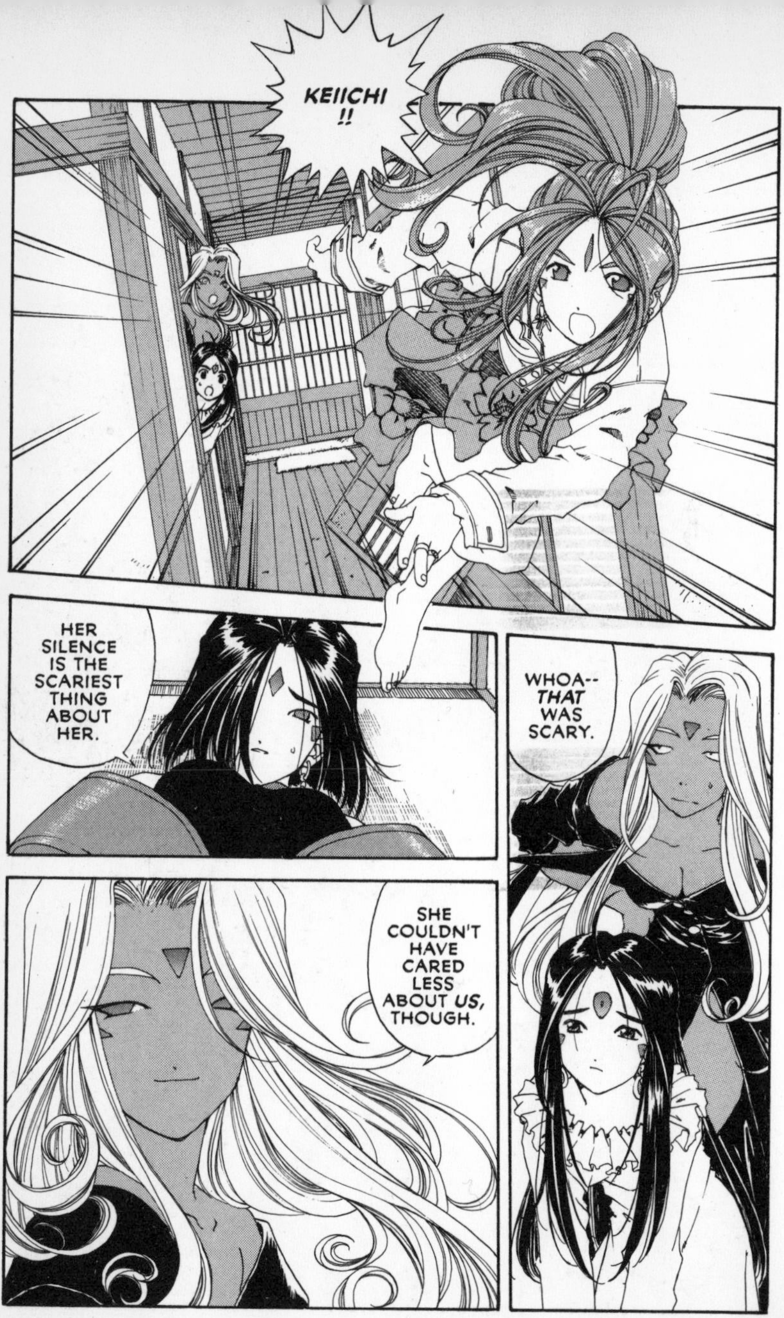
KEIICHI !!
WHOA--*THAT* WAS SCARY.
HER SILENCE IS THE SCARIEST THING ABOUT HER.
SHE COULDN'T HAVE CARED LESS ABOUT *US*, THOUGH.

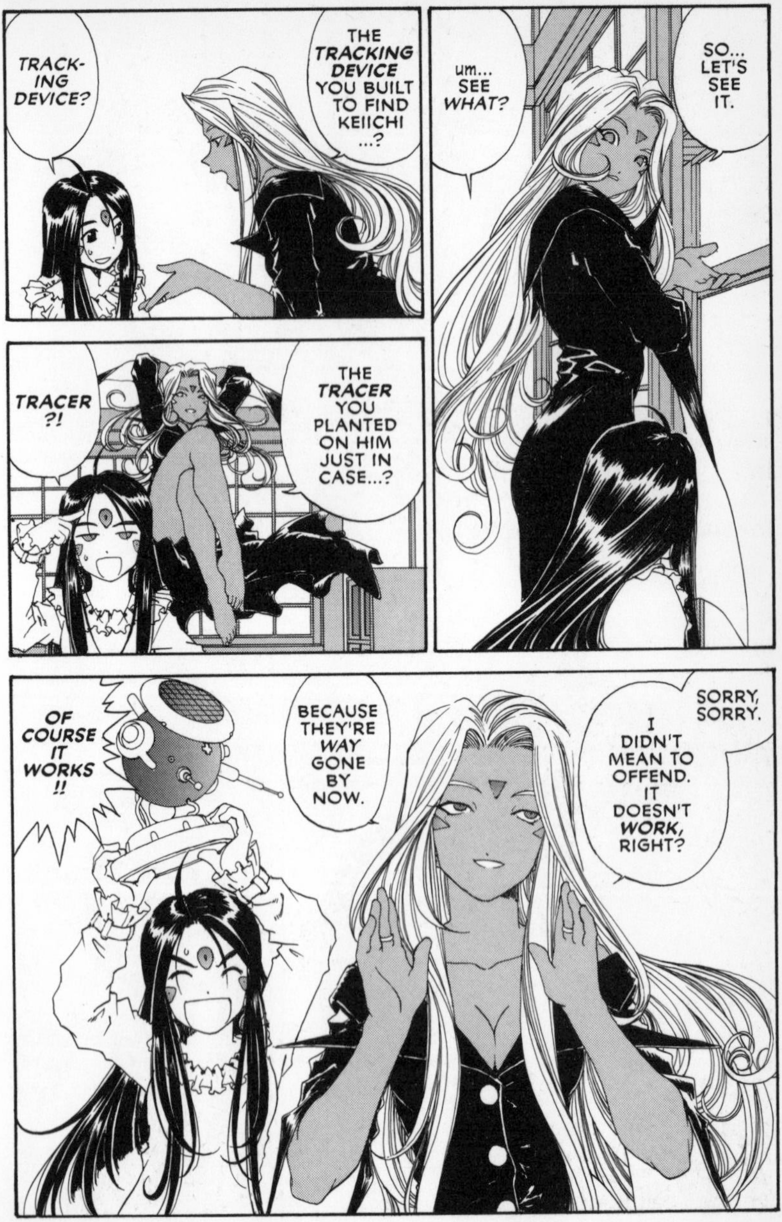
SO... LET'S SEE IT.
um... SEE WHAT?
THE TRACKING DEVICE YOU BUILT TO FIND KEIICHI ...?
TRACK-ING DEVICE?
THE TRACER YOU PLANTED ON HIM JUST IN CASE...?
TRACER ?!
SORRY, SORRY.
I DIDN'T MEAN TO OFFEND. IT DOESN'T WORK, RIGHT?
BECAUSE THEY'RE WAY GONE BY NOW.
OF COURSE IT WORKS !!

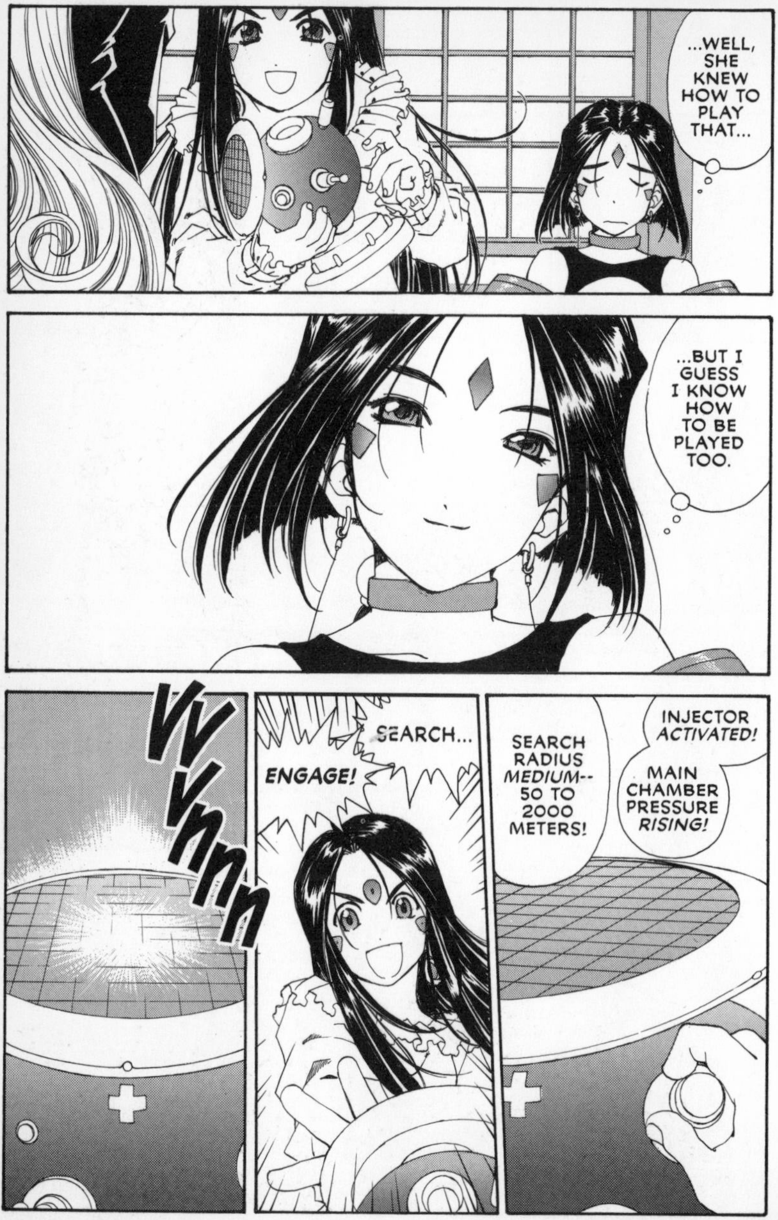
...WELL, SHE KNEW HOW TO PLAY THAT...
...BUT I GUESS I KNOW HOW TO BE PLAYED TOO.
INJECTOR ACTIVATED!
MAIN CHAMBER PRESSURE RISING!
SEARCH RADIUS MEDIUM-- 50 TO 2000 METERS!
SEARCH...
ENGAGE!
VVVNNN

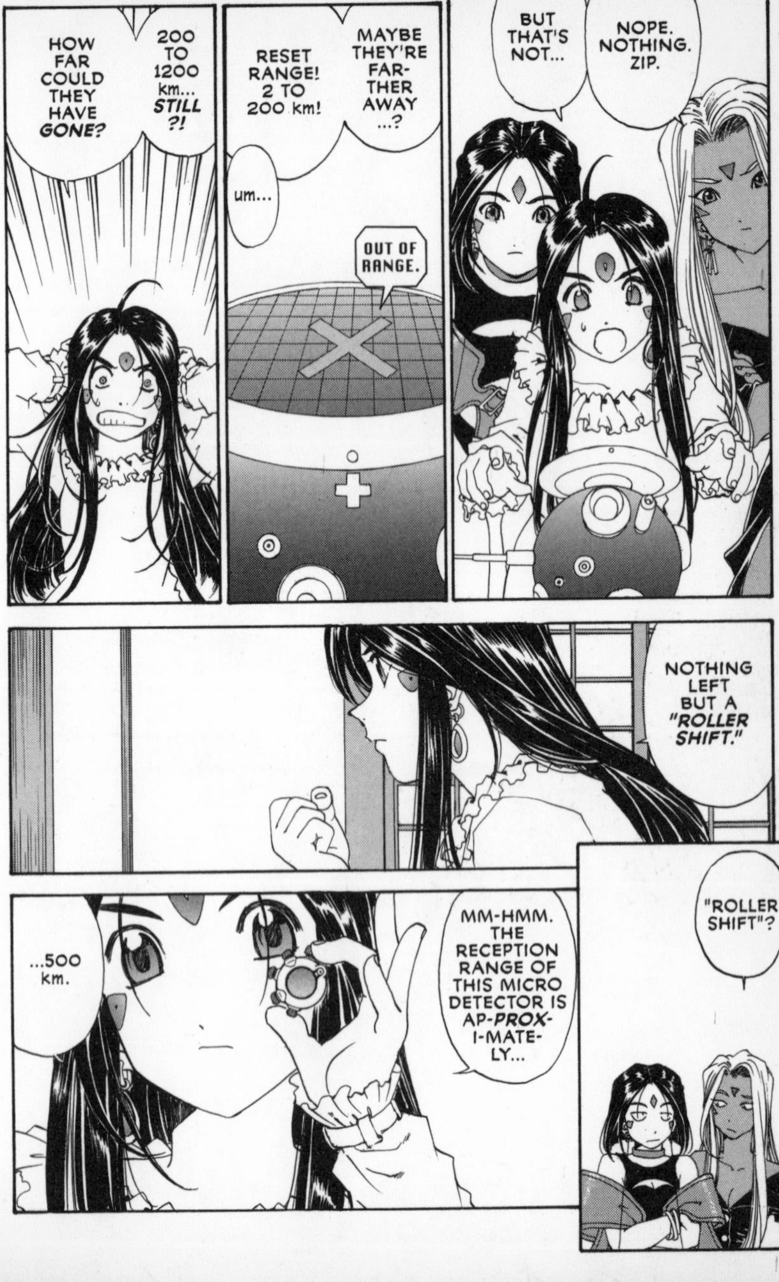
NOPE. NOTHING. ZIP.
BUT THAT'S NOT...
MAYBE THEY'RE FAR-THER AWAY ...?
RESET RANGE! 2 TO 200 km!
um...
OUT OF RANGE.
200 TO 1200 km... STILL ?!
HOW FAR COULD THEY HAVE GONE?
NOTHING LEFT BUT A "ROLLER SHIFT."
"ROLLER SHIFT"?
MM-HMM. THE RECEPTION RANGE OF THIS MICRO DETECTOR IS AP-PROX-I-MATE-LY...
...500 km.

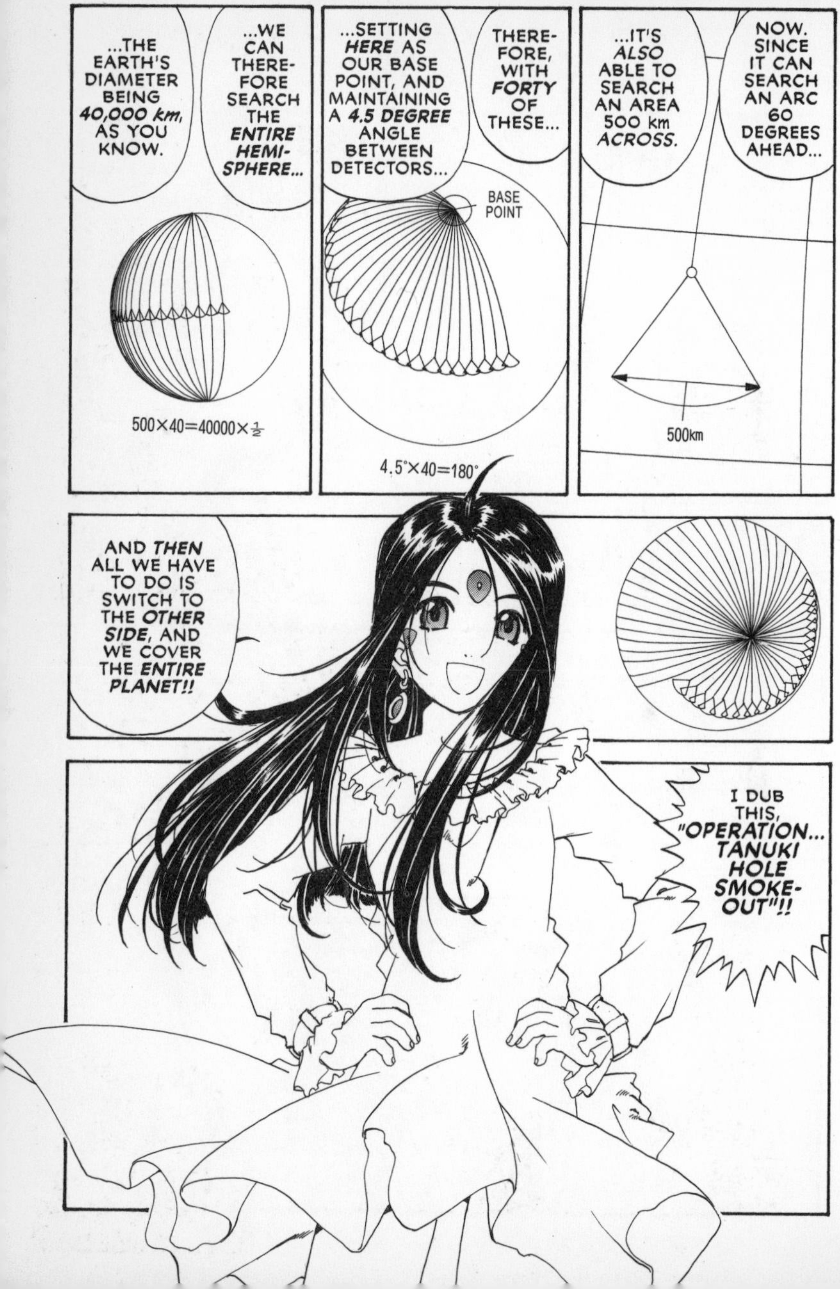
NOW. SINCE IT CAN SEARCH AN ARC 60 DEGREES AHEAD...
...IT'S *ALSO* ABLE TO SEARCH AN AREA 500 km *ACROSS.*
500km
THERE-FORE, WITH *FORTY* OF THESE...
...SETTING *HERE* AS OUR BASE POINT, AND MAINTAINING A *4.5 DEGREE* ANGLE BETWEEN DETECTORS...
BASE POINT
4.5°×40=180°
...WE CAN THERE-FORE SEARCH THE *ENTIRE HEMI-SPHERE...*
...THE EARTH'S DIAMETER BEING *40,000 km,* AS YOU KNOW.
500×40=40000×½
AND *THEN* ALL WE HAVE TO DO IS SWITCH TO THE *OTHER SIDE,* AND WE COVER THE *ENTIRE PLANET!!*
I DUB THIS, *"OPERATION... TANUKI HOLE SMOKE-OUT"!!*

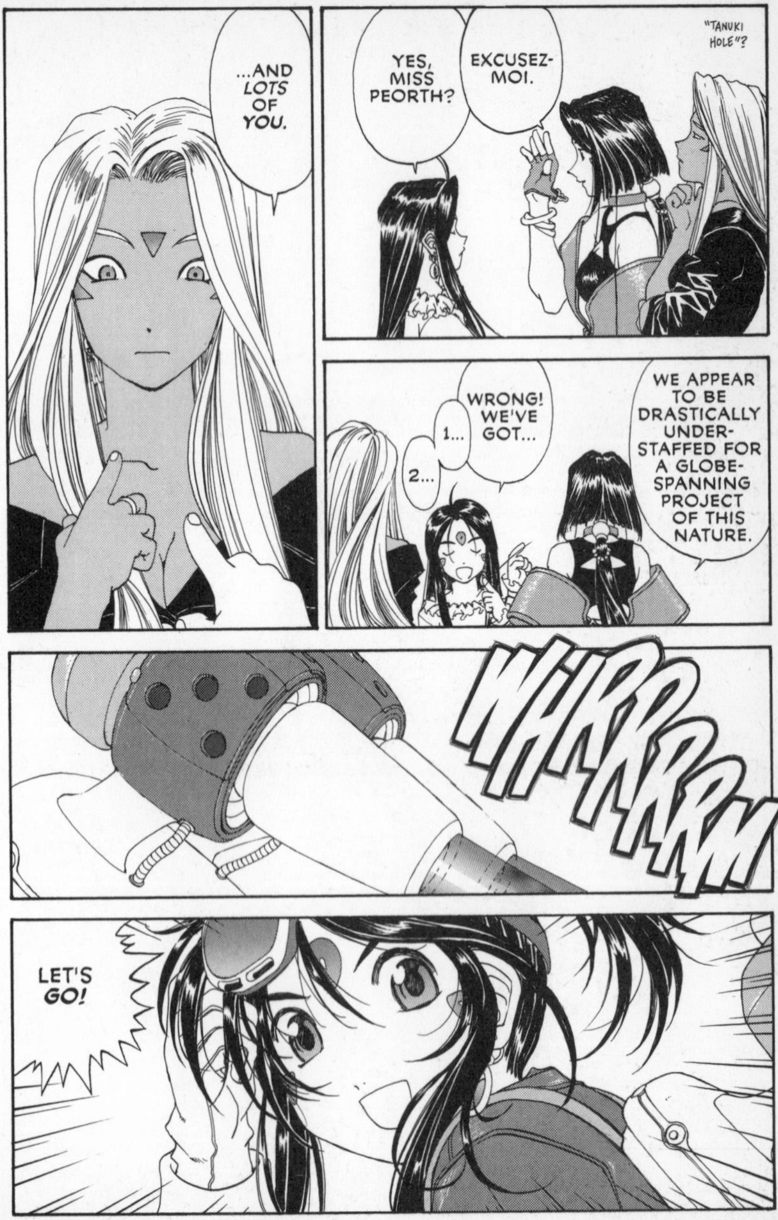
"TANUKI HOLE"?
EXCUSEZ-MOI.
YES, MISS PEORTH?
WE APPEAR TO BE DRASTICALLY UNDER-STAFFED FOR A GLOBE-SPANNING PROJECT OF THIS NATURE.
WRONG! WE'VE GOT...
1...
2...
...AND LOTS OF YOU.
WHIRRRRM
LET'S GO!

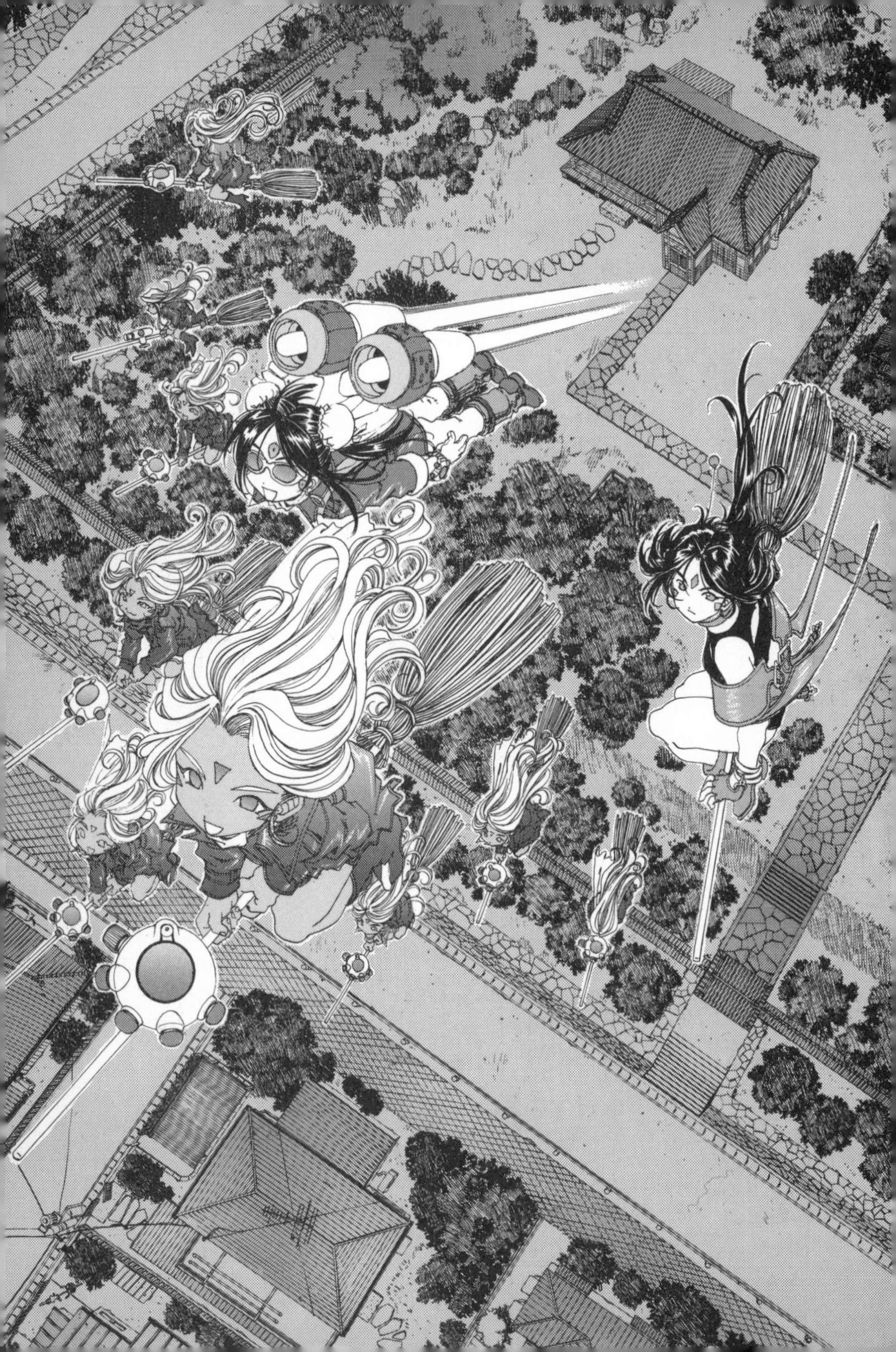

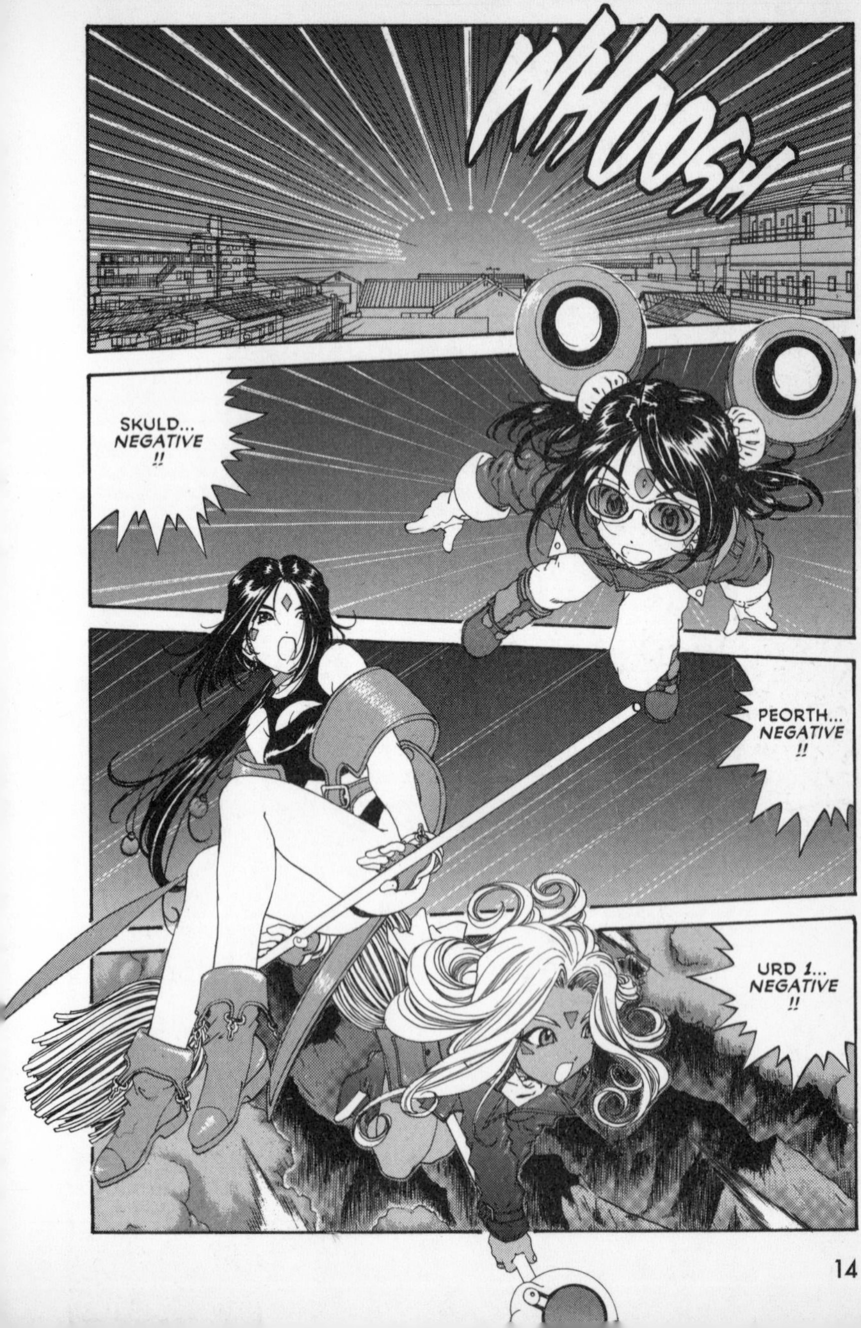
WHOOSH
SKULD... NEGATIVE !!
PEORTH... NEGATIVE !!
URD 1... NEGATIVE !!

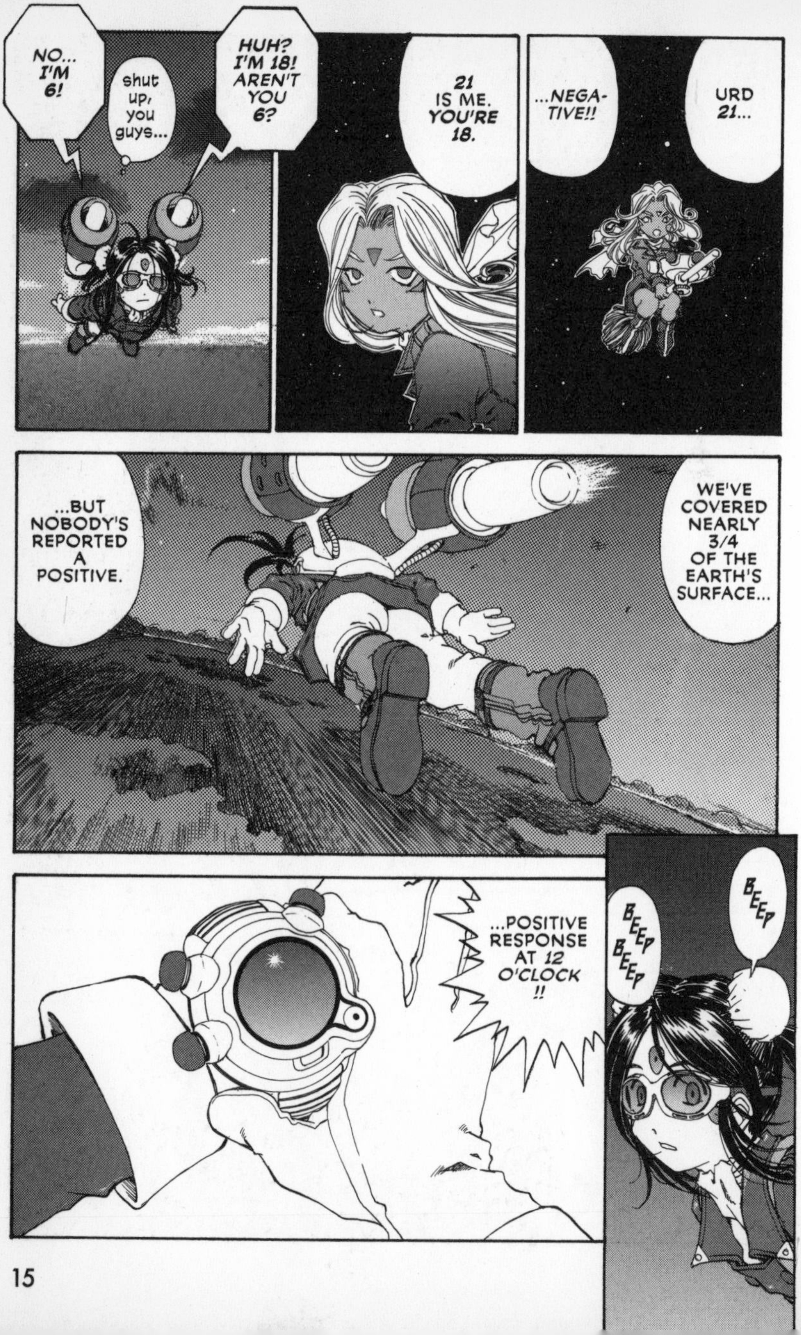
URD 21...
...NEGA-TIVE!!
21 IS ME. YOU'RE 18.
HUH? I'M 18! AREN'T YOU 6?
shut up, you guys...
NO... I'M 6!
WE'VE COVERED NEARLY 3/4 OF THE EARTH'S SURFACE...
...BUT NOBODY'S REPORTED A POSITIVE.
BEEP
BEEP BEEP
...POSITIVE RESPONSE AT 12 O'CLOCK !!

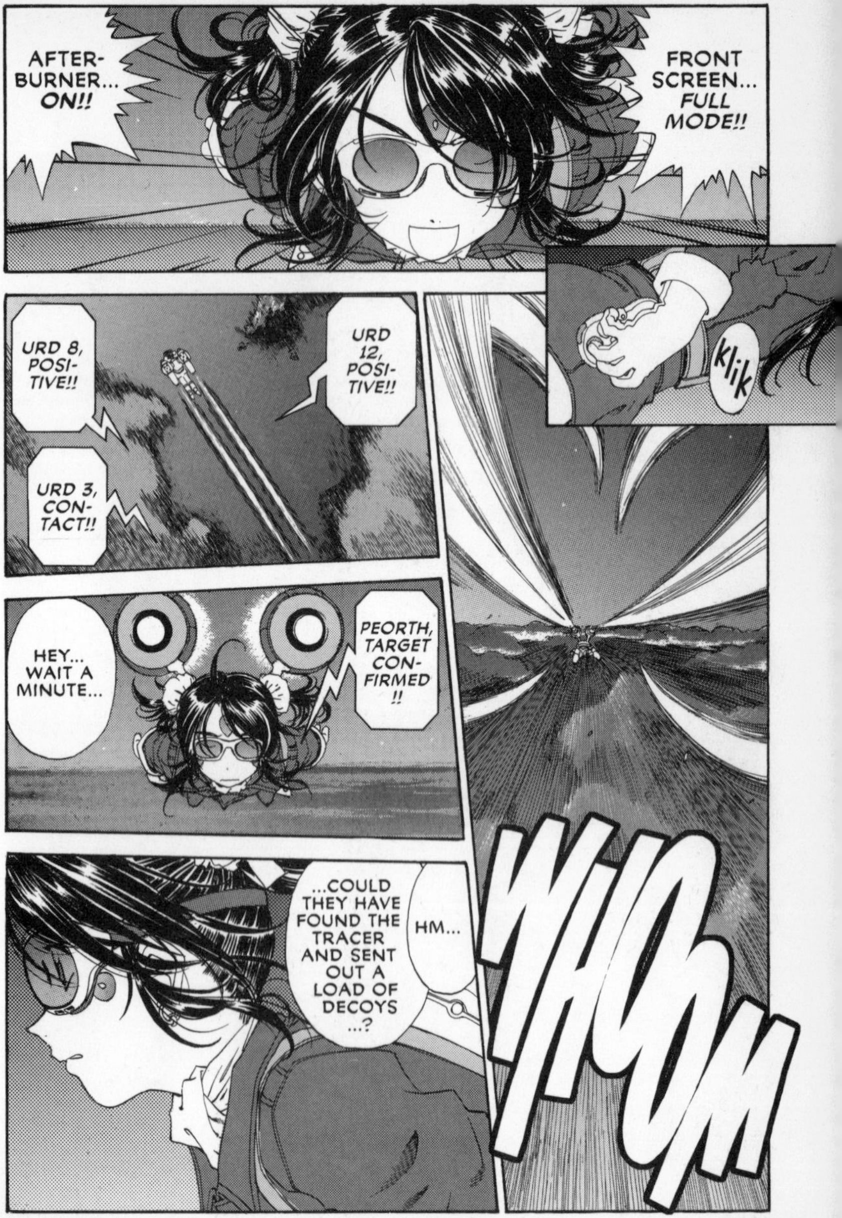
FRONT SCREEN... FULL MODE!!
AFTER-BURNER... ON!!
klik
WHOOM
URD 12, POSI-TIVE!!
URD 8, POSI-TIVE!!
URD 3, CON-TACT!!
PEORTH, TARGET CON-FIRMED !!
HEY... WAIT A MINUTE...
HM...
...COULD THEY HAVE FOUND THE TRACER AND SENT OUT A LOAD OF DECOYS ...?

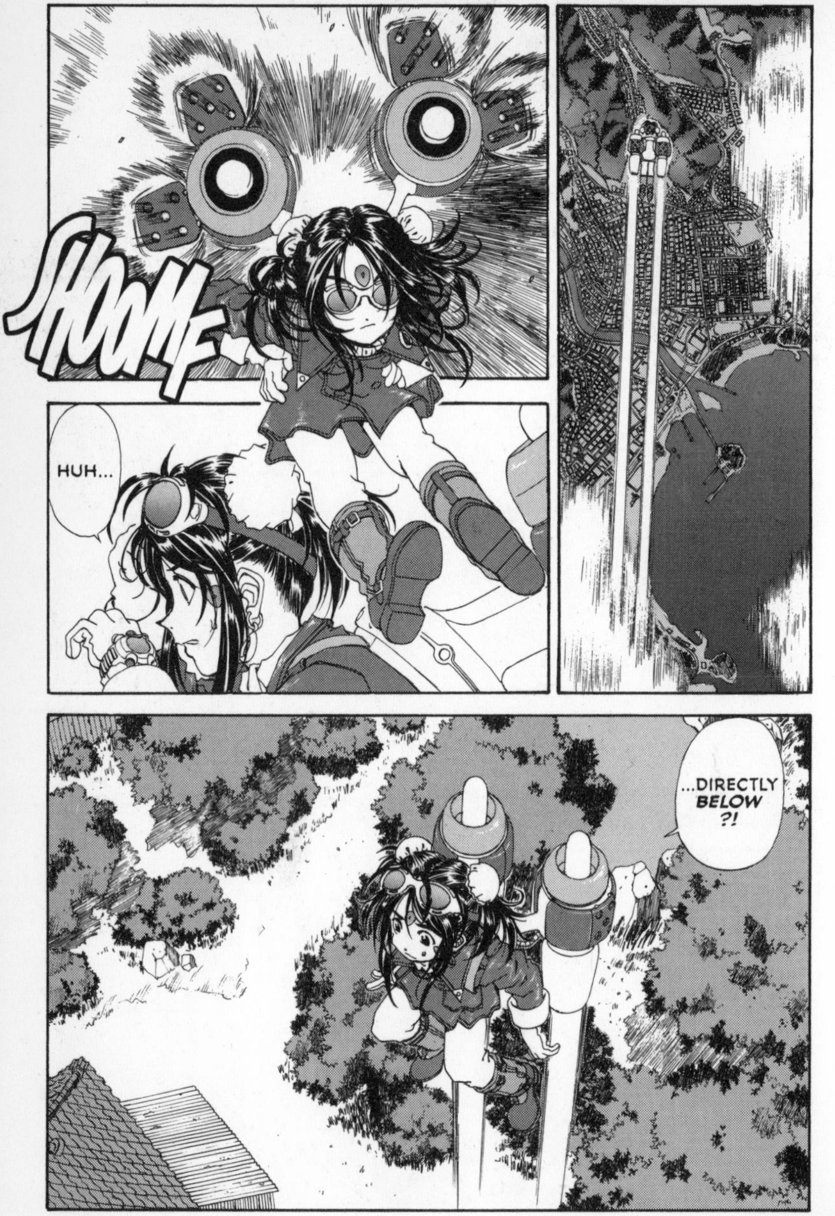
SHOOMF
HUH...
...DIRECTLY BELOW ?!

NO...

...NO, I DON'T *BELIEVE* IT!

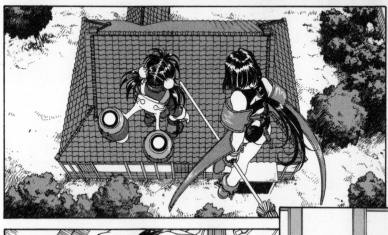

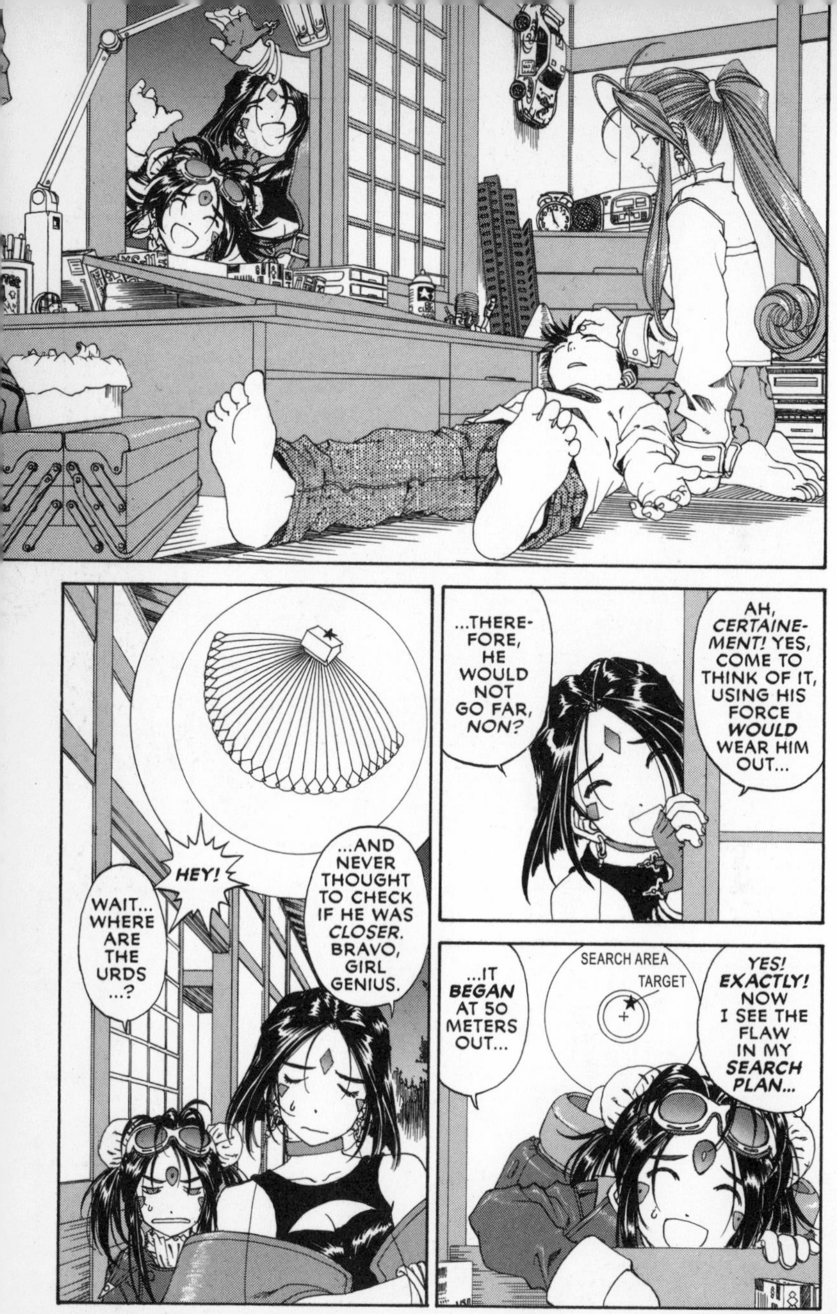
AH, CERTAINEMENT! YES, COME TO THINK OF IT, USING HIS FORCE WOULD WEAR HIM OUT...
...THEREFORE, HE WOULD NOT GO FAR, NON?
YES! EXACTLY! NOW I SEE THE FLAW IN MY SEARCH PLAN...
SEARCH AREA
TARGET
...IT BEGAN AT 50 METERS OUT...
...AND NEVER THOUGHT TO CHECK IF HE WAS CLOSER. BRAVO, GIRL GENIUS.
HEY!
WAIT... WHERE ARE THE URDS ...?

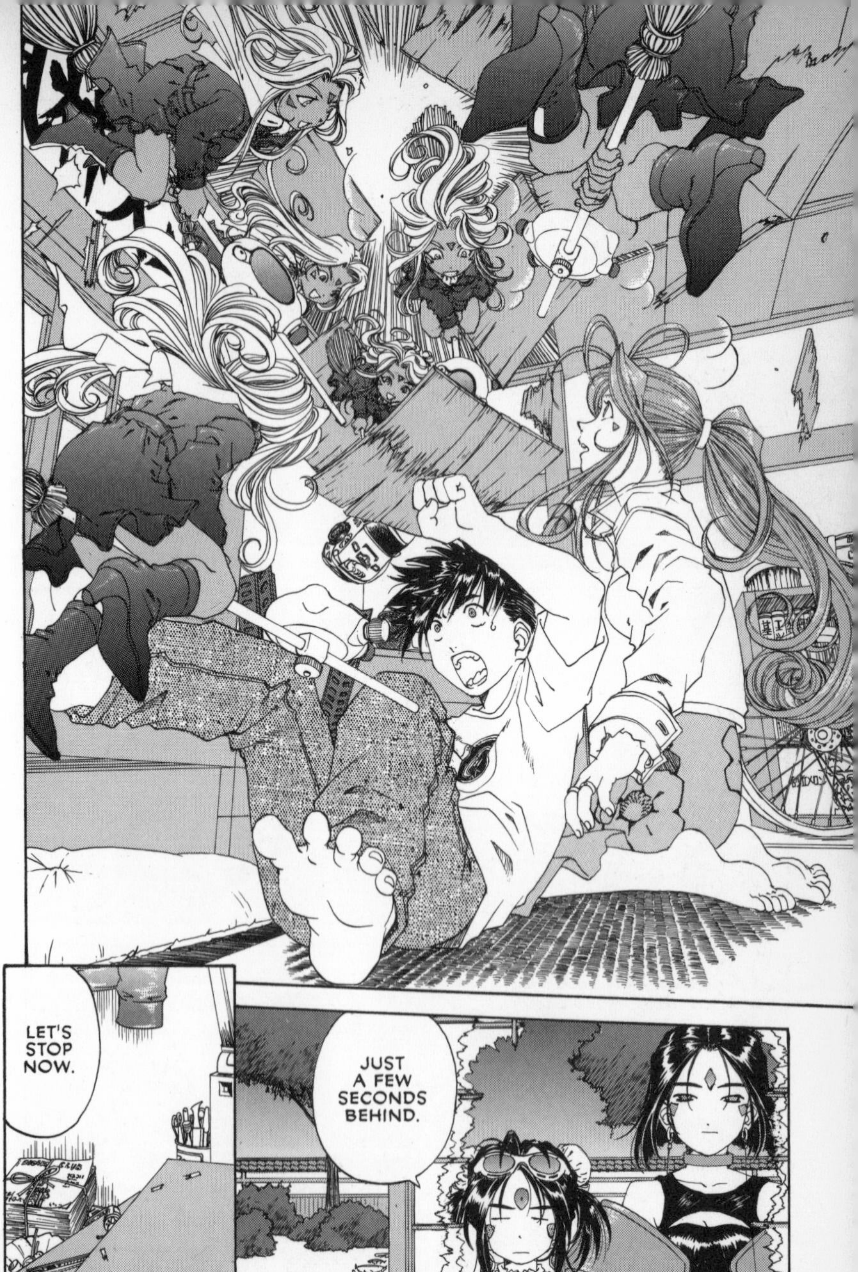
JUST A FEW SECONDS BEHIND.
LET'S STOP NOW.

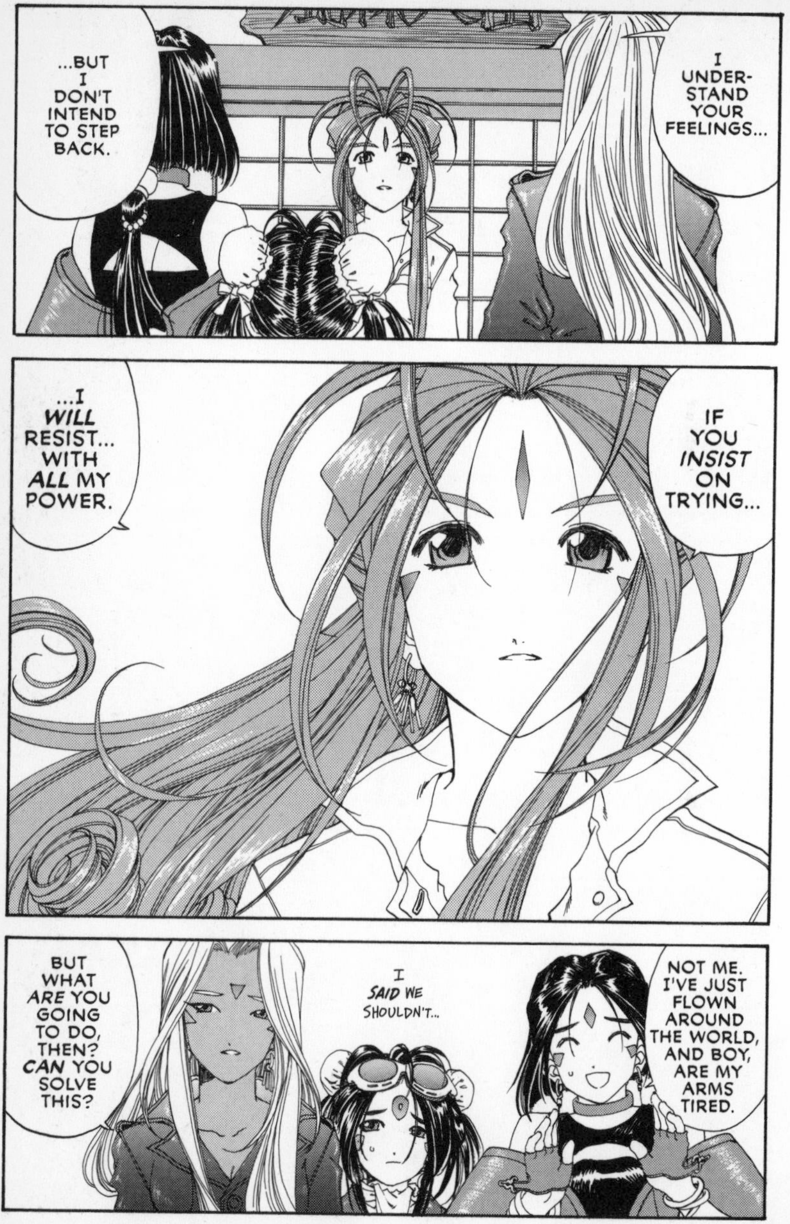
I UNDERSTAND YOUR FEELINGS...
...BUT I DON'T INTEND TO STEP BACK.
IF YOU *INSIST* ON TRYING...
...I *WILL* RESIST... WITH *ALL* MY POWER.
NOT ME. I'VE JUST FLOWN AROUND THE WORLD, AND BOY, ARE MY ARMS TIRED.
I *SAID* WE SHOULDN'T...
BUT WHAT *ARE* YOU GOING TO DO, THEN? *CAN* YOU SOLVE THIS?

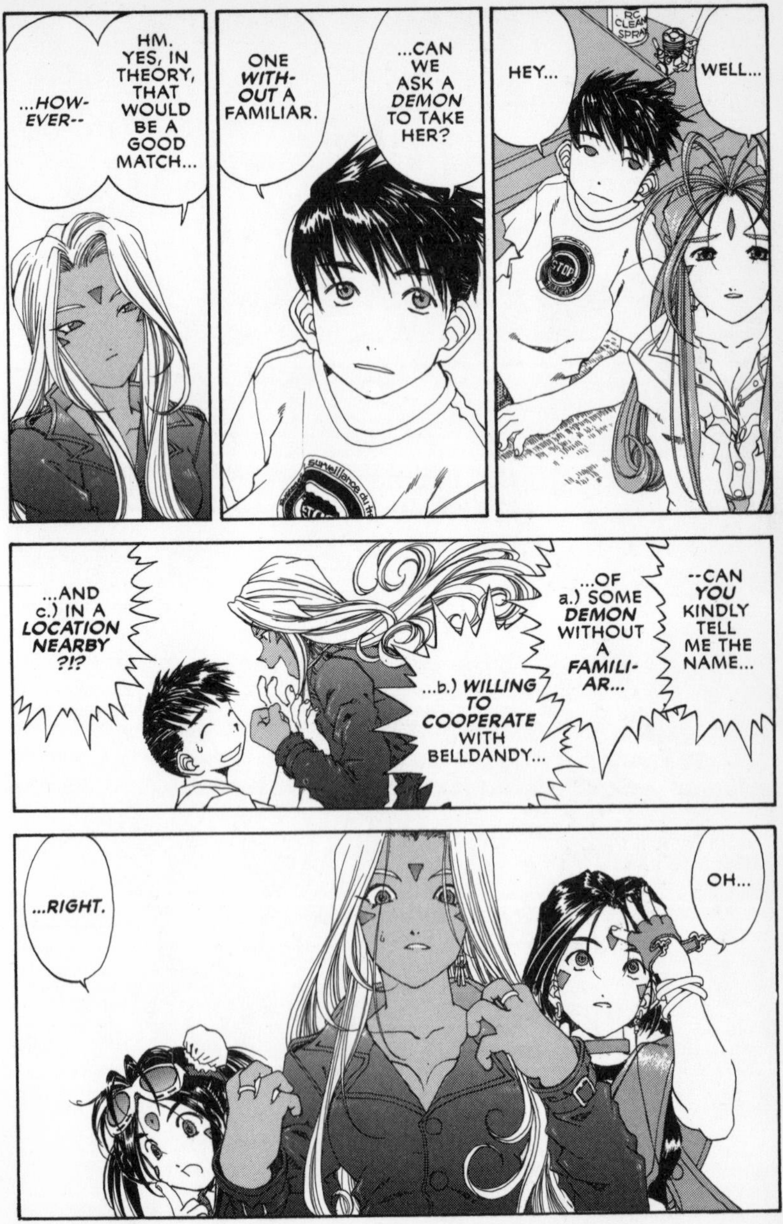
WELL...
HEY...
...CAN WE ASK A DEMON TO TAKE HER?
ONE WITHOUT A FAMILIAR.
HM. YES, IN THEORY, THAT WOULD BE A GOOD MATCH...
...HOWEVER--
--CAN YOU KINDLY TELL ME THE NAME...
...OF a.) SOME DEMON WITHOUT A FAMILIAR...
...b.) WILLING TO COOPERATE WITH BELLDANDY...
...AND c.) IN A LOCATION NEARBY?!?
OH...
...RIGHT.

CHAPTER 171

Kiss Me Goodbye

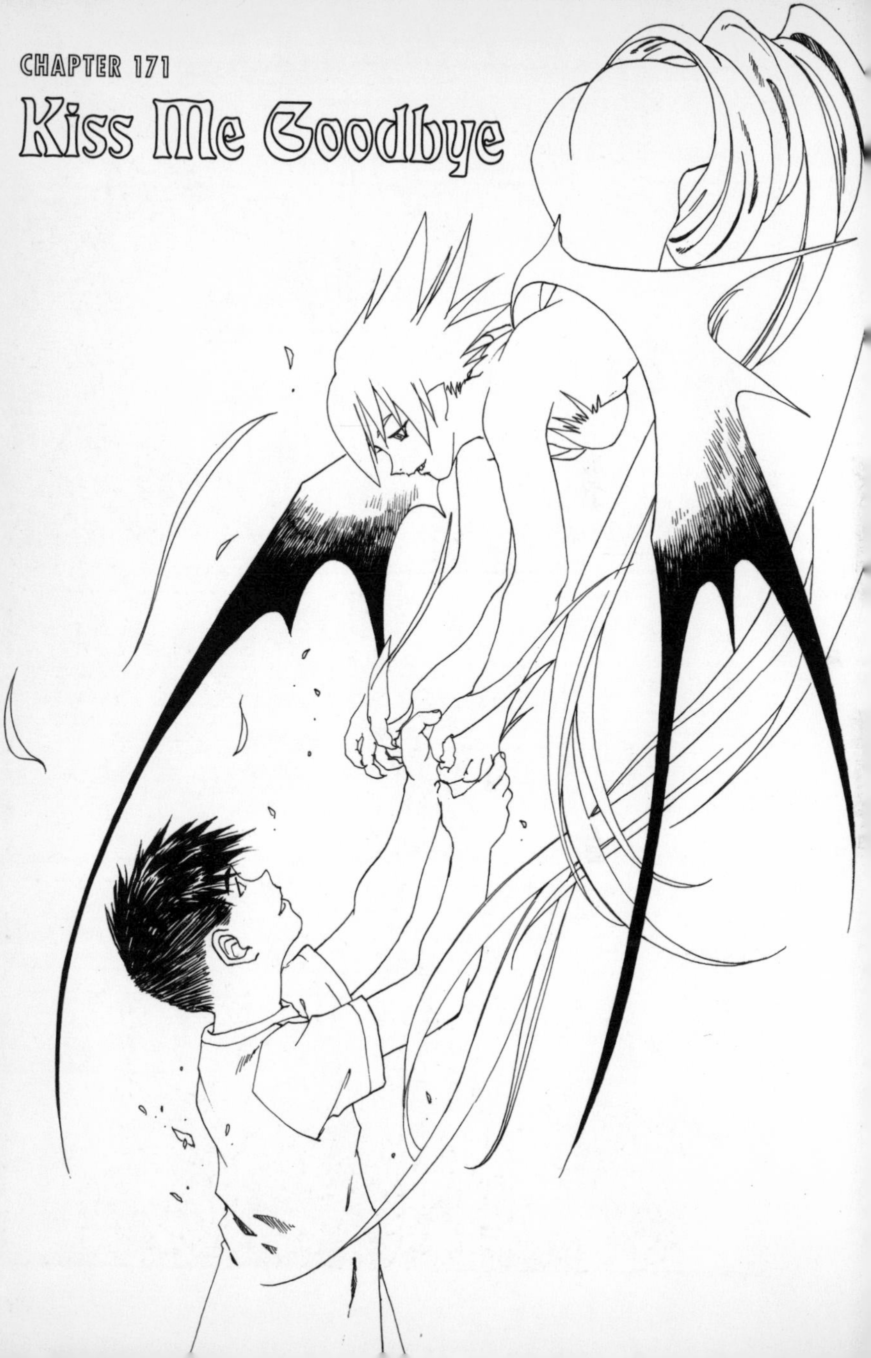

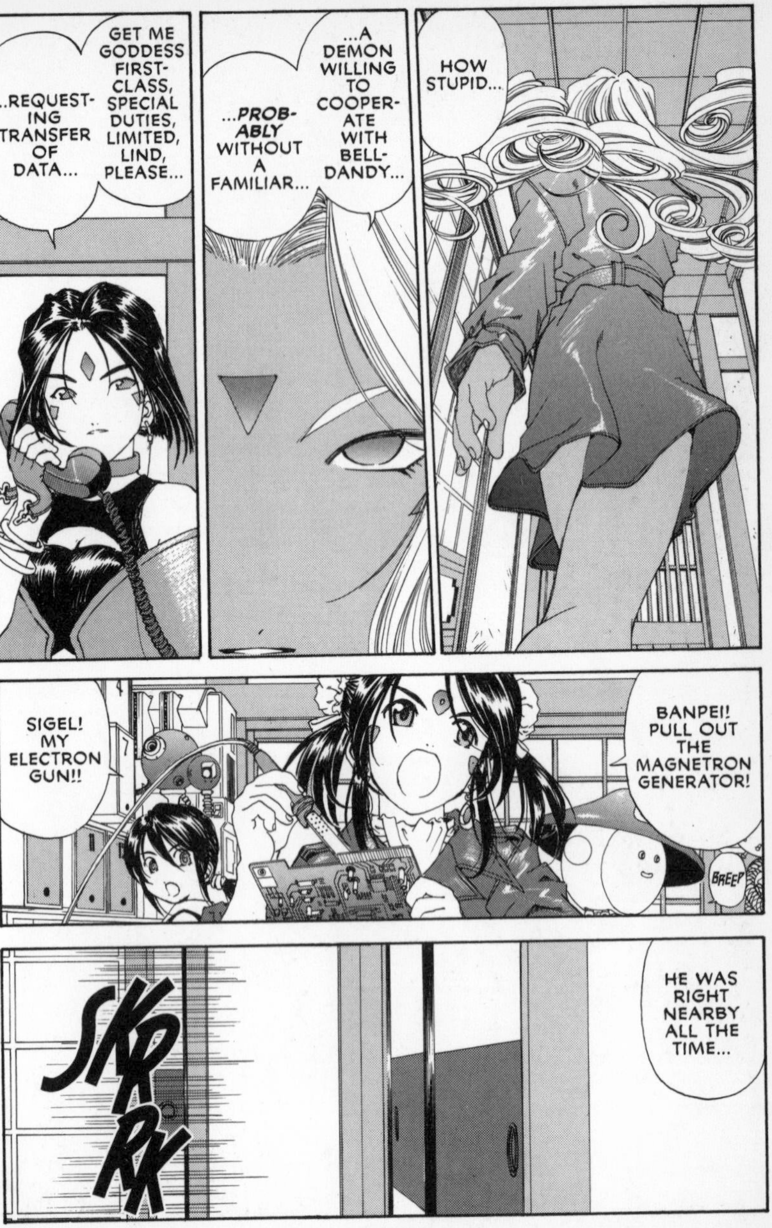
HOW STUPID...
...A DEMON WILLING TO COOPER-ATE WITH BELL-DANDY...
...*PROB-ABLY* WITHOUT A FAMILIAR...
GET ME GODDESS FIRST-CLASS, SPECIAL DUTIES, LIMITED, LIND, PLEASE...
...REQUEST-ING TRANSFER OF DATA...
BANPEI! PULL OUT THE MAGNETRON GENERATOR!
BREEP
SIGEL! MY ELECTRON GUN!!
HE WAS RIGHT NEARBY ALL THE TIME...
SKRK

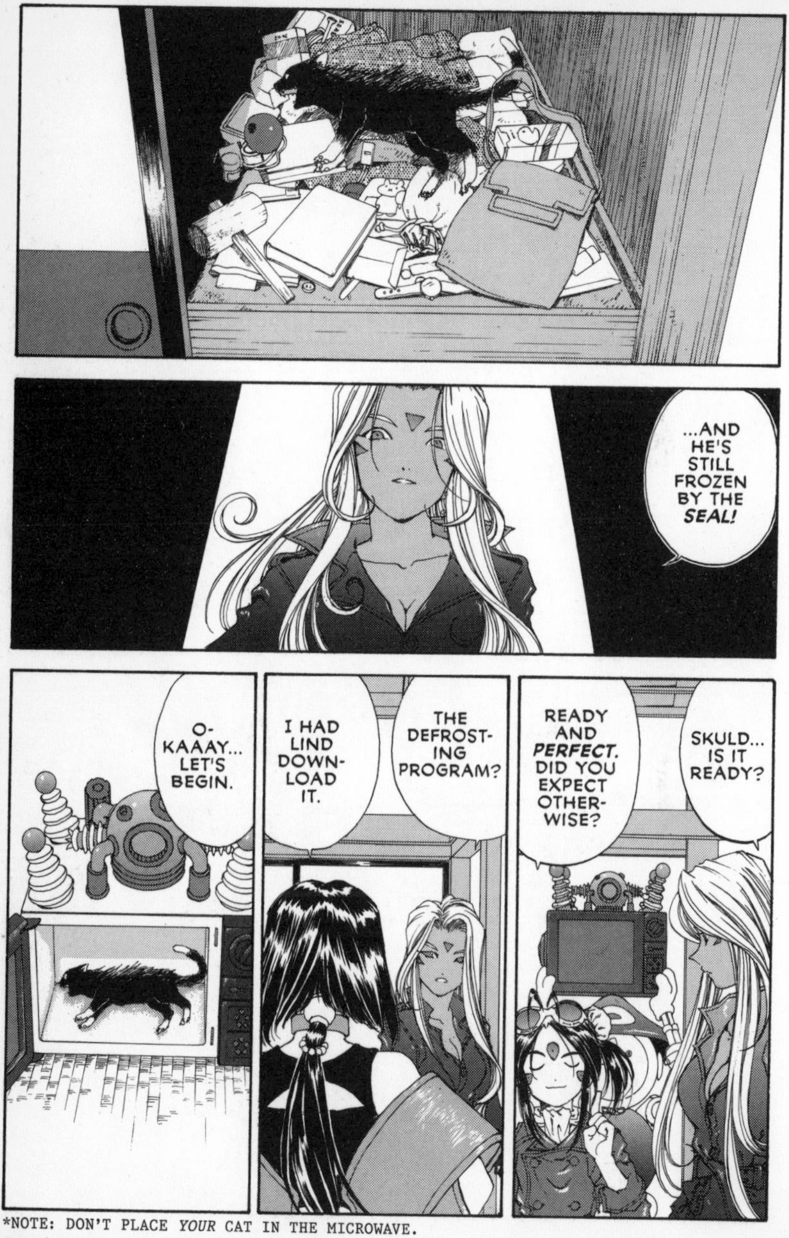
...AND HE'S STILL FROZEN BY THE *SEAL!*
SKULD... IS IT READY?
READY AND *PERFECT.* DID YOU EXPECT OTHER-WISE?
THE DEFROST-ING PROGRAM?
I HAD LIND DOWN-LOAD IT.
O-KAAAY... LET'S BEGIN.

*NOTE: DON'T PLACE *YOUR* CAT IN THE MICROWAVE.

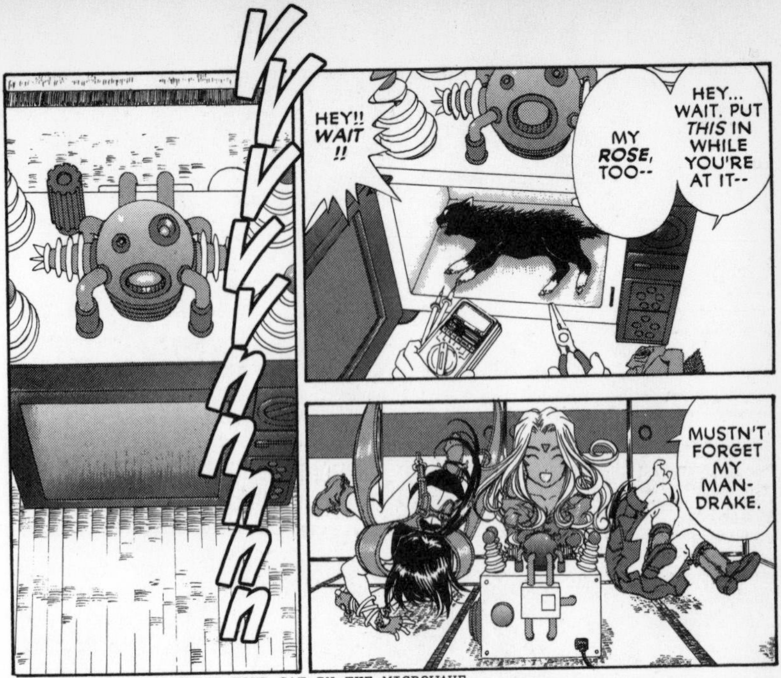
HEY... WAIT. PUT THIS IN WHILE YOU'RE AT IT--
MY ROSE, TOO--
HEY!! WAIT !!
MUSTN'T FORGET MY MAN-DRAKE.
VVVVVVnnnnn

*NOTE: DON'T *EVER* PLACE YOUR CAT IN THE MICROWAVE.

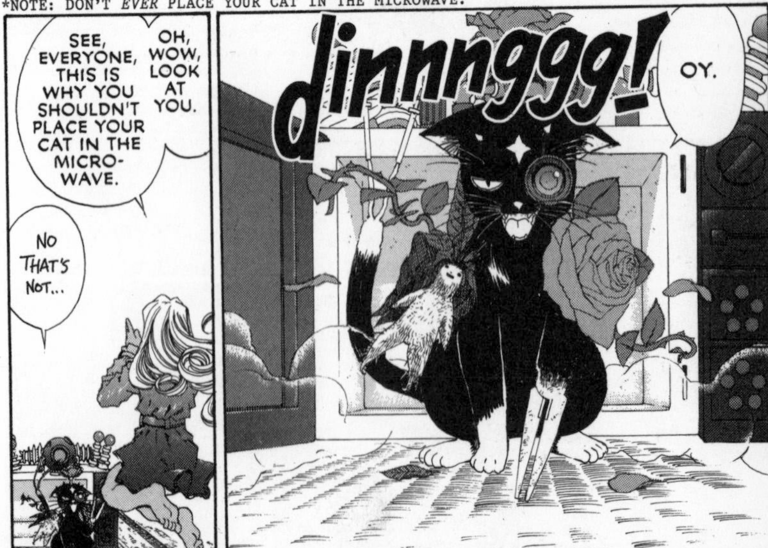
dinnnggg!
OY.
OH, WOW, LOOK AT YOU.
SEE, EVERYONE, THIS IS WHY YOU SHOULDN'T PLACE YOUR CAT IN THE MICRO-WAVE.
NO THAT'S NOT...

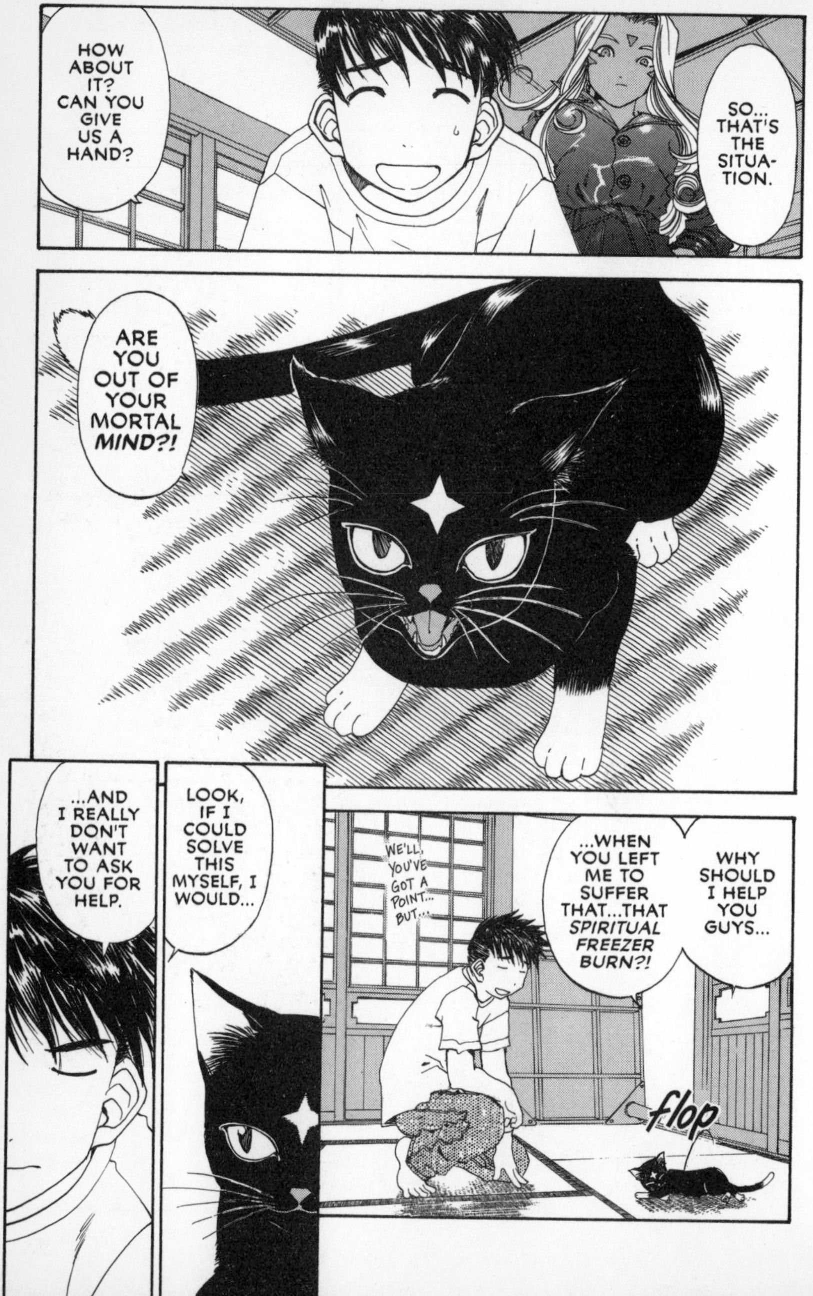
SO... THAT'S THE SITUATION.
HOW ABOUT IT? CAN YOU GIVE US A HAND?
ARE YOU OUT OF YOUR MORTAL *MIND?!*
WHY SHOULD I HELP YOU GUYS...
...WHEN YOU LEFT ME TO SUFFER THAT...THAT *SPIRITUAL FREEZER BURN?!*
WE'LL, YOU'VE GOT A POINT... BUT...
flop
LOOK, IF I COULD SOLVE THIS MYSELF, I WOULD...
...AND I REALLY DON'T WANT TO ASK YOU FOR HELP.

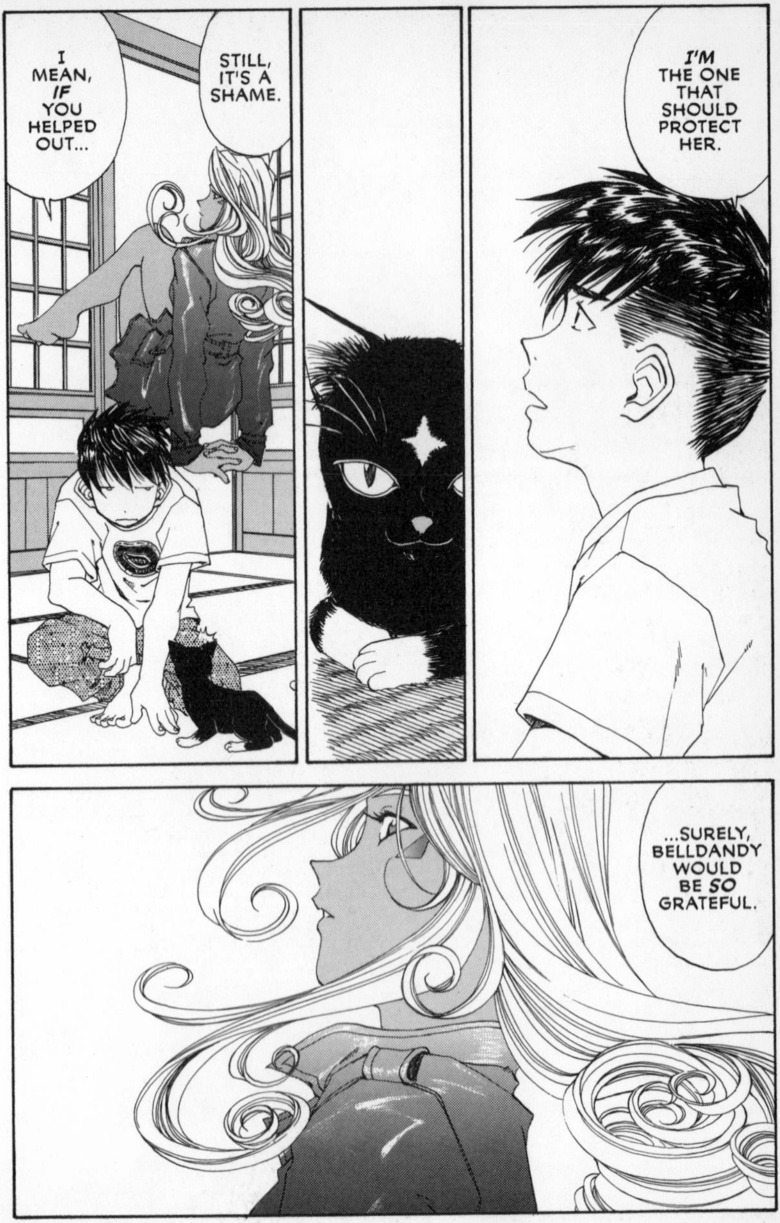
I'M THE ONE THAT SHOULD PROTECT HER.
STILL, IT'S A SHAME.
I MEAN, IF YOU HELPED OUT...
...SURELY, BELLDANDY WOULD BE SO GRATEFUL.

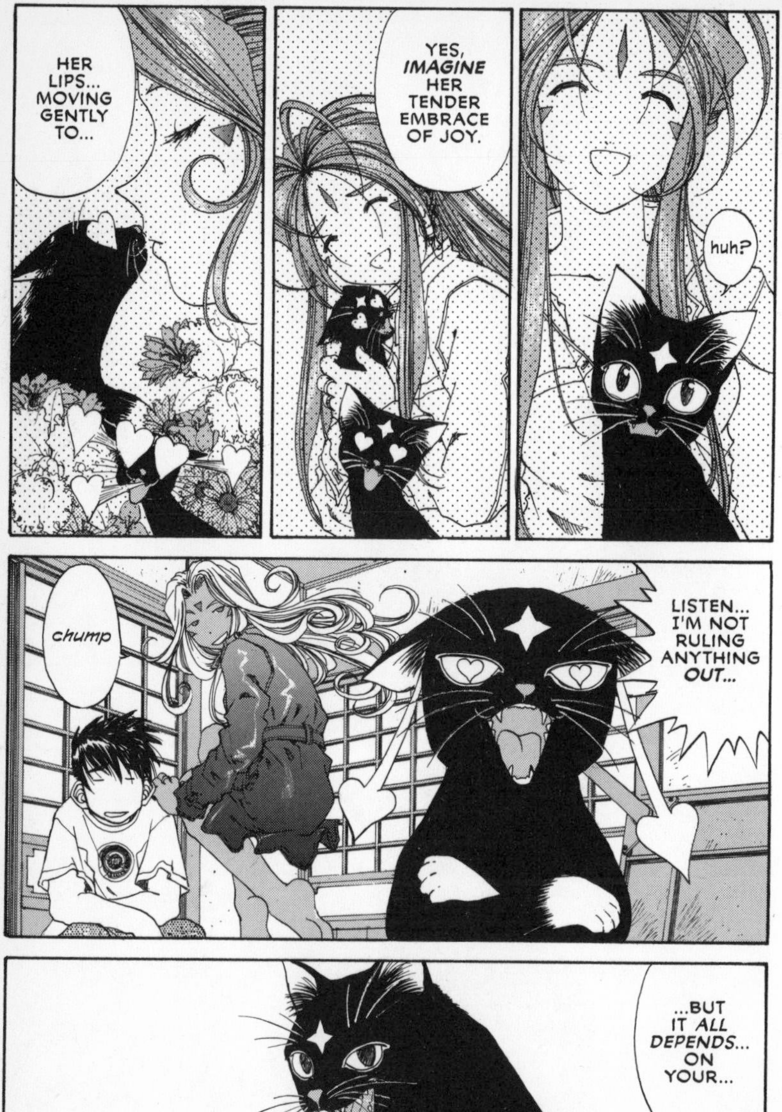
huh?
YES, IMAGINE HER TENDER EMBRACE OF JOY.
HER LIPS... MOVING GENTLY TO...
LISTEN... I'M NOT RULING ANYTHING OUT...
chump
...BUT IT ALL DEPENDS... ON YOUR...

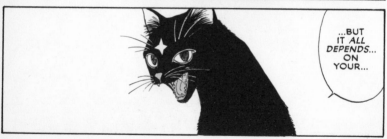

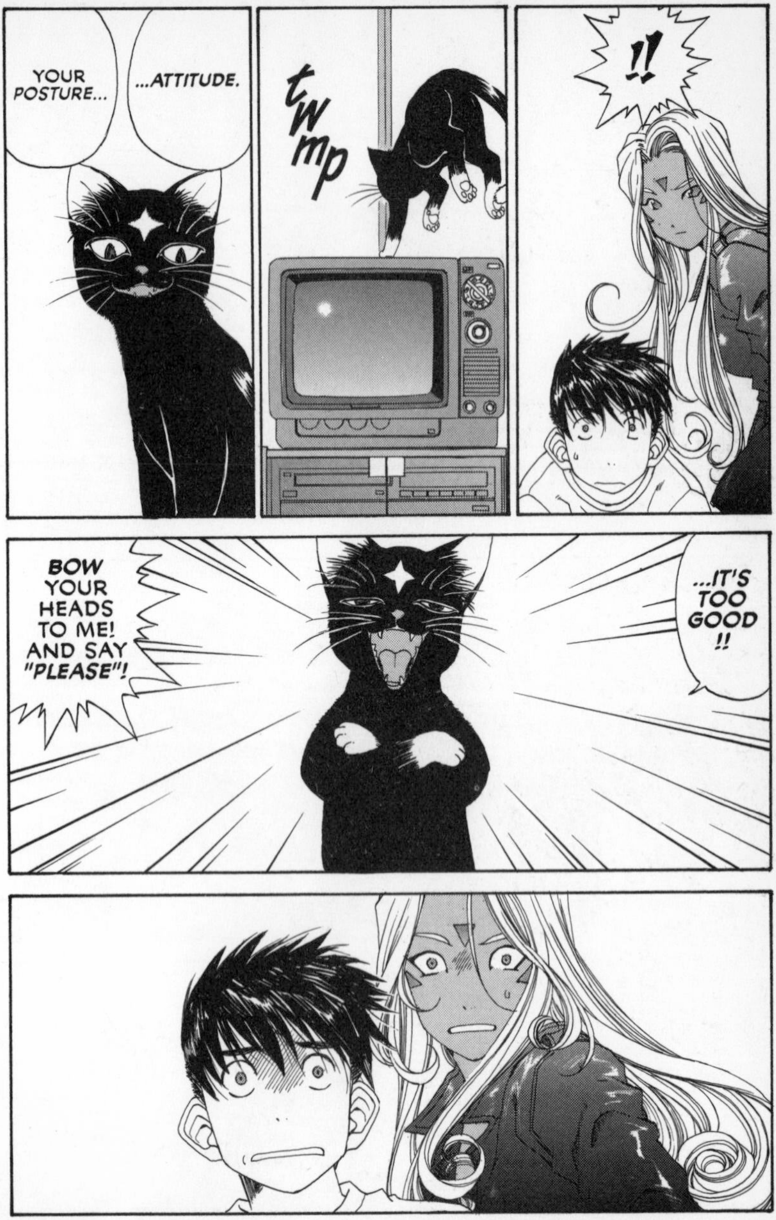

YOUR POSTURE...
...ATTITUDE.
twmp
!!
BOW YOUR HEADS TO ME! AND SAY "PLEASE"!
...IT'S TOO GOOD !!

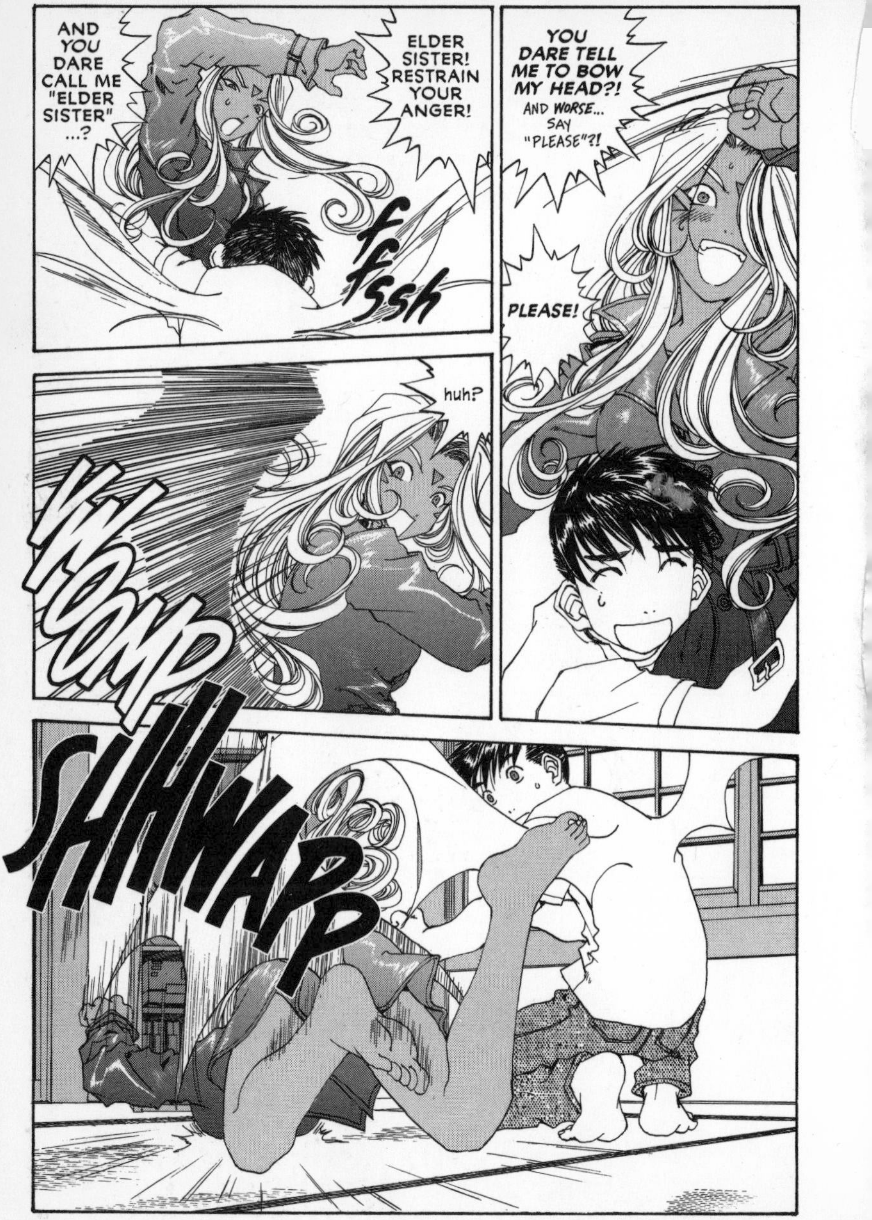
YOU DARE TELL ME TO BOW MY HEAD?!
AND WORSE... SAY "PLEASE"?!
PLEASE!
ELDER SISTER! RESTRAIN YOUR ANGER!
AND YOU DARE CALL ME "ELDER SISTER" ...?
ffssh
huh?
WHOOMP
SHHWAP

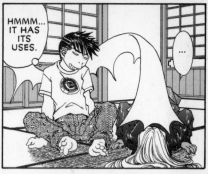

...
HMMM... IT HAS ITS USES.
PLEASE HELP US!!
HM... YES, YES, THAT'S MORE LIKE IT.
AND *YET*... THERE IS A *PROBLEM.*
WHAT?
DON'T PLAY DUMB.
IN ORDER TO GIVE ME THE *FAMILI-AR*...
...*YOU* HAVE TO REVEAL MY *IDENTITY.*
OH... YEAH!
HMMM... WHAT SHOULD WE DO ABOUT *THAT...?*
....

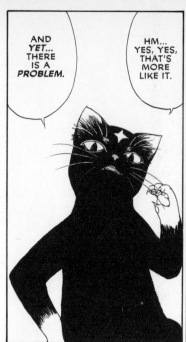

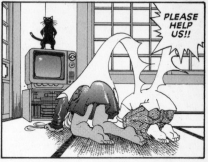

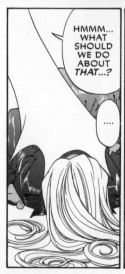

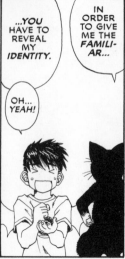

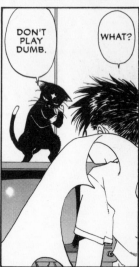

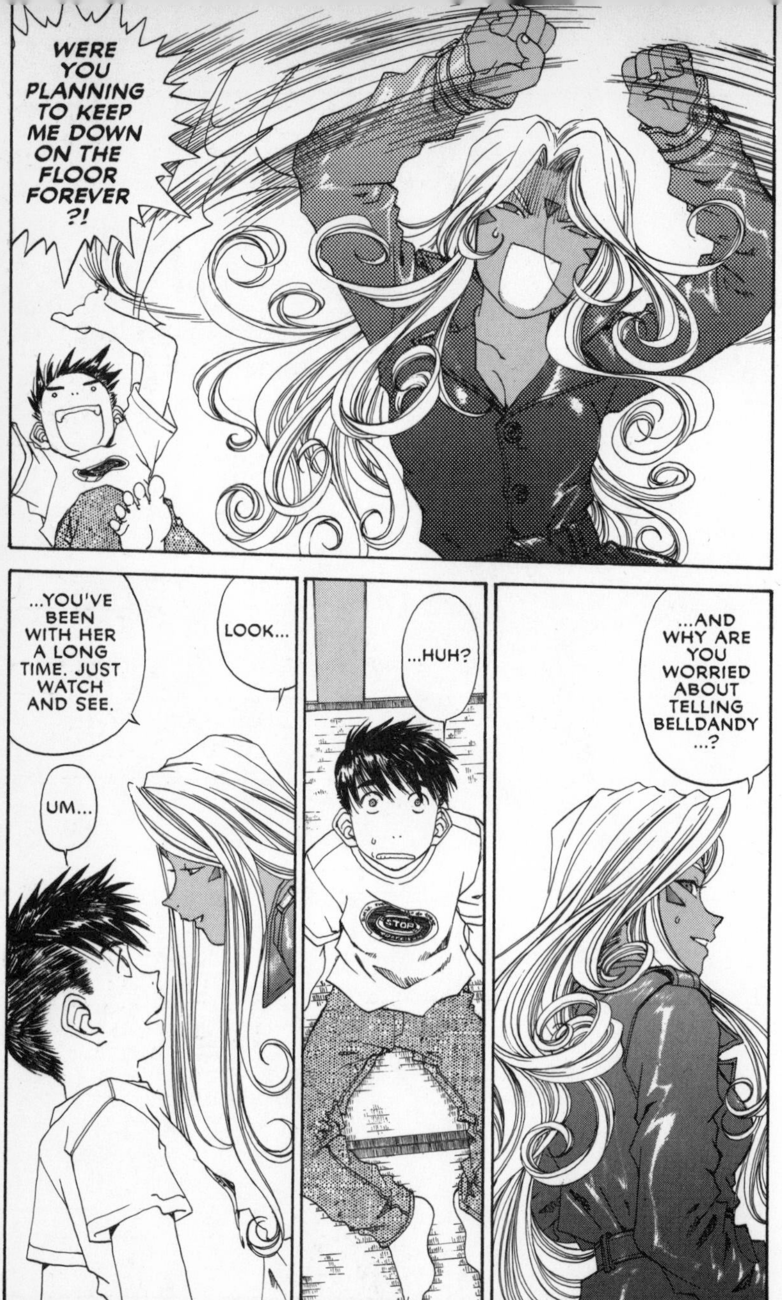
WERE YOU PLANNING TO KEEP ME DOWN ON THE FLOOR FOREVER ?!
...AND WHY ARE YOU WORRIED ABOUT TELLING BELLDANDY ...?
...HUH?
LOOK...
...YOU'VE BEEN WITH HER A LONG TIME. JUST WATCH AND SEE.
UM...

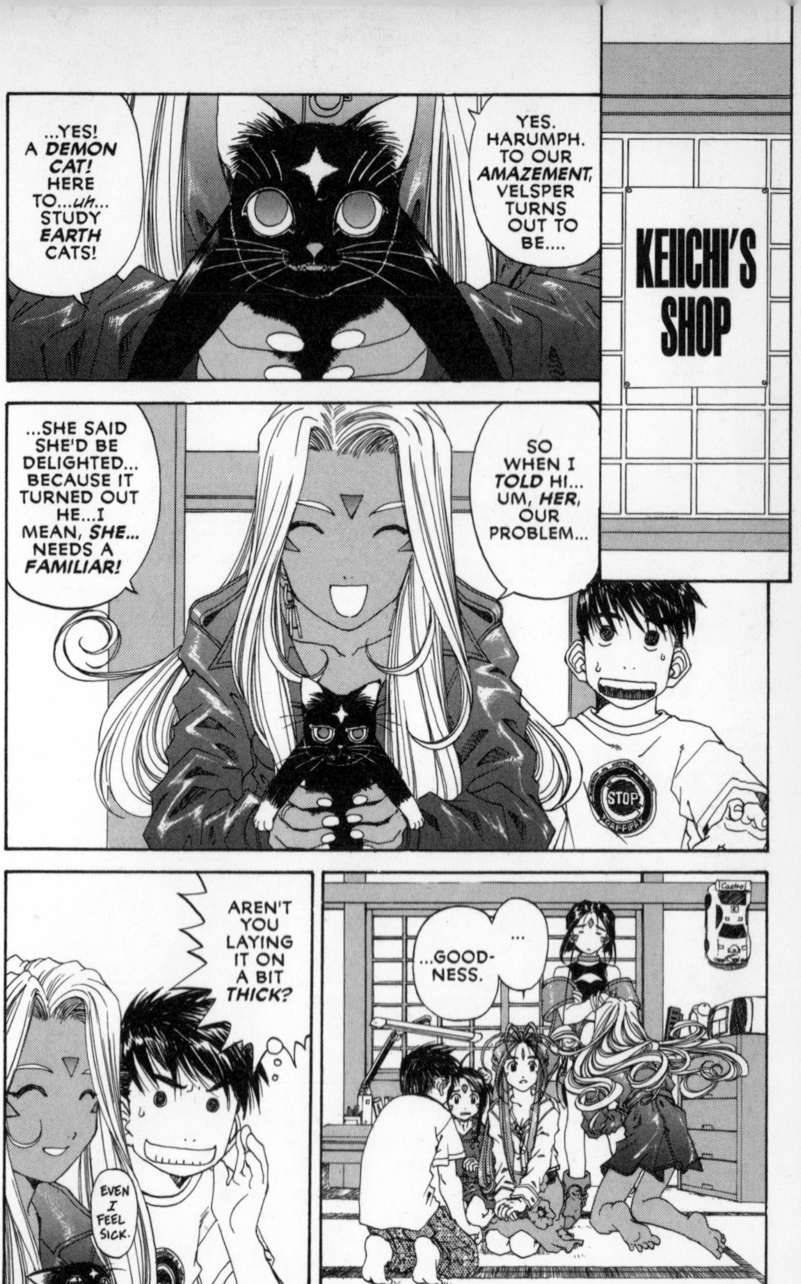
KEIICHI'S SHOP
YES. HARUMPH. TO OUR AMAZEMENT, VELSPER TURNS OUT TO BE....
...YES! A DEMON CAT! HERE TO...uh... STUDY EARTH CATS!
SO WHEN I TOLD HI... UM, HER, OUR PROBLEM...
...SHE SAID SHE'D BE DELIGHTED... BECAUSE IT TURNED OUT HE...I MEAN, SHE... NEEDS A FAMILIAR!
...
...GOOD-NESS.
AREN'T YOU LAYING IT ON A BIT THICK?
EVEN I FEEL SICK.

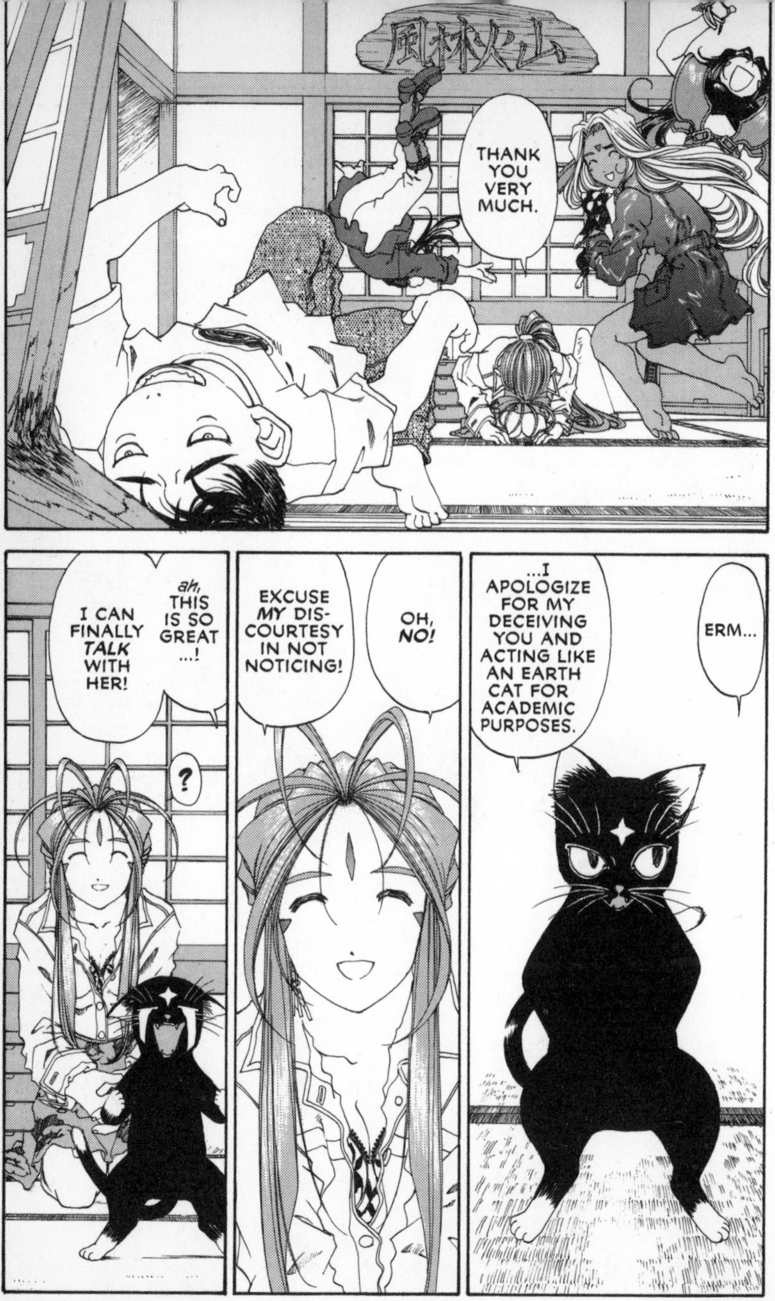
風林火山
THANK YOU VERY MUCH.
ERM...
...I APOLOGIZE FOR MY DECEIVING YOU AND ACTING LIKE AN EARTH CAT FOR ACADEMIC PURPOSES.
OH, *NO!*
EXCUSE *MY* DIS-COURTESY IN NOT NOTICING!
ah, THIS IS SO GREAT ...!
I CAN FINALLY *TALK* WITH HER!
?

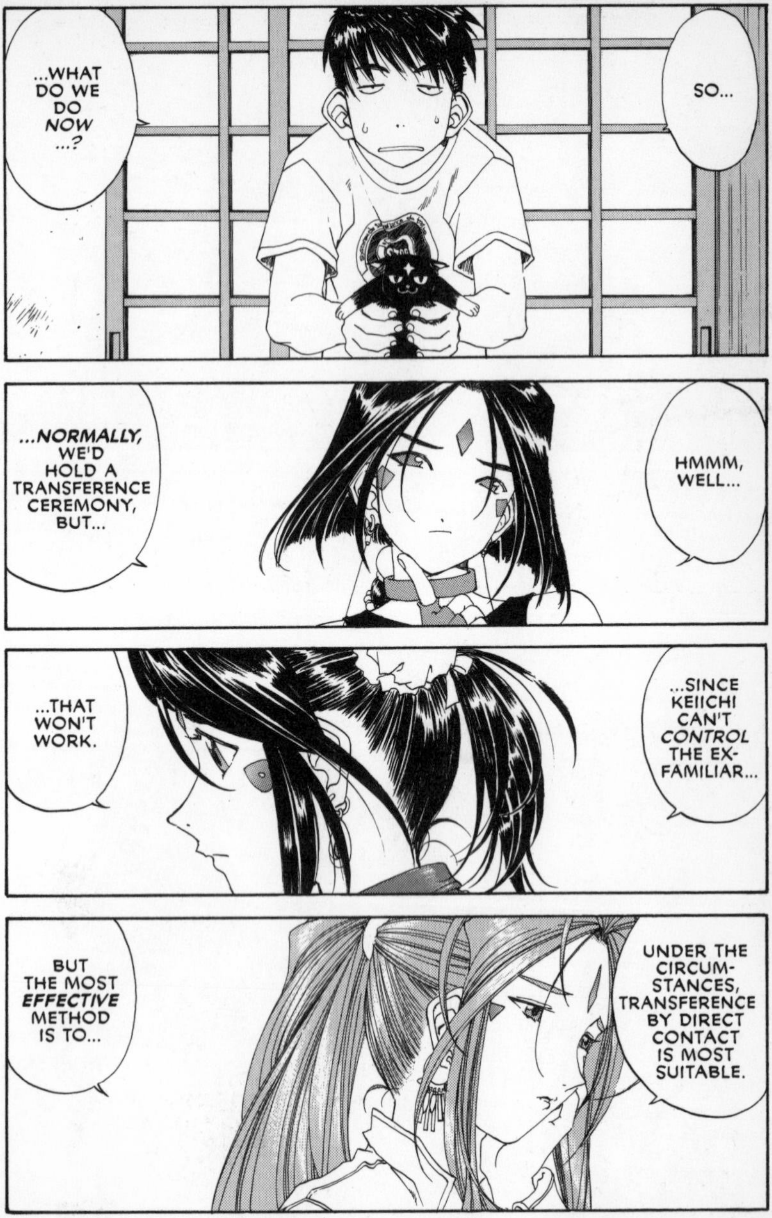
SO...
...WHAT DO WE DO *NOW* ...?
HMMM, WELL...
...NORMALLY, WE'D HOLD A TRANSFERENCE CEREMONY, BUT...
...SINCE KEIICHI CAN'T *CONTROL* THE EX-FAMILIAR...
...THAT WON'T WORK.
UNDER THE CIRCUMSTANCES, TRANSFERENCE BY DIRECT CONTACT IS MOST SUITABLE.
BUT THE MOST ***EFFECTIVE*** METHOD IS TO...

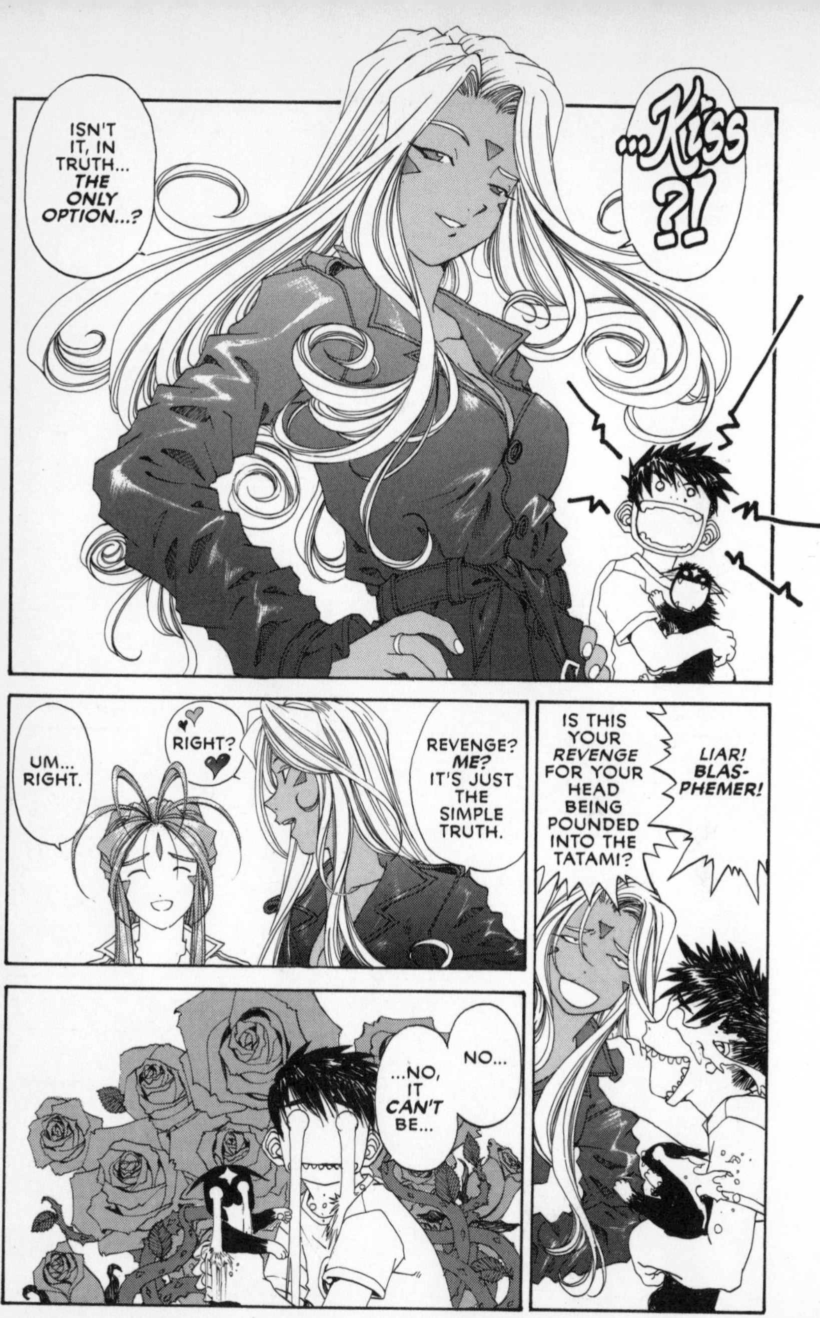
...Kiss ?!
ISN'T IT, IN TRUTH... *THE ONLY OPTION...?*
IS THIS YOUR *REVENGE* FOR YOUR HEAD BEING POUNDED INTO THE TATAMI?
LIAR! BLASPHEMER!
REVENGE? *ME?* IT'S JUST THE SIMPLE TRUTH.
RIGHT?
UM... RIGHT.
NO...
...NO, IT *CAN'T* BE...

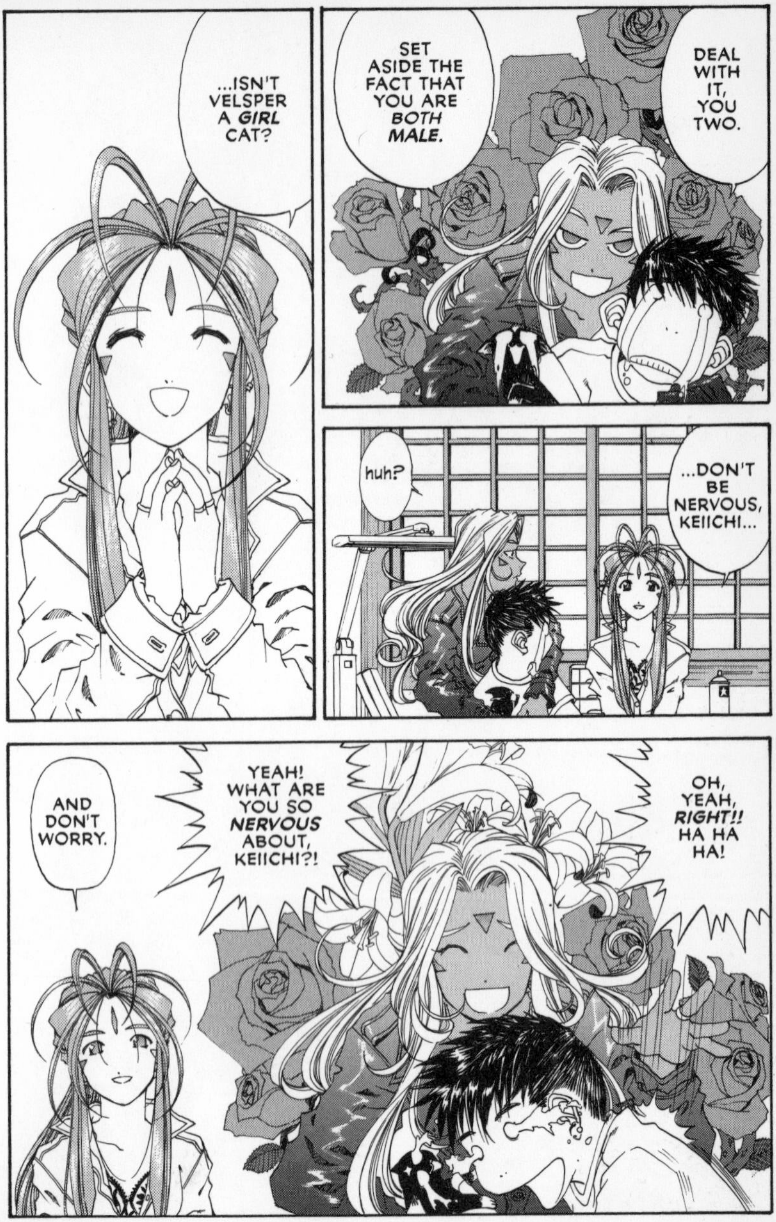
DEAL WITH IT, YOU TWO.
SET ASIDE THE FACT THAT YOU ARE *BOTH MALE.*
...DON'T BE NERVOUS, KEIICHI...
huh?
...ISN'T VELSPER A *GIRL* CAT?
OH, YEAH, *RIGHT!!* HA HA HA!
YEAH! WHAT ARE YOU SO *NERVOUS* ABOUT, KEIICHI?!
AND DON'T WORRY.

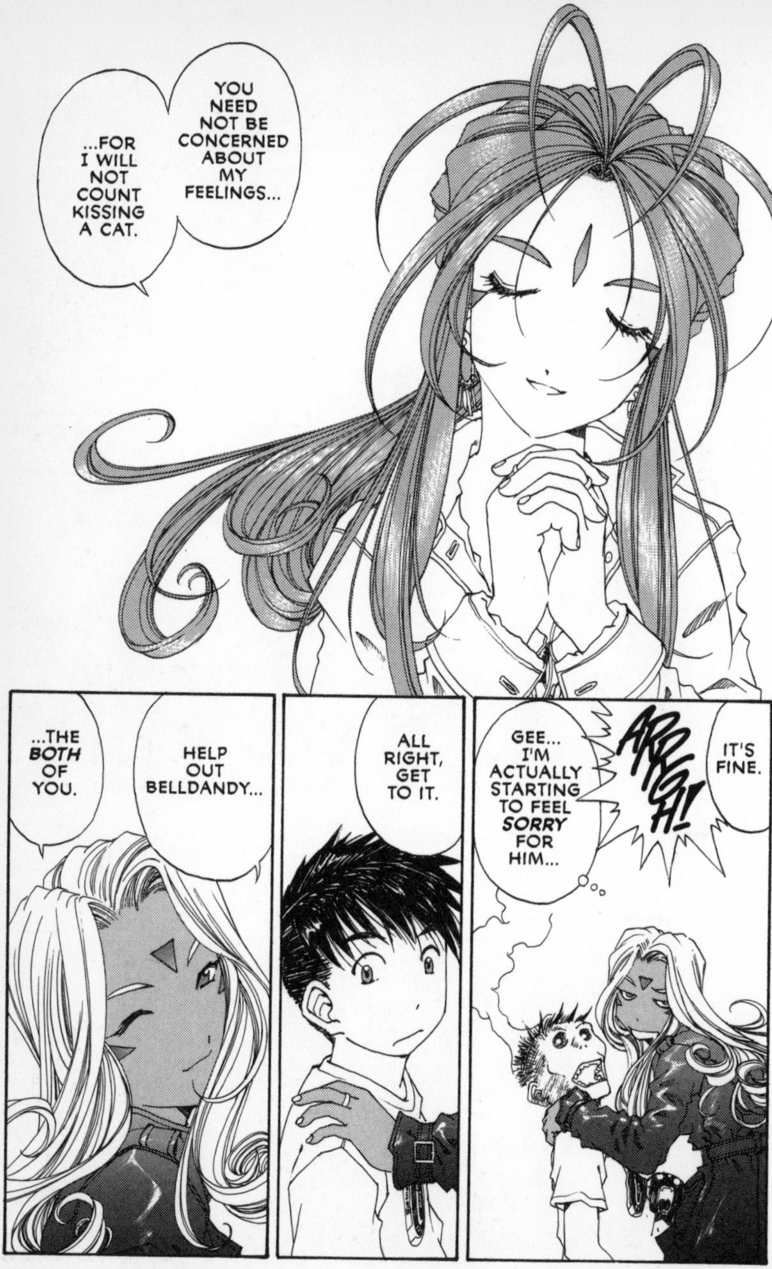

YOU NEED NOT BE CONCERNED ABOUT MY FEELINGS...
...FOR I WILL NOT COUNT KISSING A CAT.
IT'S FINE.
ARRGH!
GEE... I'M ACTUALLY STARTING TO FEEL *SORRY* FOR HIM...
ALL RIGHT, GET TO IT.
HELP OUT BELLDANDY...
...THE *BOTH* OF YOU.

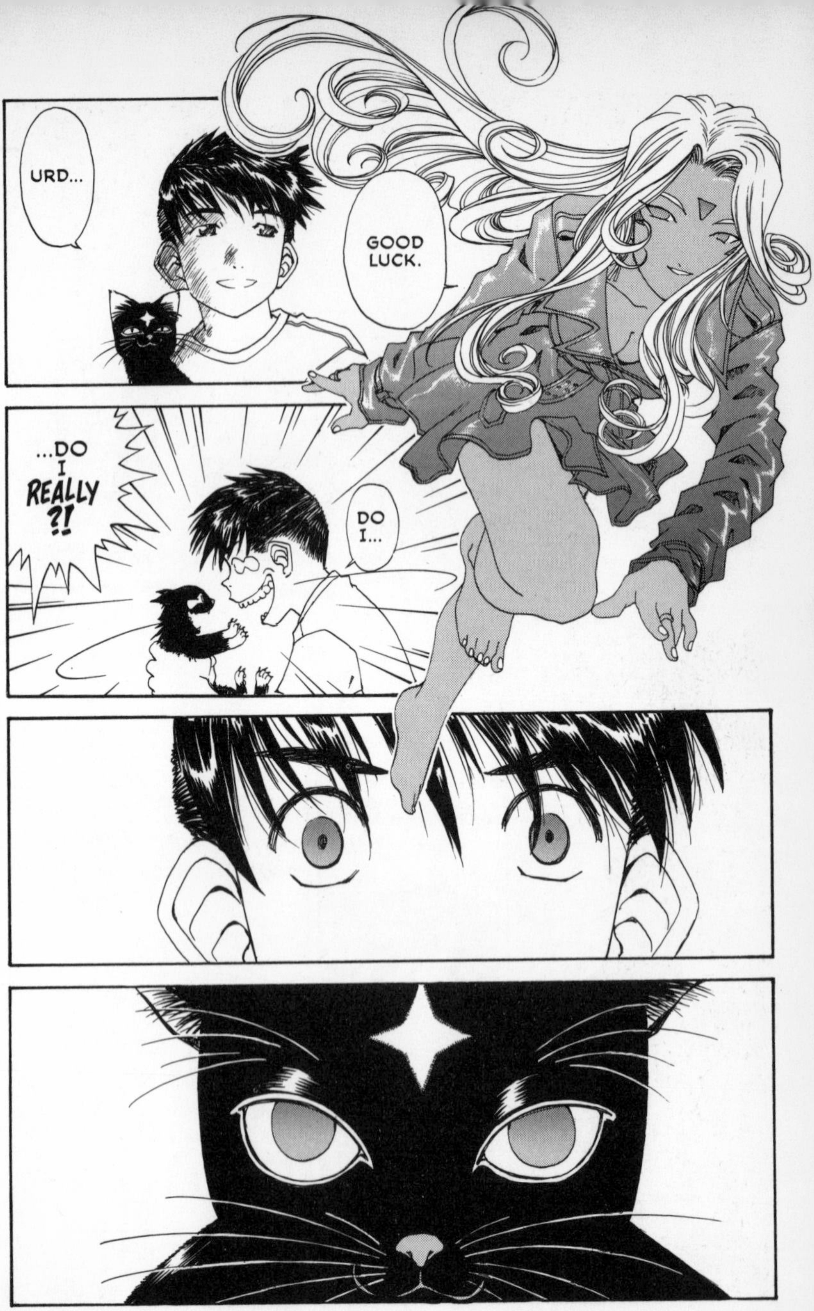
GOOD LUCK.
URD...
DO I...
...DO I REALLY ?!

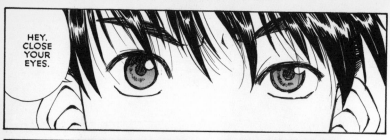

HEY. CLOSE YOUR EYES.

YOU FIRST, BUDDY.

mmmmm

groan

...ON SO MANY DIFFERENT LEVELS!!!

NO! IT'S WRONG...

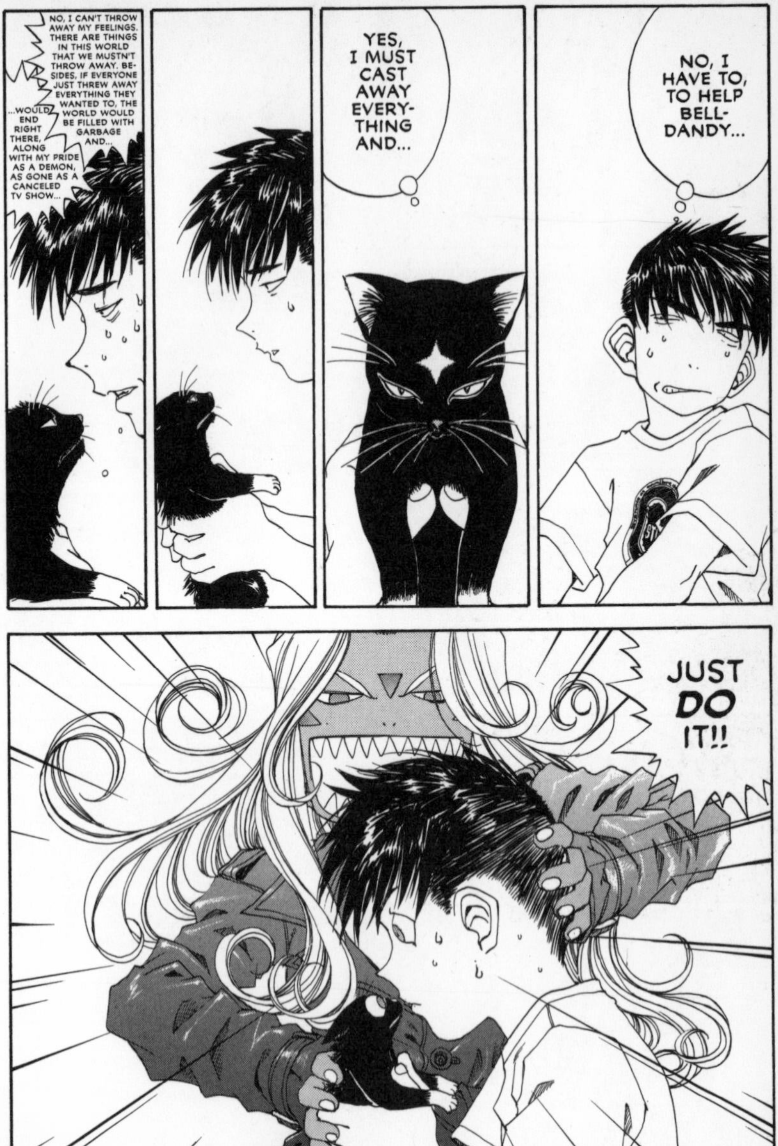
NO, I HAVE TO, TO HELP BELL-DANDY...
YES, I MUST CAST AWAY EVERY-THING AND...
NO, I CAN'T THROW AWAY MY FEELINGS. THERE ARE THINGS IN THIS WORLD THAT WE MUSTN'T THROW AWAY. BE-SIDES, IF EVERYONE JUST THREW AWAY EVERYTHING THEY WANTED TO, THE WORLD WOULD BE FILLED WITH GARBAGE AND...
...WOULD END RIGHT THERE, ALONG WITH MY PRIDE AS A DEMON, AS GONE AS A CANCELED TV SHOW...
JUST *DO* IT!!

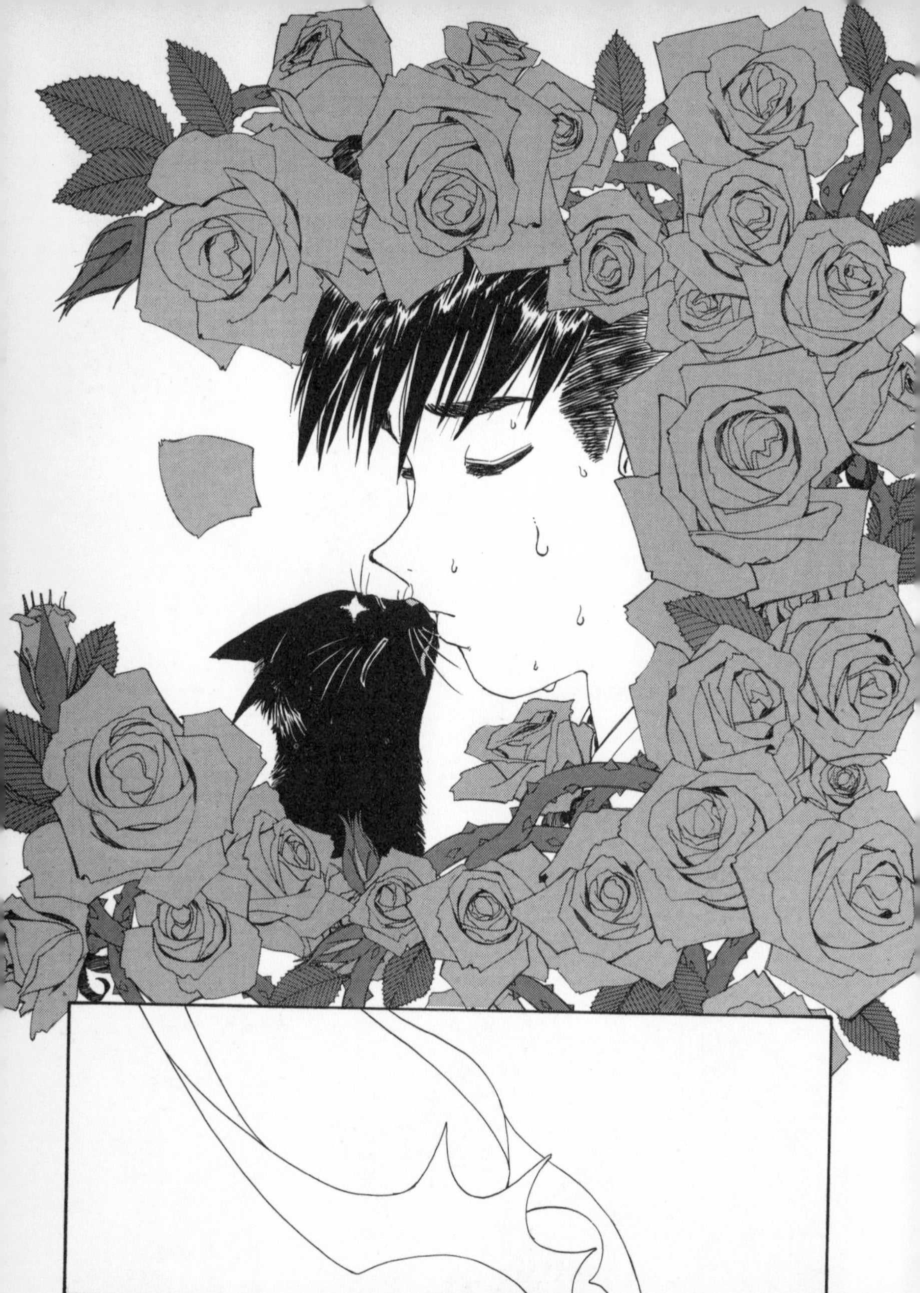

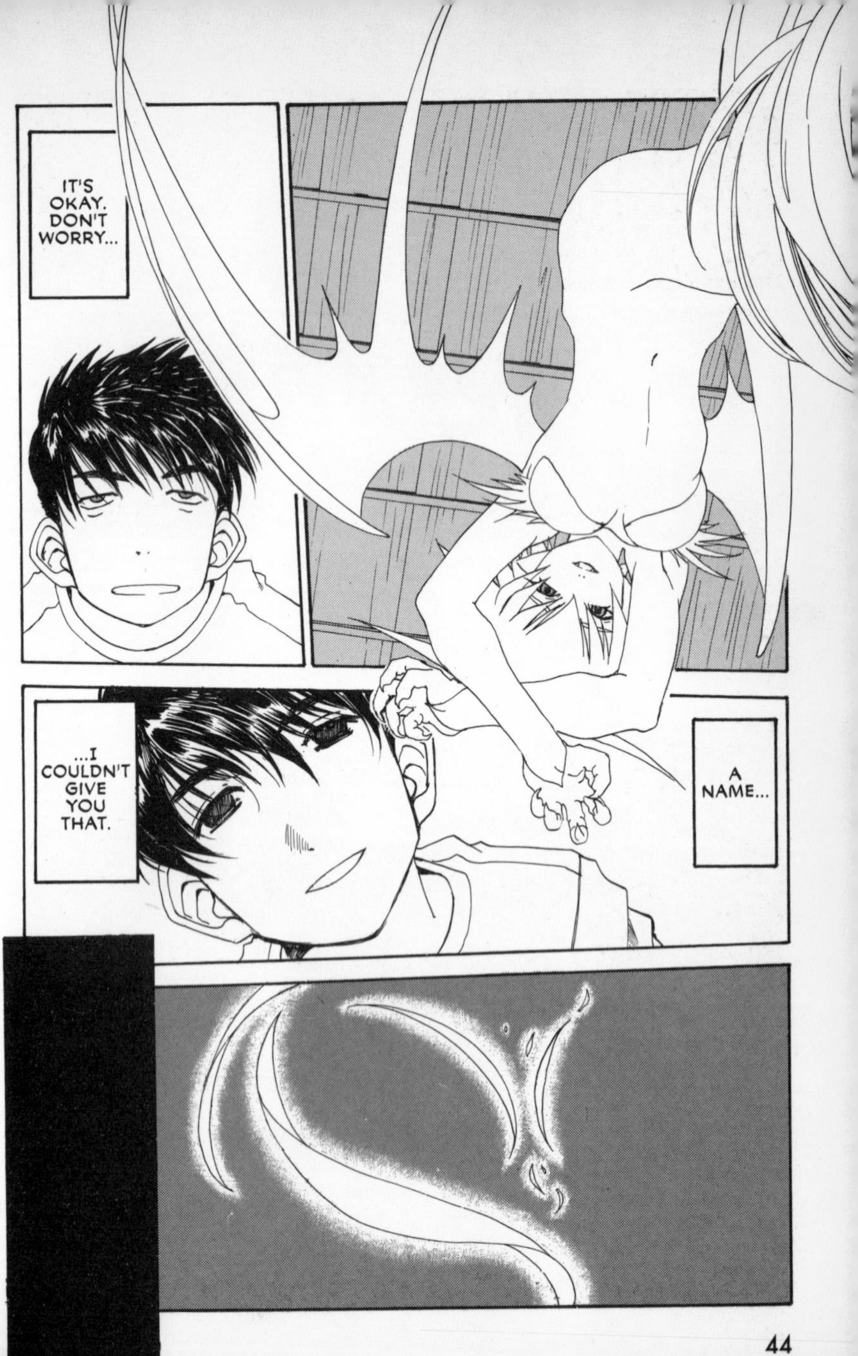
IT'S OKAY. DON'T WORRY...
A NAME...
...I COULDN'T GIVE YOU THAT.

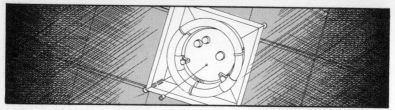

EVERY-
THING'S
OKAY.

THE
ANGEL
...?

KEIICHI...

SHE'S
SAFELY
TRANS-
FERRED
TO
VELSPER.

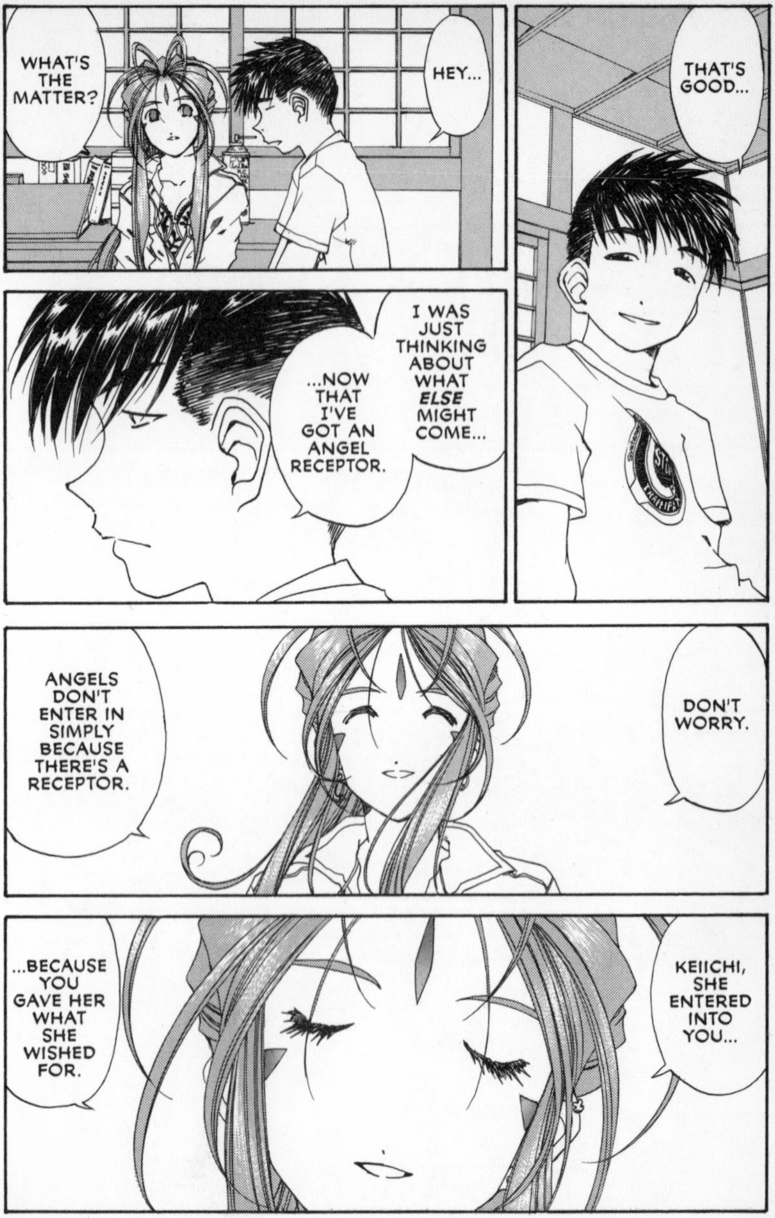
THAT'S GOOD...
HEY...
WHAT'S THE MATTER?
I WAS JUST THINKING ABOUT WHAT *ELSE* MIGHT COME...
...NOW THAT I'VE GOT AN ANGEL RECEPTOR.
DON'T WORRY.
ANGELS DON'T ENTER IN SIMPLY BECAUSE THERE'S A RECEPTOR.
KEIICHI, SHE ENTERED INTO YOU...
...BECAUSE YOU GAVE HER WHAT SHE WISHED FOR.

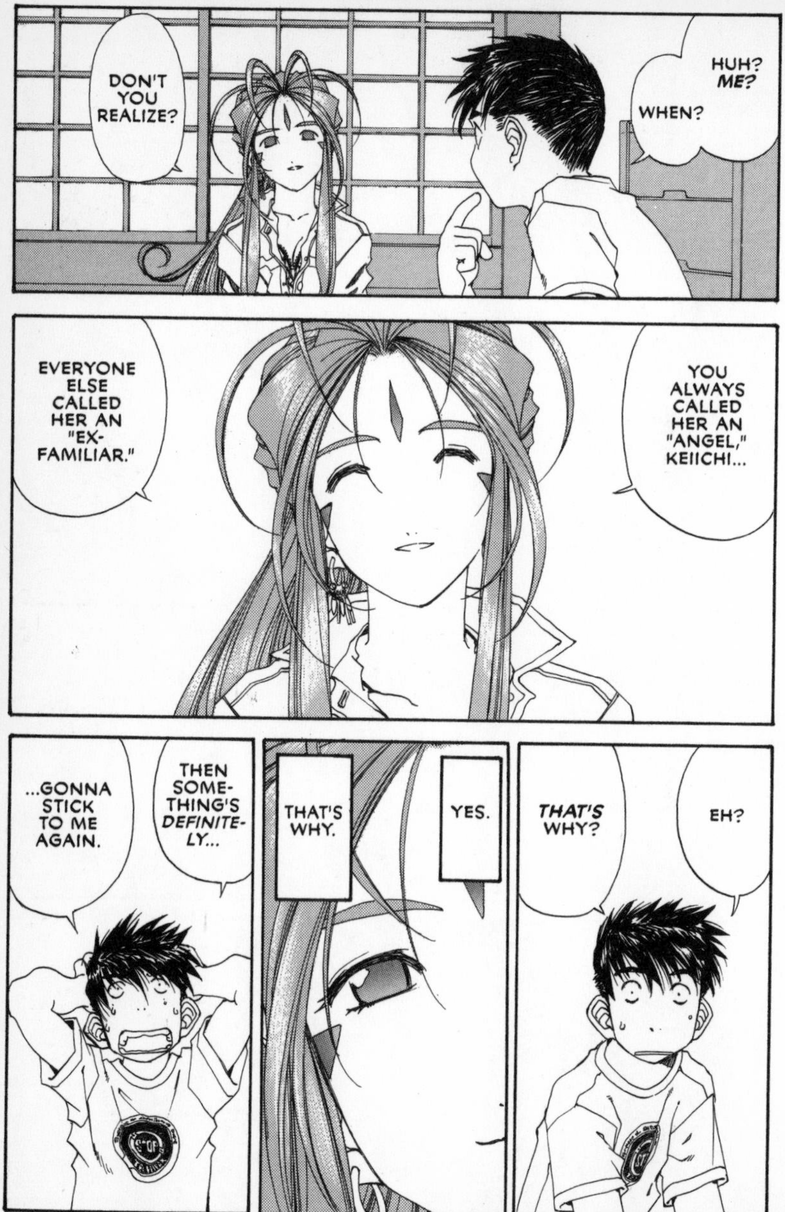
HUH? *ME?*
WHEN?
DON'T YOU REALIZE?
YOU ALWAYS CALLED HER AN "ANGEL," KEIICHI...
EVERYONE ELSE CALLED HER AN "EX-FAMILIAR."
EH?
THAT'S WHY?
YES.
THAT'S WHY.
THEN SOMETHING'S *DEFINITELY*...
...GONNA STICK TO ME AGAIN.

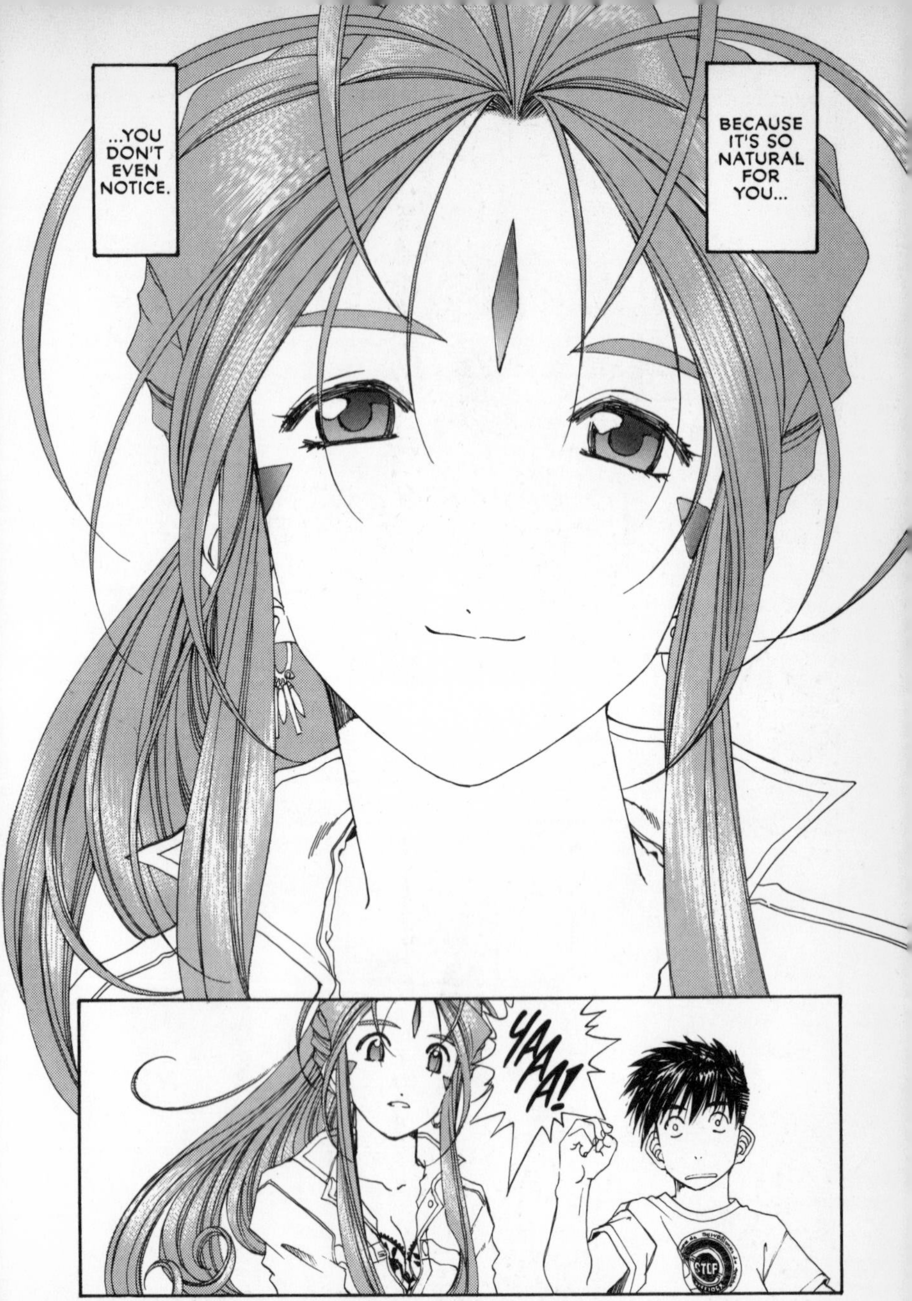
BECAUSE IT'S SO NATURAL FOR YOU...
...YOU DON'T EVEN NOTICE.
YAAAA!

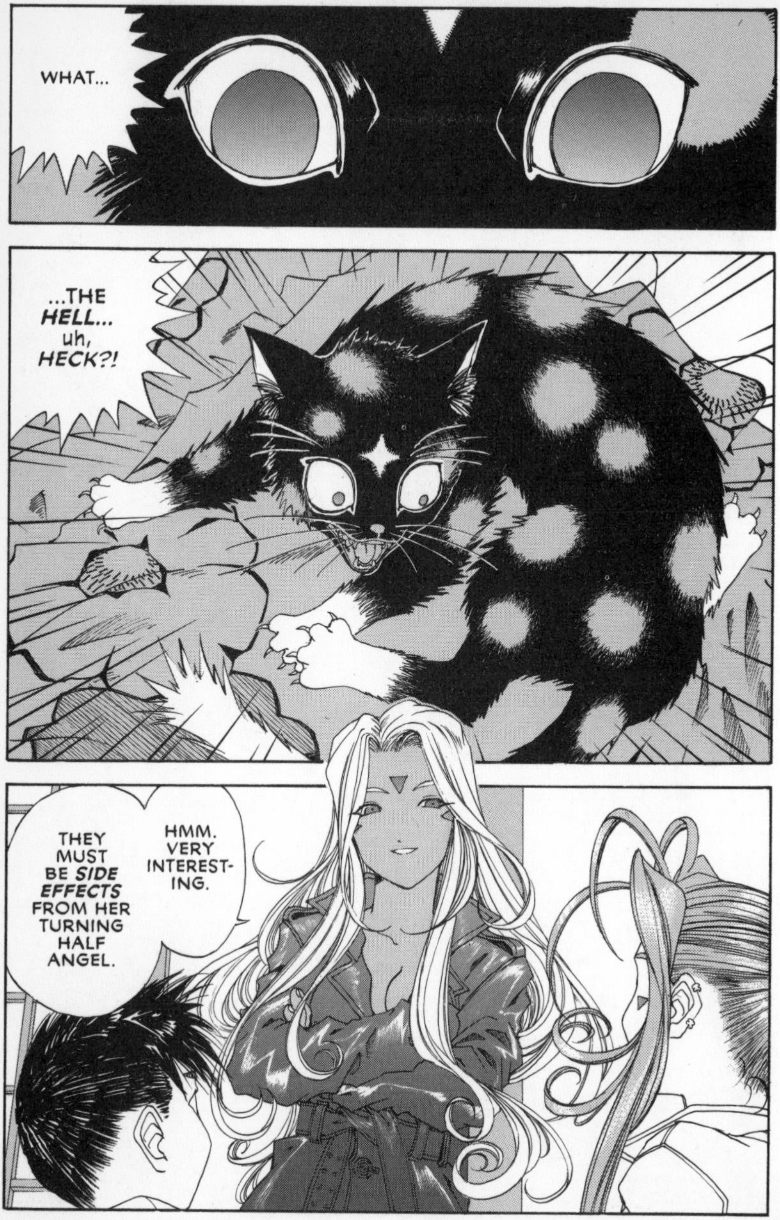
WHAT...
...THE HELL... uh, HECK?!
HMM. VERY INTEREST-ING.
THEY MUST BE SIDE EFFECTS FROM HER TURNING HALF ANGEL.

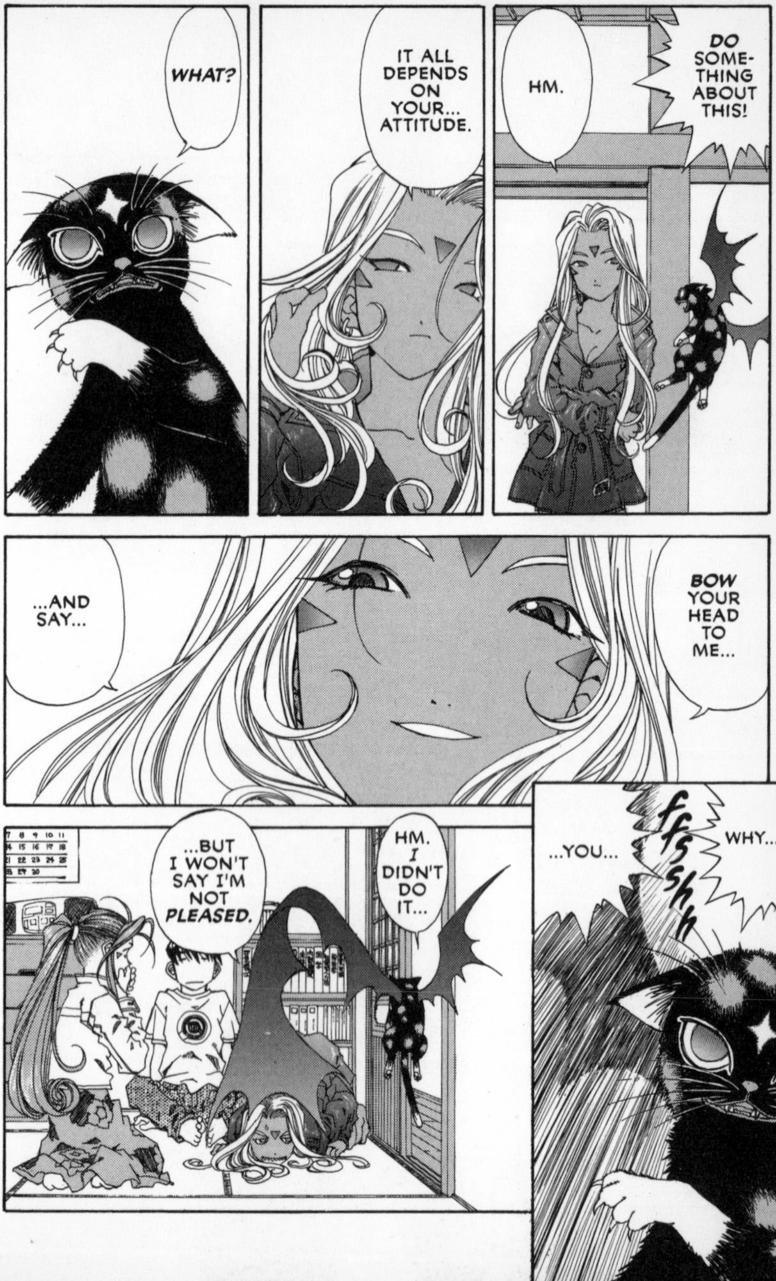
DO SOMETHING ABOUT THIS!
HM.
IT ALL DEPENDS ON YOUR... ATTITUDE.
WHAT?
BOW YOUR HEAD TO ME...
...AND SAY...
WHY...
ffsshh
...YOU...
HM. I DIDN'T DO IT...
...BUT I WON'T SAY I'M NOT PLEASED.

CHAPTER 172

Shoot or Die!

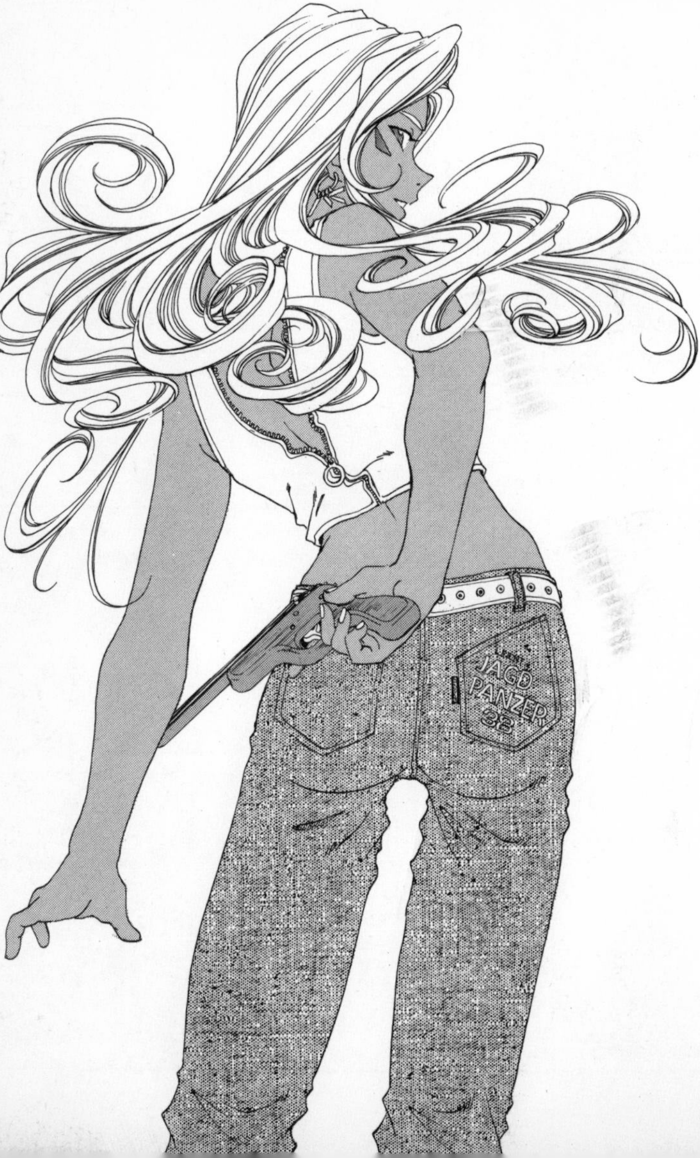
JAGD PANZER 38

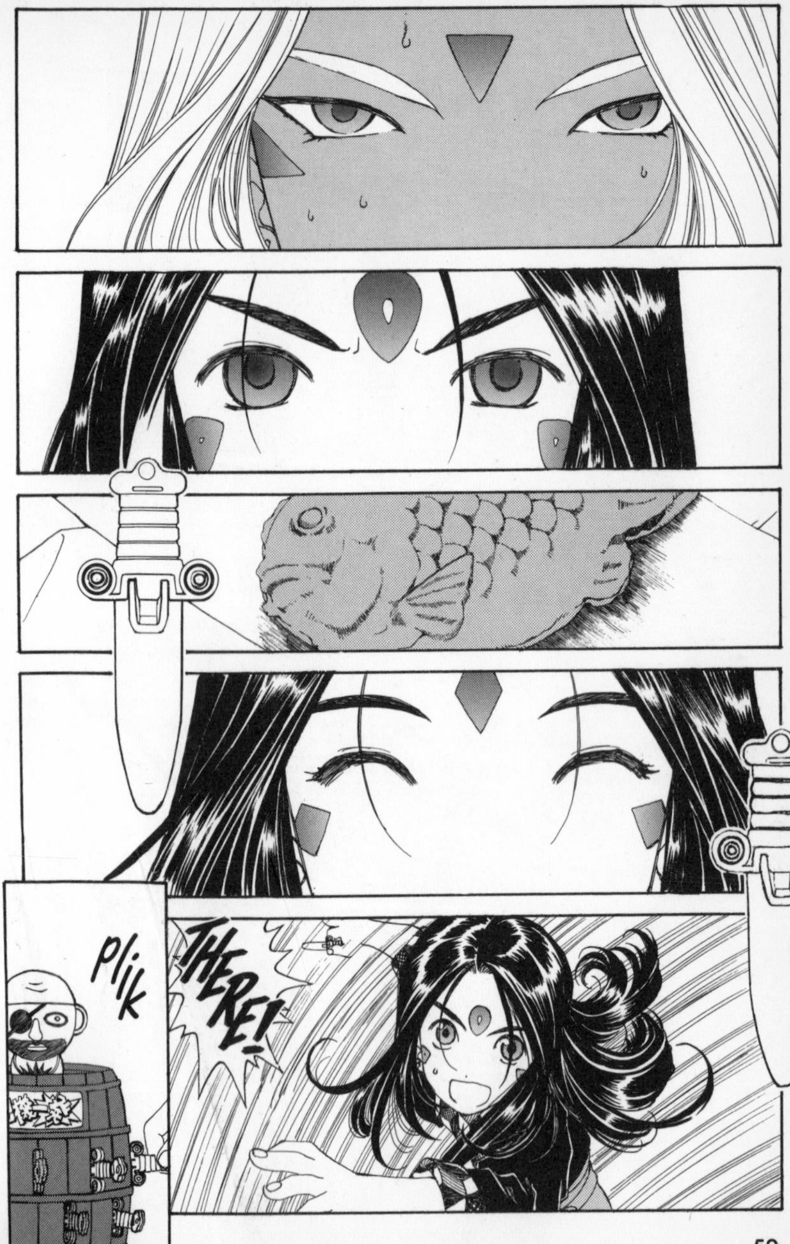
THERE!
plik

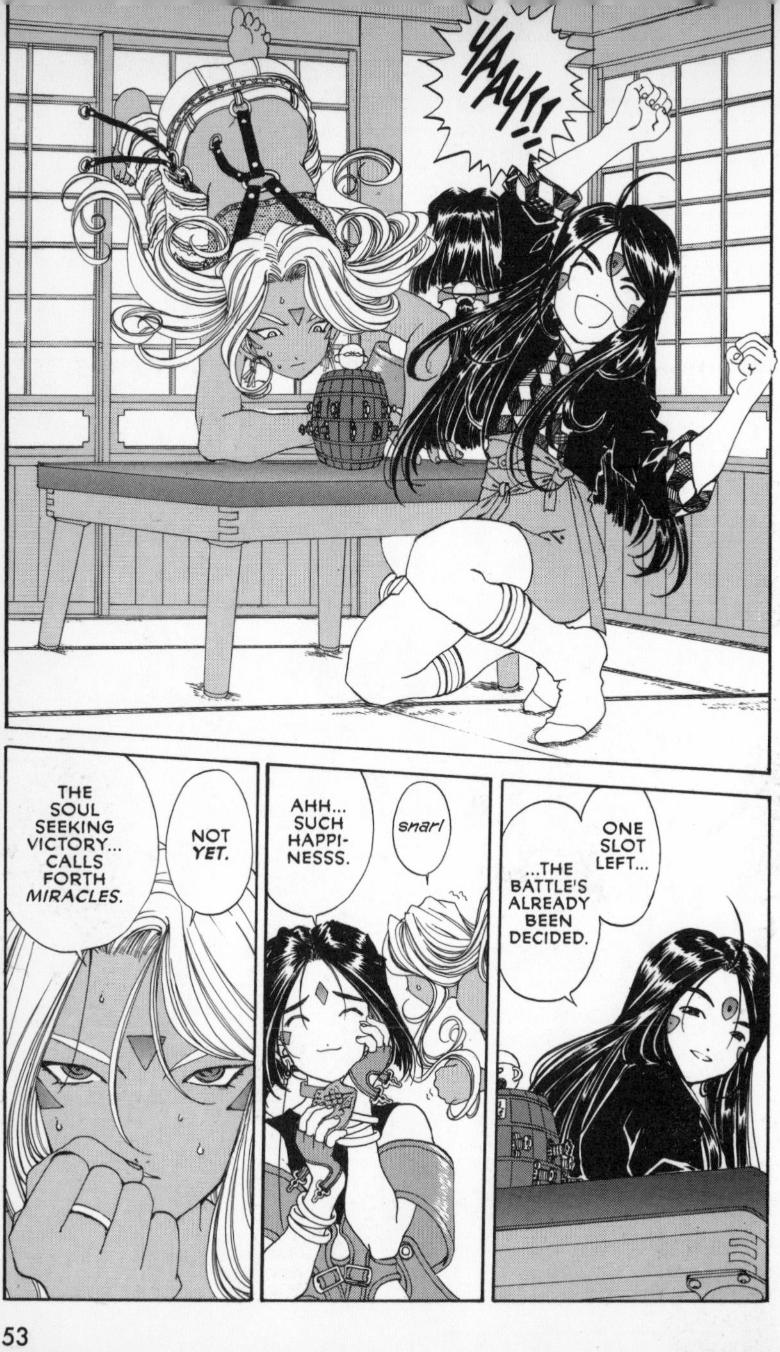

YAAY!!!
ONE SLOT LEFT...
...THE BATTLE'S ALREADY BEEN DECIDED.
snarl
AHH... SUCH HAPPI-NESSS.
NOT *YET.*
THE SOUL SEEKING VICTORY... CALLS FORTH *MIRACLES.*

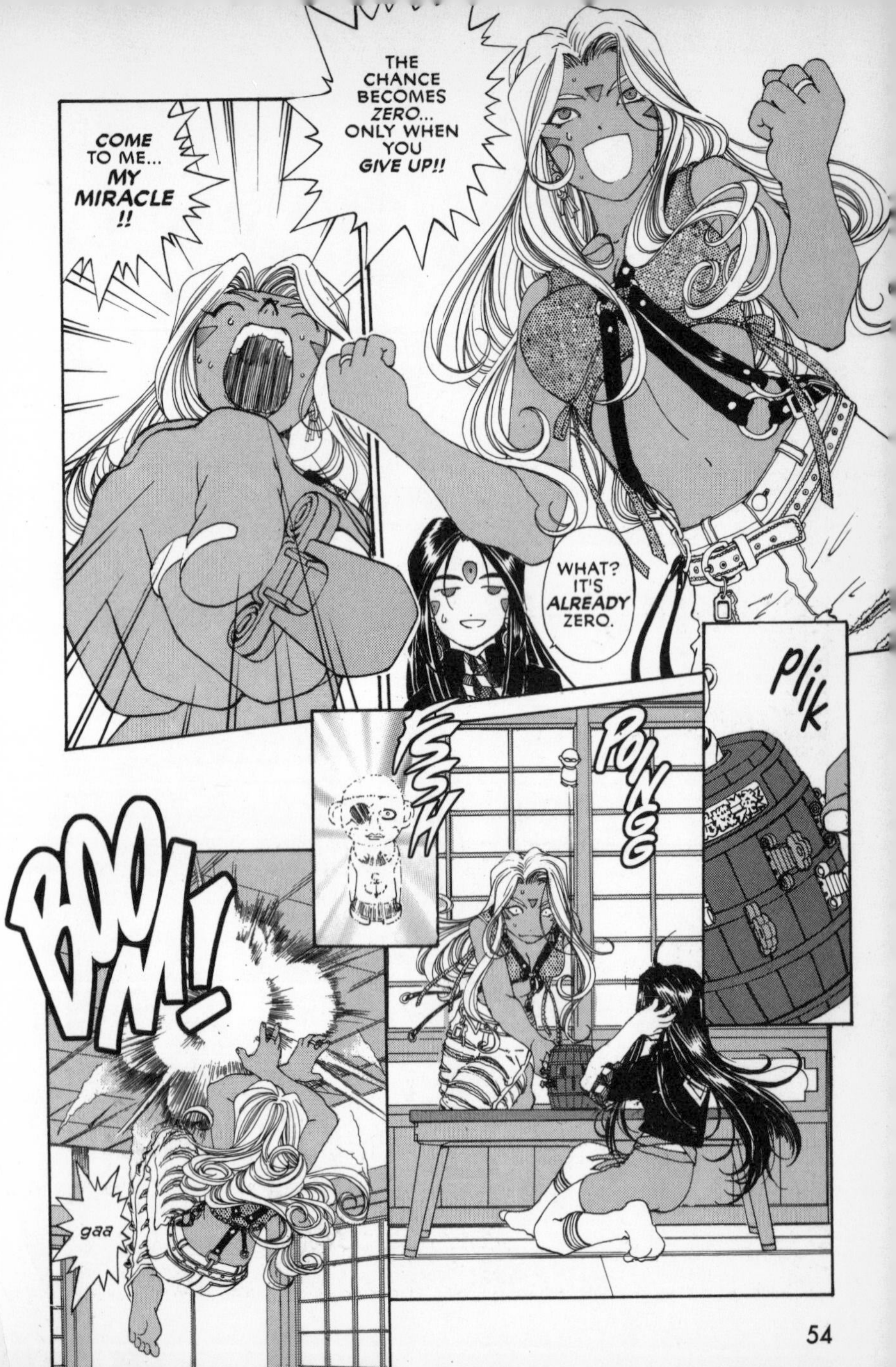
THE CHANCE BECOMES *ZERO*... ONLY WHEN YOU *GIVE UP!!*
COME TO ME... MY MIRACLE !!
WHAT? IT'S *ALREADY* ZERO.
plik
POINGG
FSSH
BOOM!
gaa

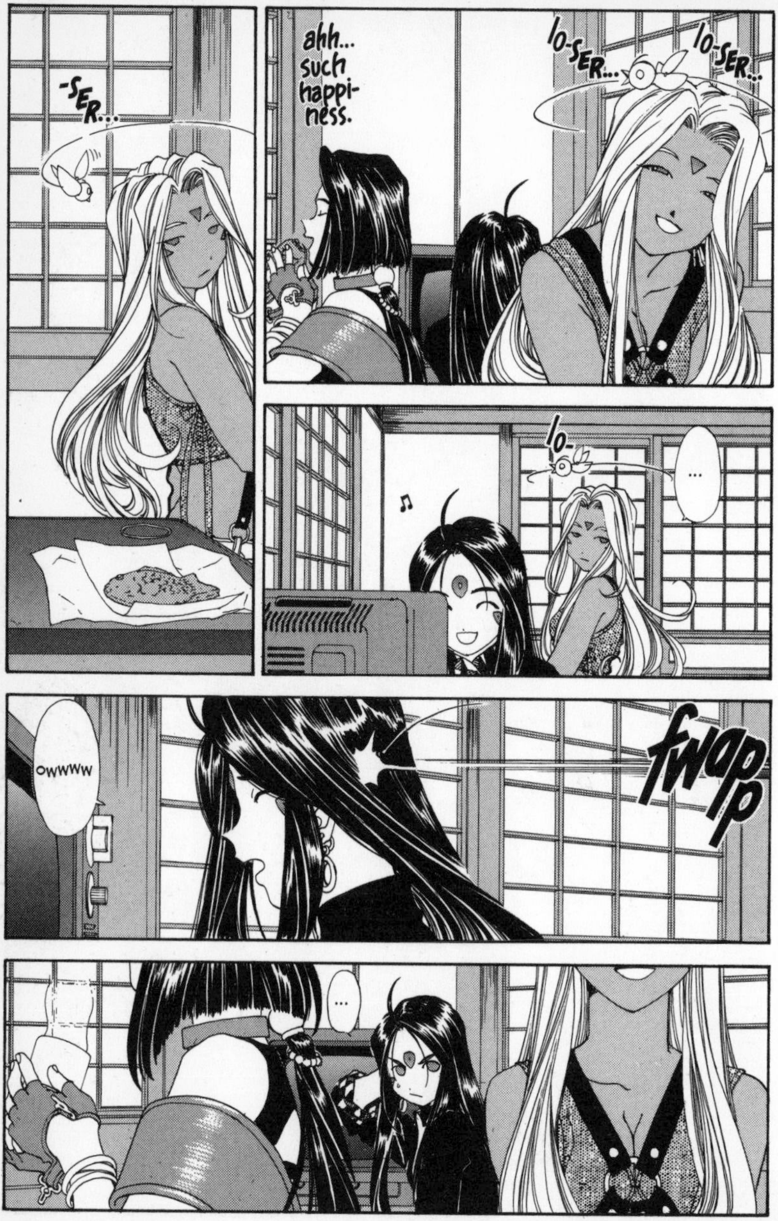

lo-SER...
lo-SER...
ahh... such happiness.
...
lo-
♪
-SER...
fwap
owwww
...

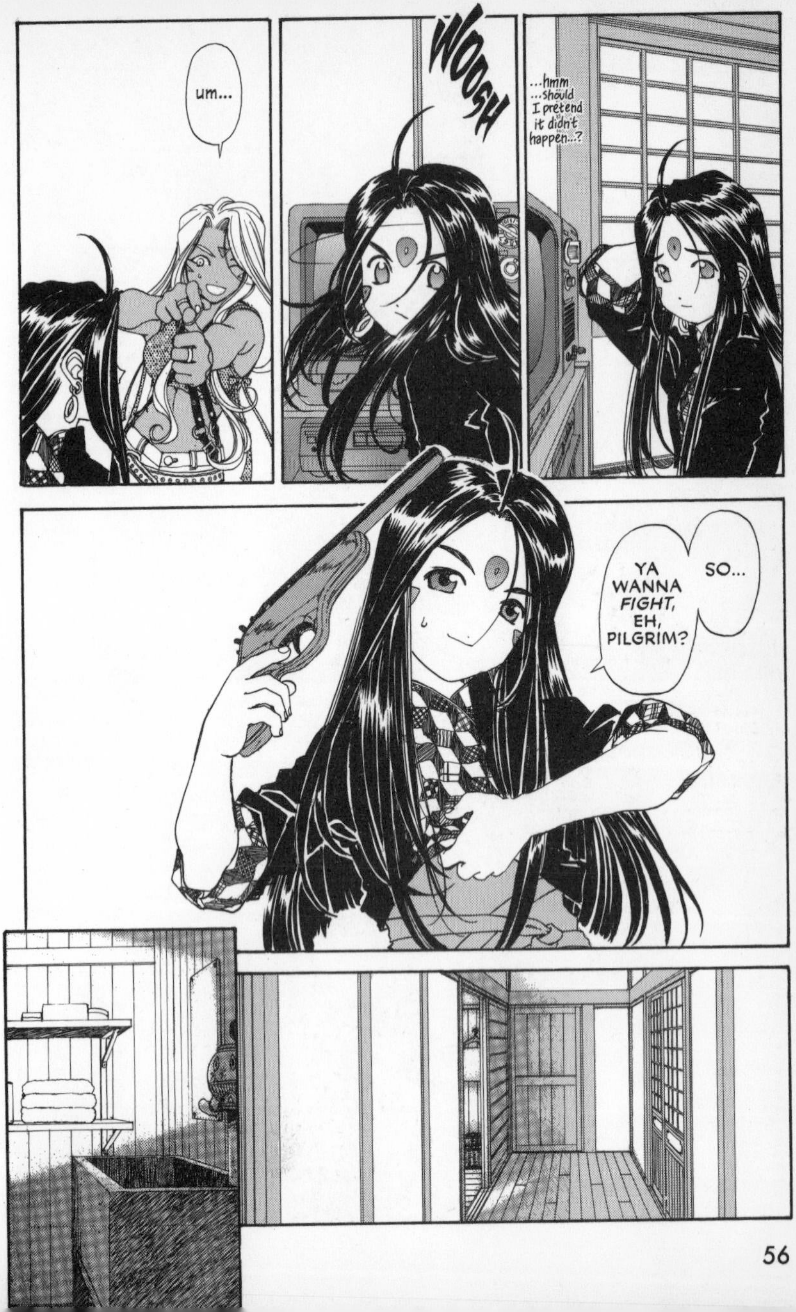
...hmm ...should I pretend it didn't happen...?
WOOSH
um...
SO...
YA WANNA FIGHT, EH, PILGRIM?

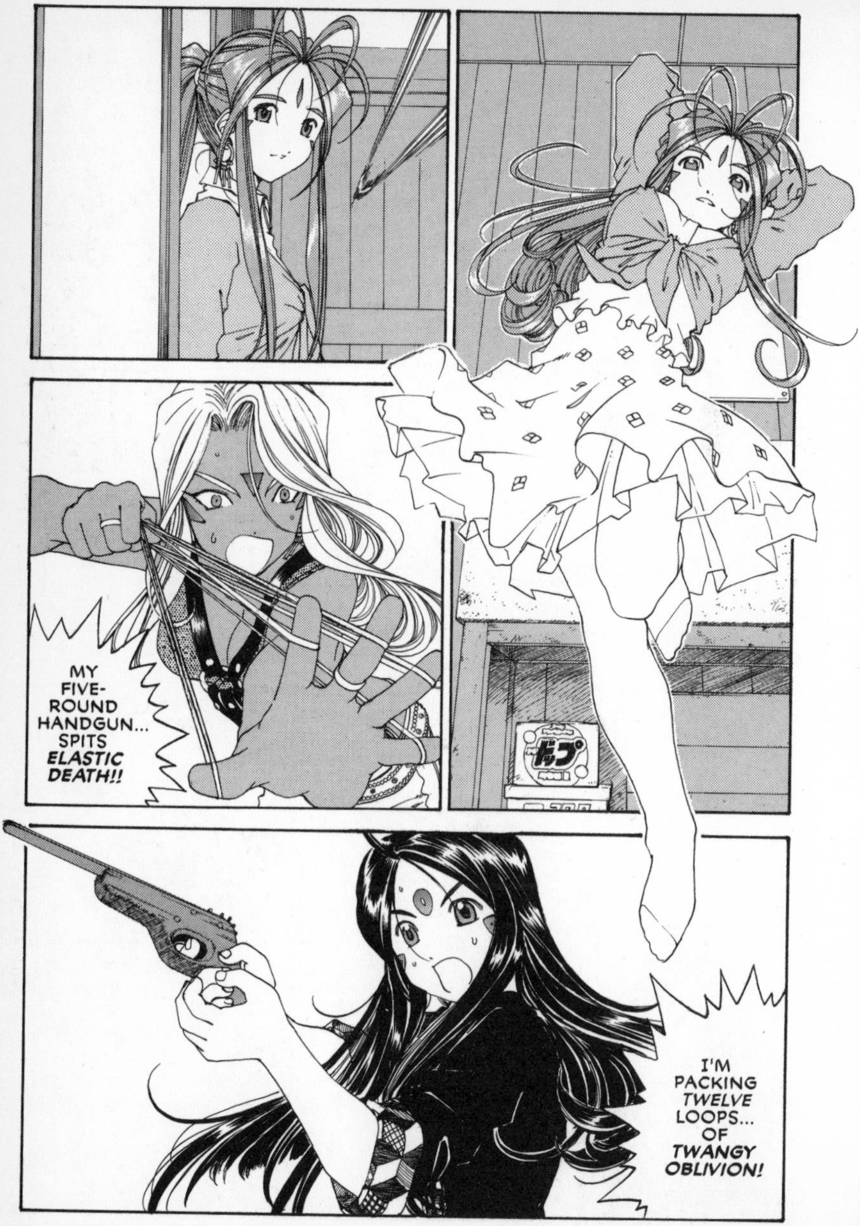
MY FIVE-ROUND HANDGUN... SPITS *ELASTIC DEATH!!*
I'M PACKING *TWELVE* LOOPS... OF *TWANGY OBLIVION!*

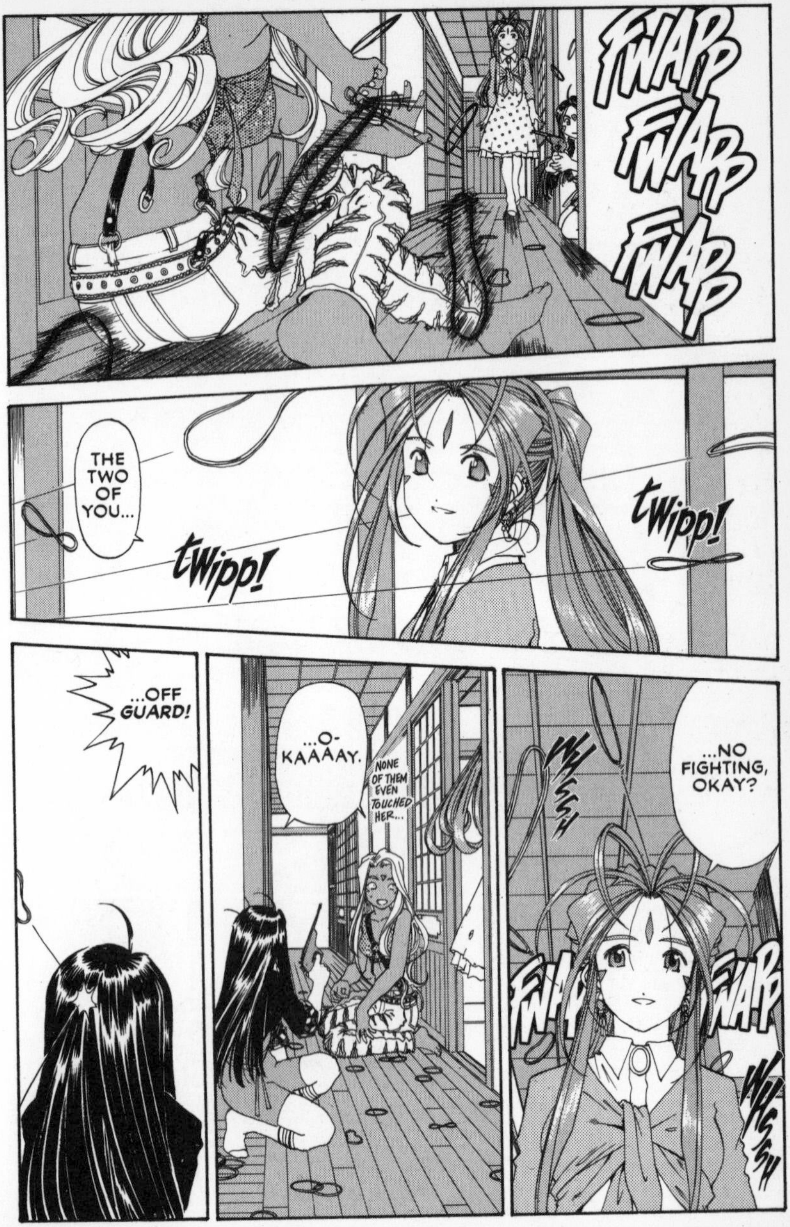
FWAPP
FWAPP
FWAPP
THE TWO OF YOU...
tWipp!
tWipp!
...NO FIGHTING, OKAY?
...O-KAAAAY.
NONE OF THEM EVEN TOUCHED HER...
...OFF GUARD!

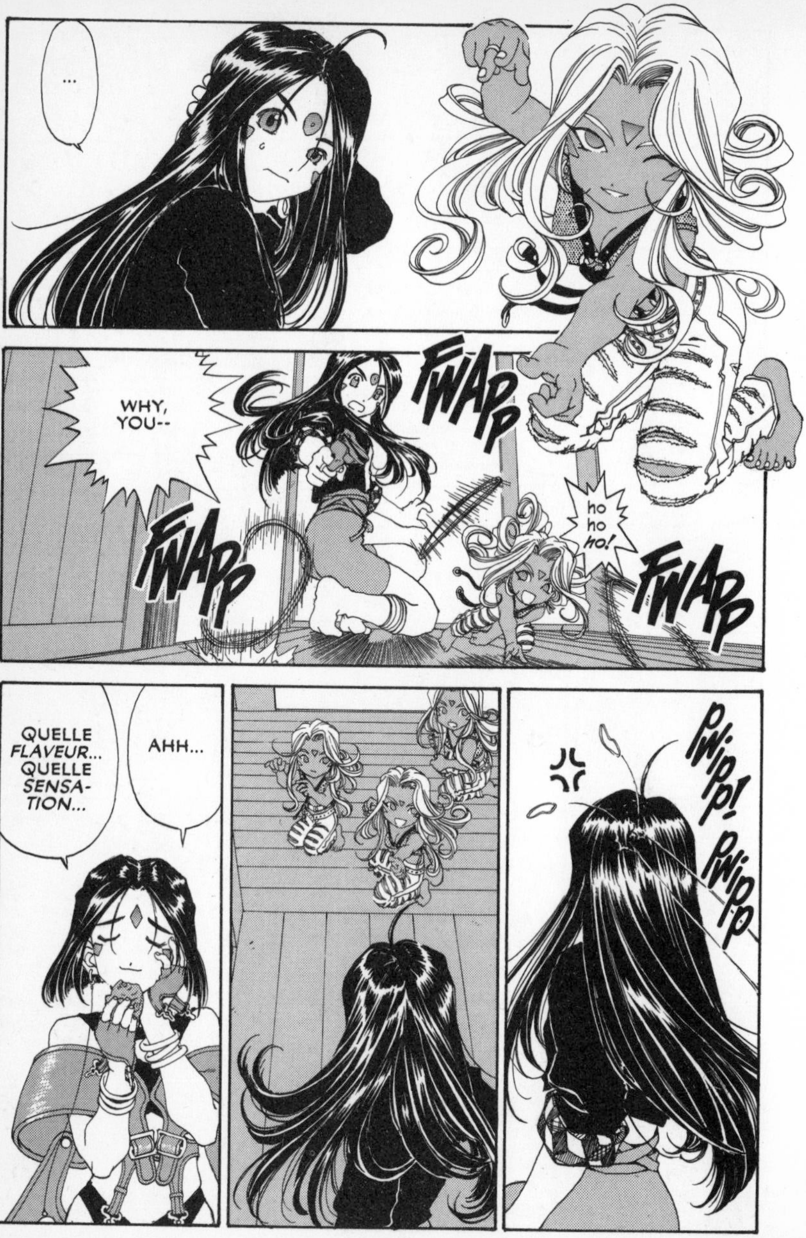
...
FWAPP
WHY, YOU--
ho ho ho!
FWAPP
FWAPP
PWIPP!
PWIPP
AHH...
QUELLE FLAVEUR... QUELLE SENSATION...

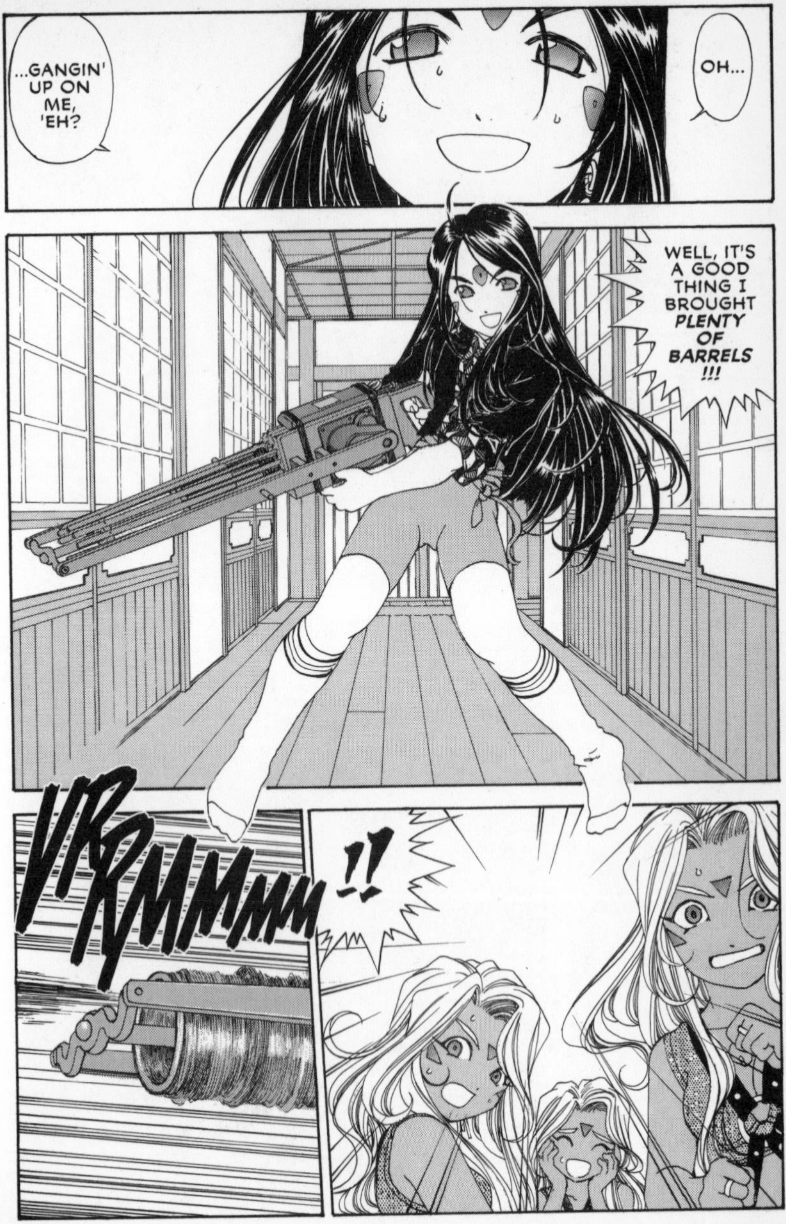
OH...
...GANGIN' UP ON ME, 'EH?
WELL, IT'S A GOOD THING I BROUGHT ***PLENTY OF BARRELS*** !!!
VRRMMMM!!

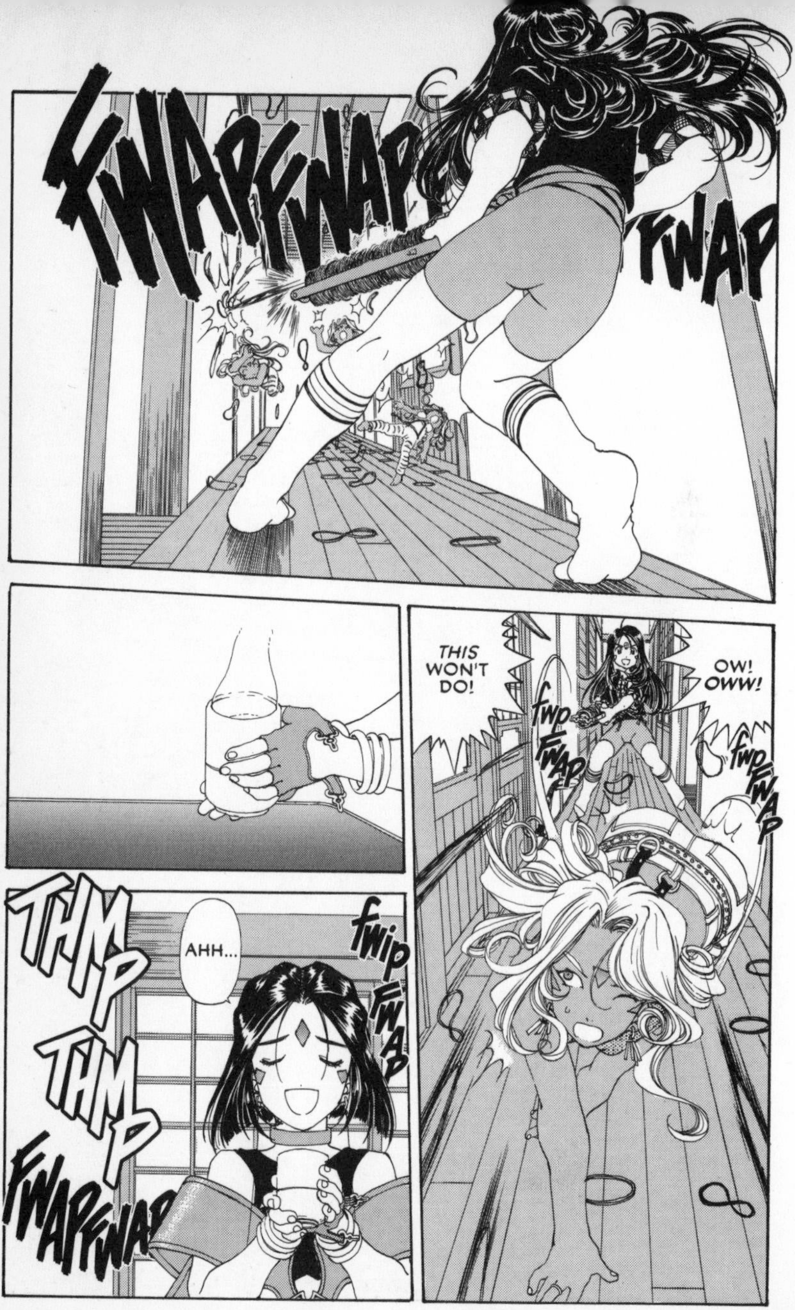
FWAP
FWAPFWAP
OW! OWW!
fwpFWAP
THIS WON'T DO!
fwpFWAP
fwipFWAP
AHH...
THMP THMP
FWAPFWAP

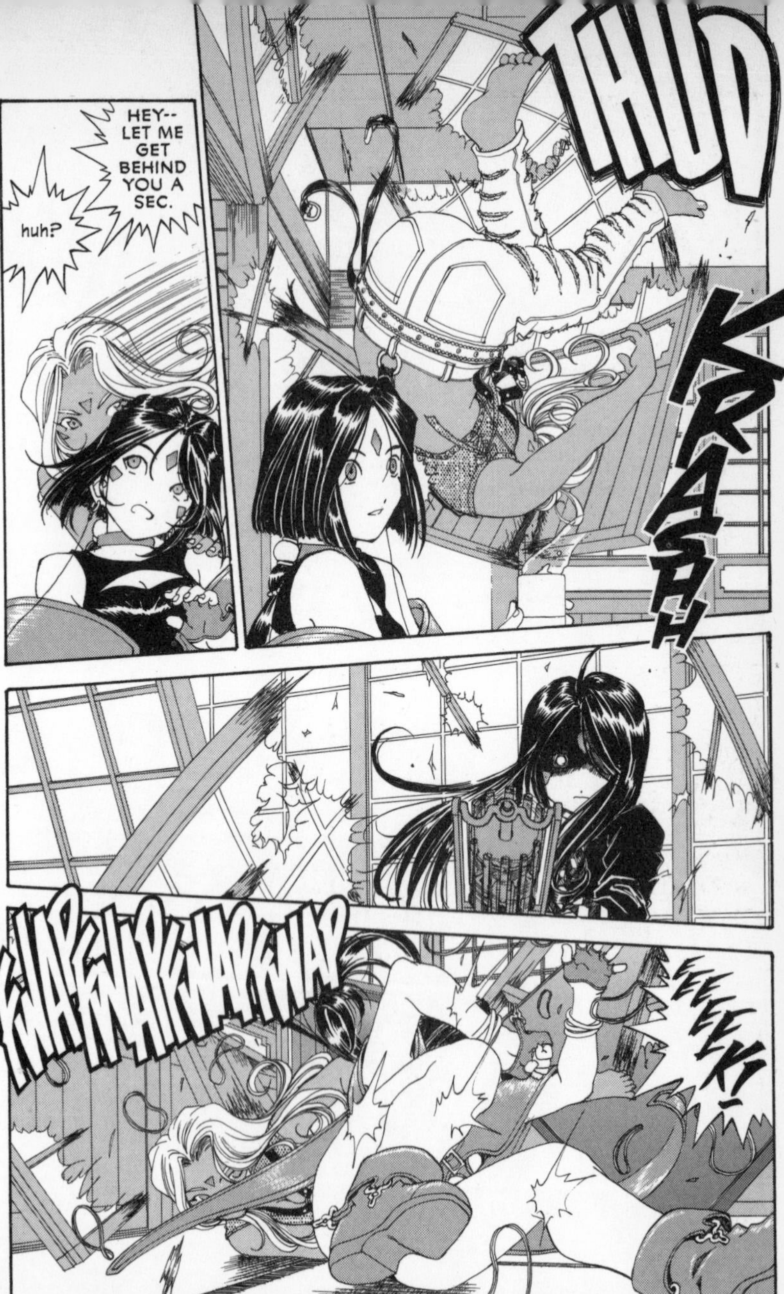
THUD
KRASHH!
HEY-- LET ME GET BEHIND YOU A SEC.
huh?
EEEEEK!
FWAPFWAPFWAPFWAP

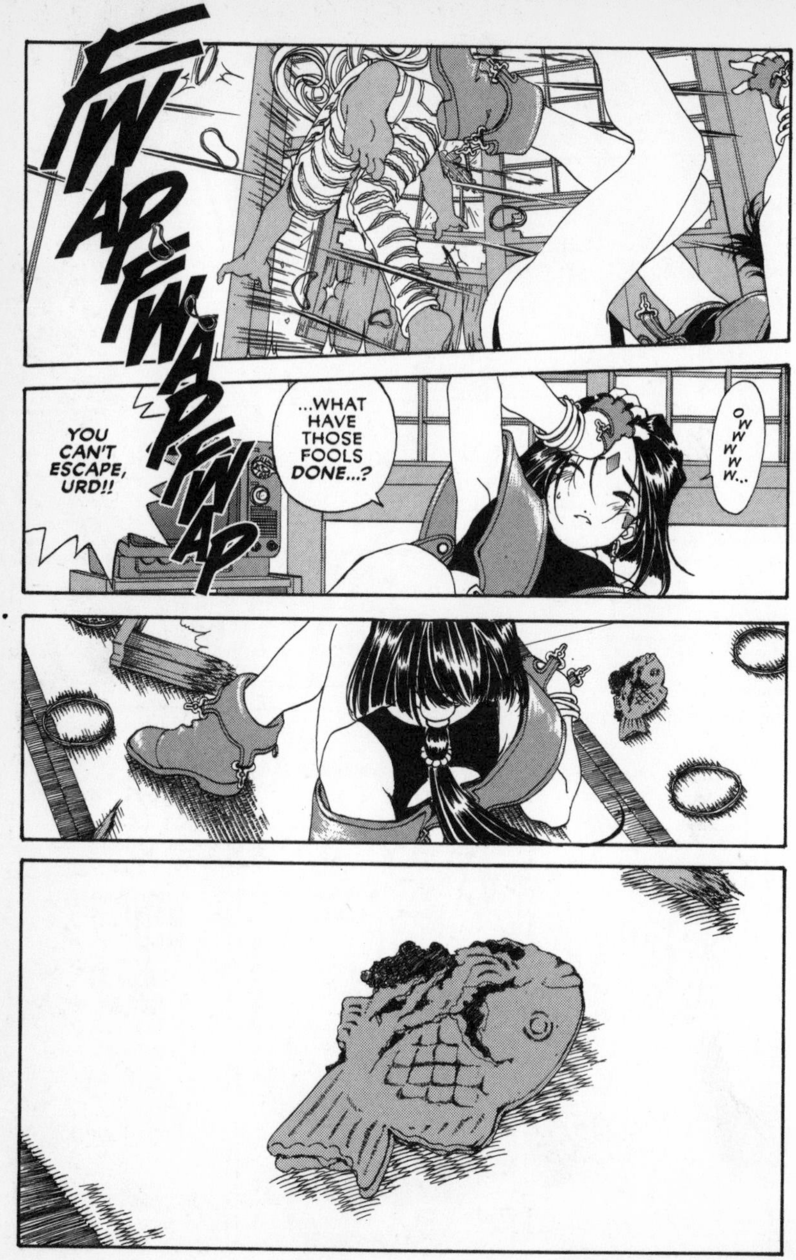
FWAP FWAP FWAP FWAP
OWWWWW...
...WHAT HAVE THOSE FOOLS DONE...?
YOU CAN'T ESCAPE, URD!!

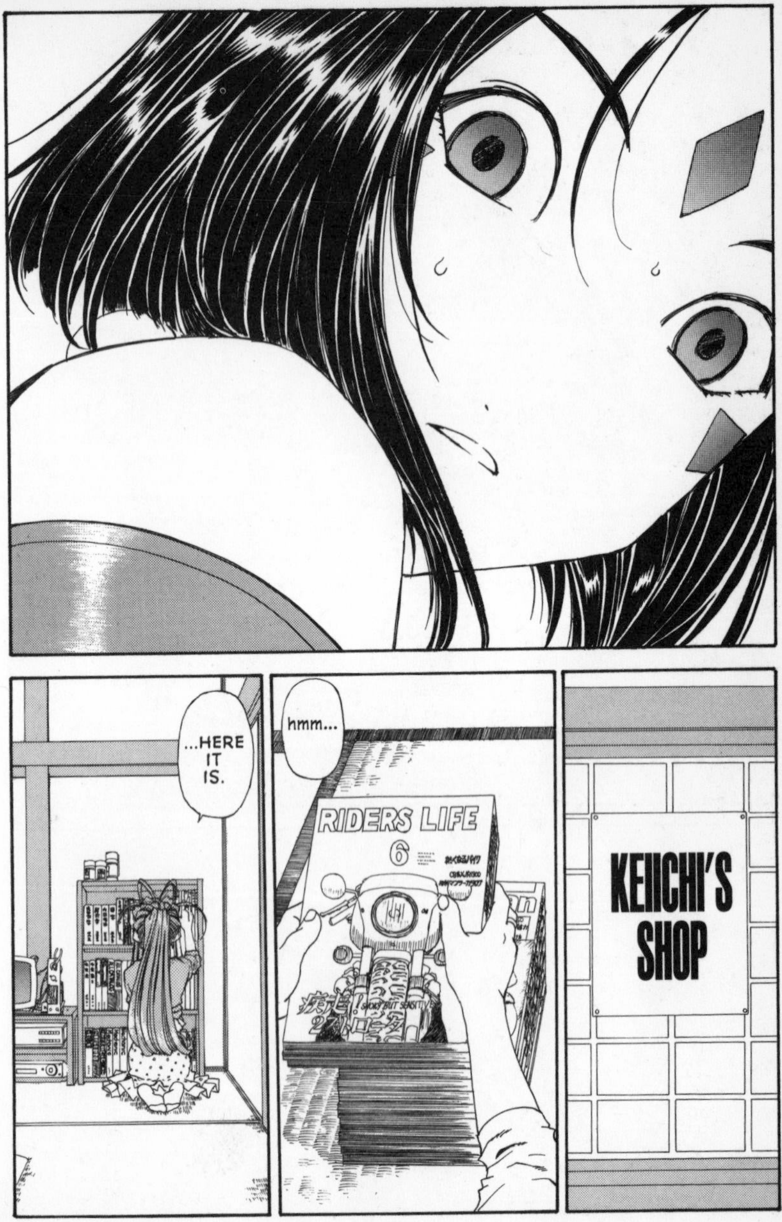
KEIICHI'S SHOP
hmm...
RIDERS LIFE
6
...HERE IT IS.

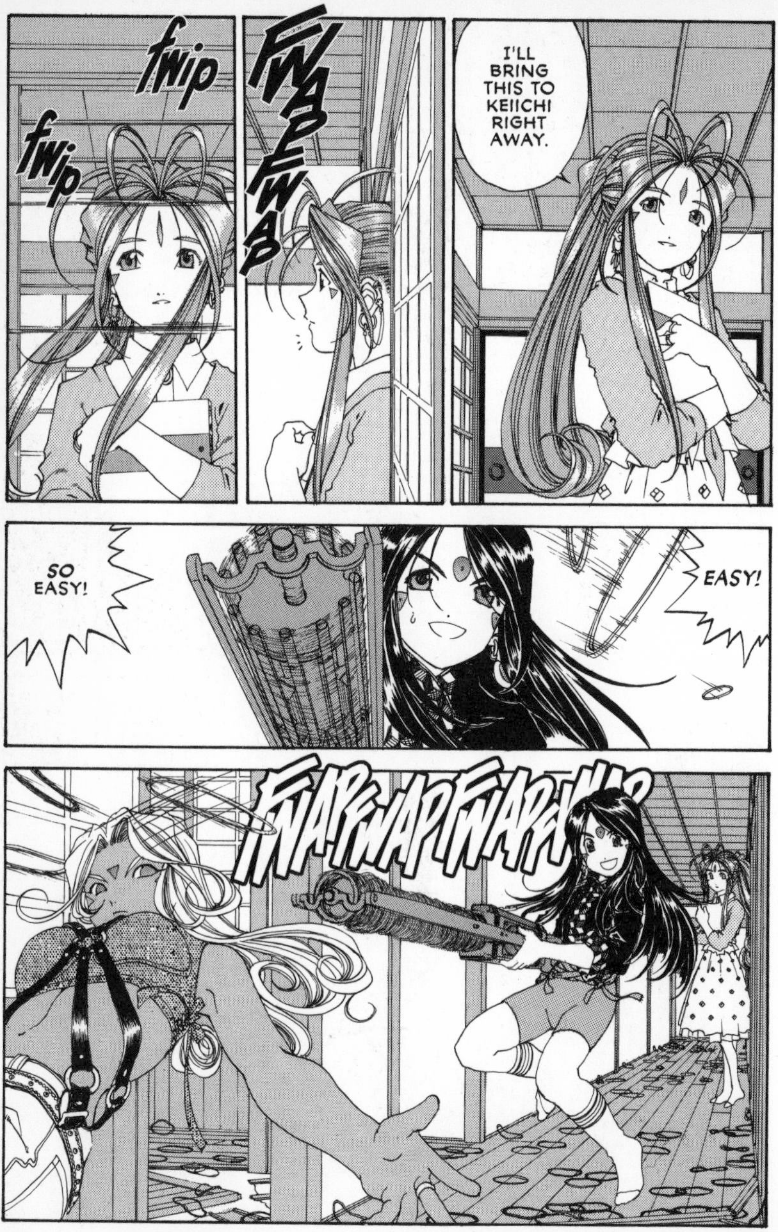
I'LL BRING THIS TO KEIICHI RIGHT AWAY.
FWAP FWAP
fwip
fwip
EASY!
SO EASY!
FWAP FWAP FWAP FWAP

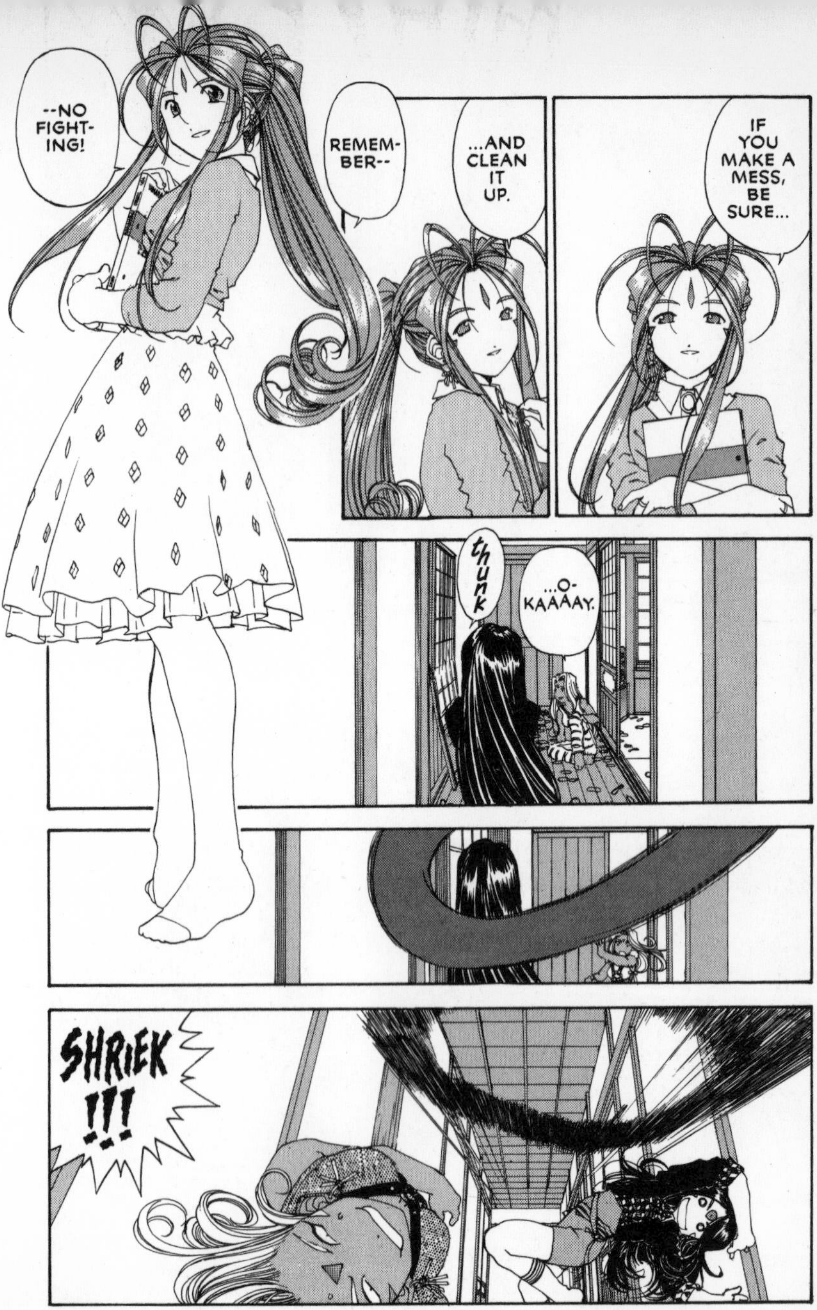
IF YOU MAKE A MESS, BE SURE...
...AND CLEAN IT UP.
REMEMBER--
--NO FIGHTING!
...O-KAAAAY.
thunk
SHRIEK!!!

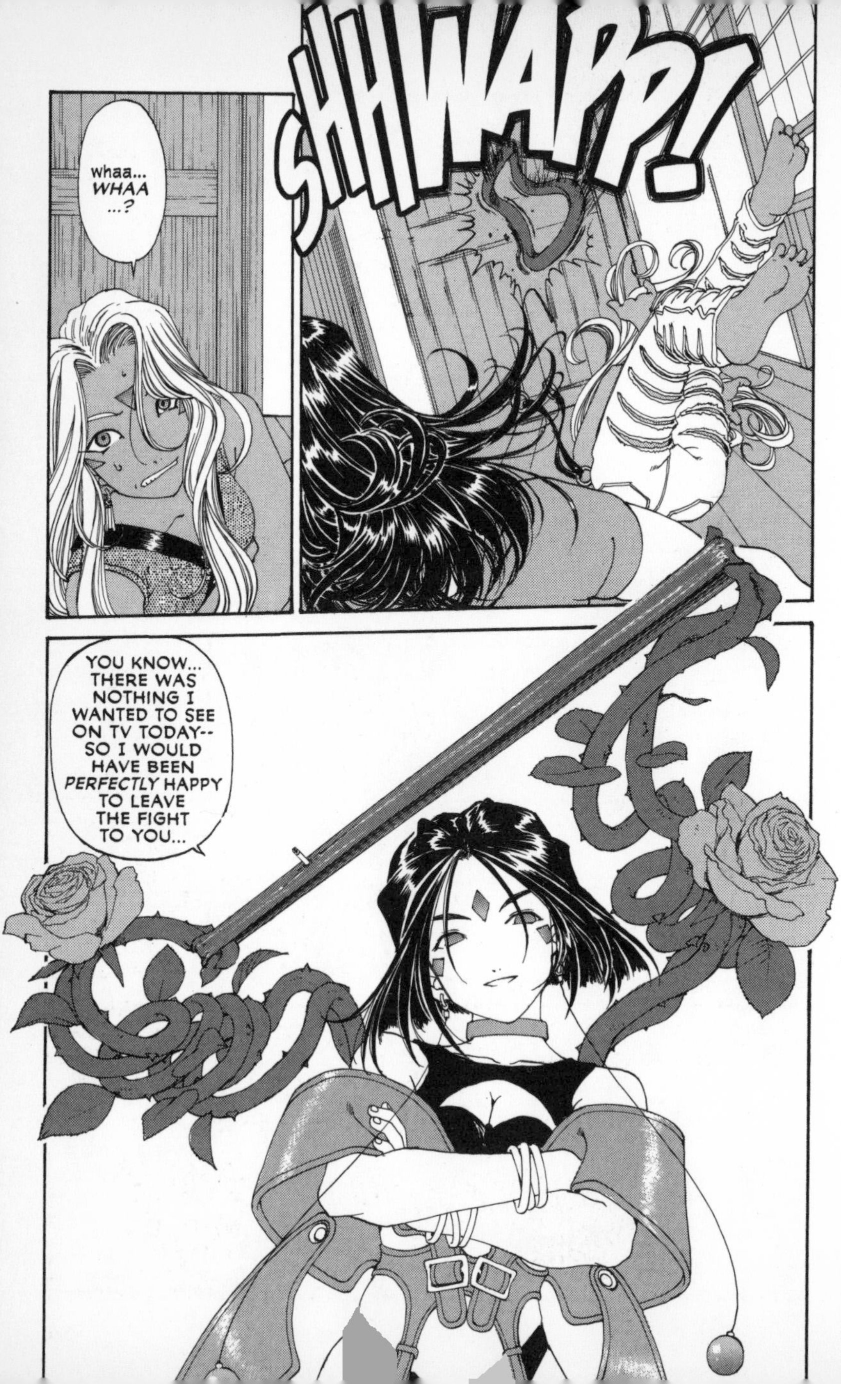
SHHWAPP!
whaa... WHAA ...?
YOU KNOW... THERE WAS NOTHING I WANTED TO SEE ON TV TODAY-- SO I WOULD HAVE BEEN *PERFECTLY* HAPPY TO LEAVE THE FIGHT TO YOU...

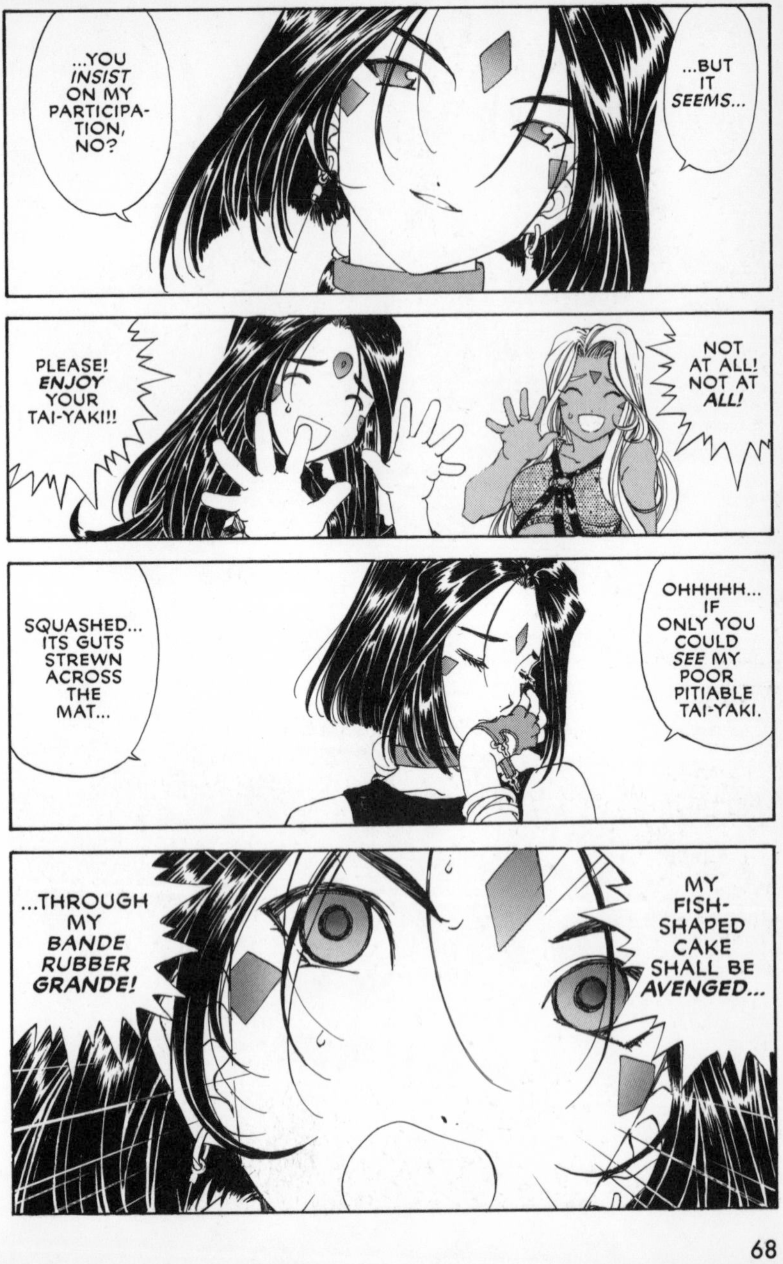
...BUT IT SEEMS...
...YOU INSIST ON MY PARTICIPATION, NO?
NOT AT ALL! NOT AT ALL!
PLEASE! ENJOY YOUR TAI-YAKI!!
OHHHHH... IF ONLY YOU COULD SEE MY POOR PITIABLE TAI-YAKI.
SQUASHED... ITS GUTS STREWN ACROSS THE MAT...
MY FISH-SHAPED CAKE SHALL BE AVENGED...
...THROUGH MY BANDE RUBBER GRANDE!

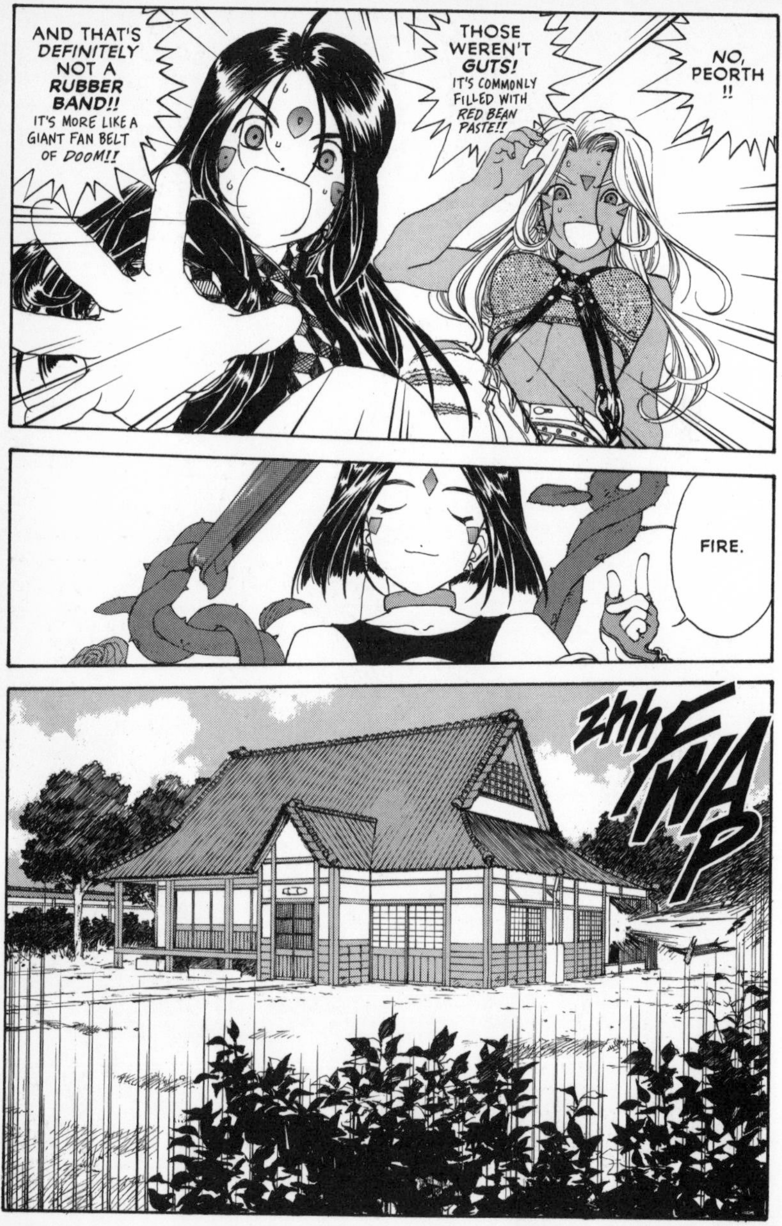
NO, PEORTH !!
THOSE WEREN'T GUTS! IT'S COMMONLY FILLED WITH RED BEAN PASTE!!
AND THAT'S DEFINITELY NOT A RUBBER BAND!! IT'S MORE LIKE A GIANT FAN BELT OF DOOM!!
FIRE.
ZHHFWAP

OH MY GODDESS!
S K U L D

CHAPTER 173

Horseshoes and Handgrenades

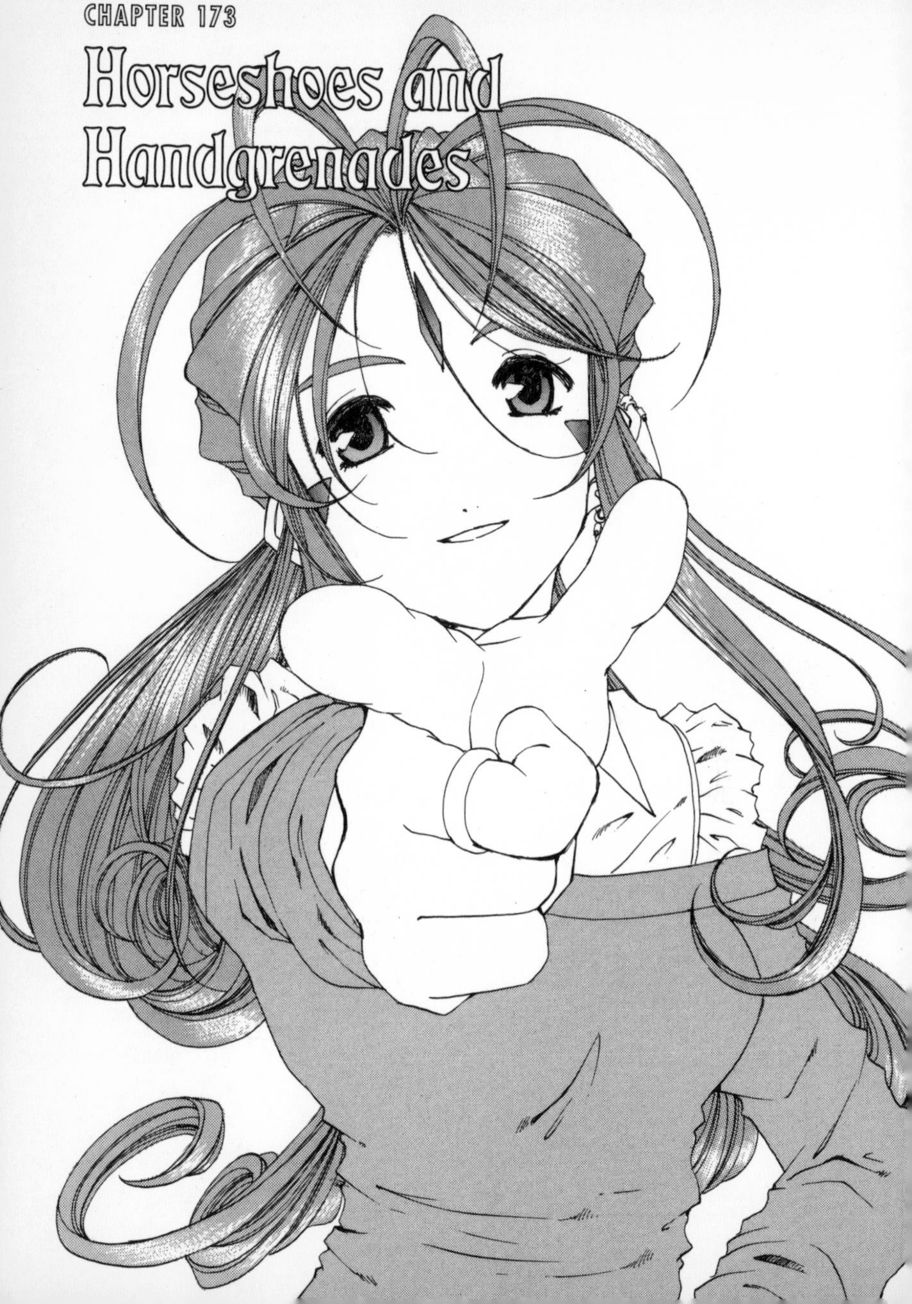

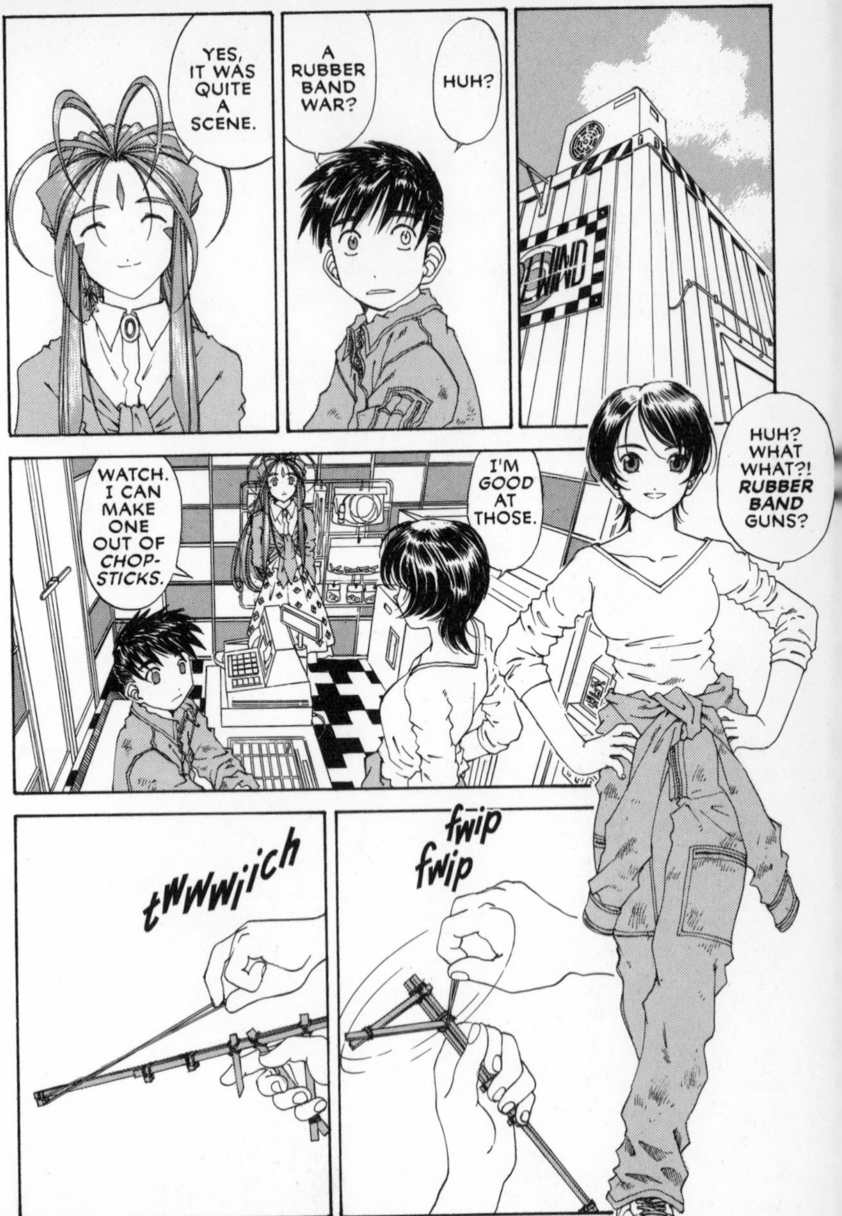
HUH?
A RUBBER BAND WAR?
YES, IT WAS QUITE A SCENE.
HUH? WHAT WHAT?! **RUBBER BAND** GUNS?
I'M *GOOD* AT THOSE.
WATCH. I CAN MAKE ONE OUT OF *CHOP-STICKS.*
fwip fwip
twwwiich

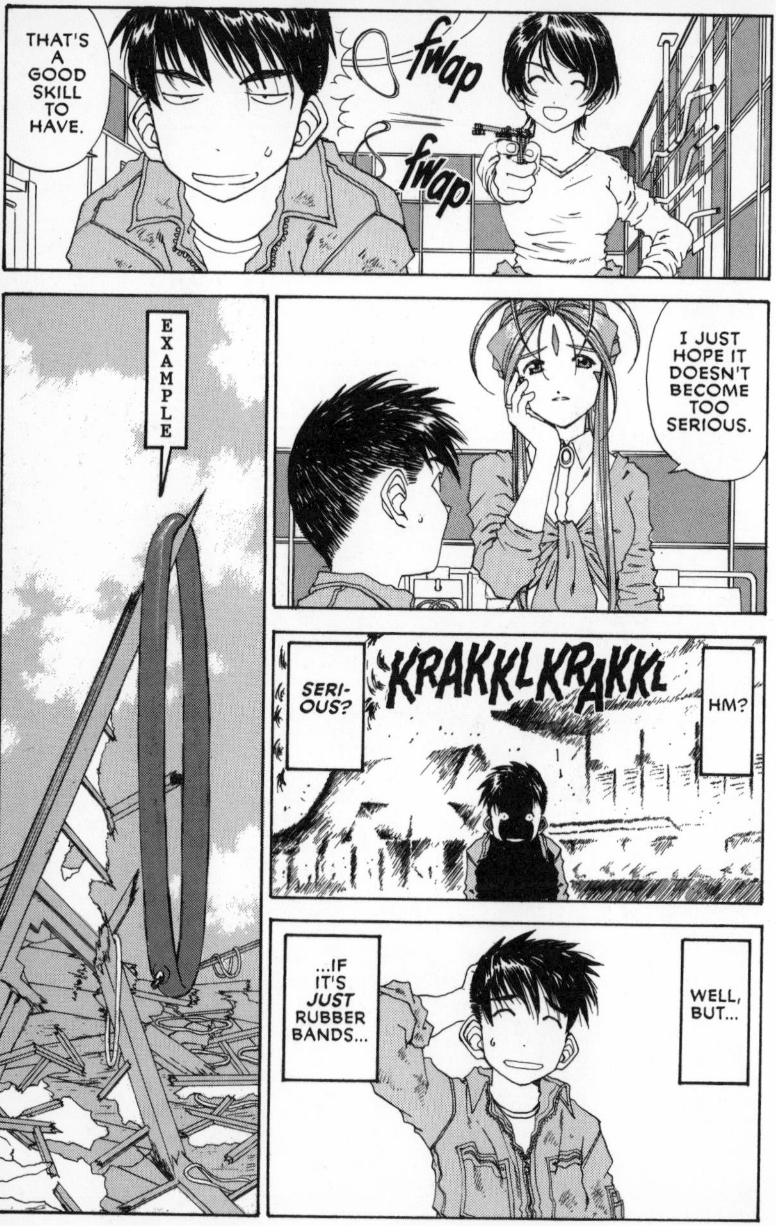
fwap
fwap
THAT'S A GOOD SKILL TO HAVE.
I JUST HOPE IT DOESN'T BECOME TOO SERIOUS.
HM?
KRAKKL KRAKKL
SERI-OUS?
WELL, BUT...
...IF IT'S *JUST* RUBBER BANDS...
EXAMPLE

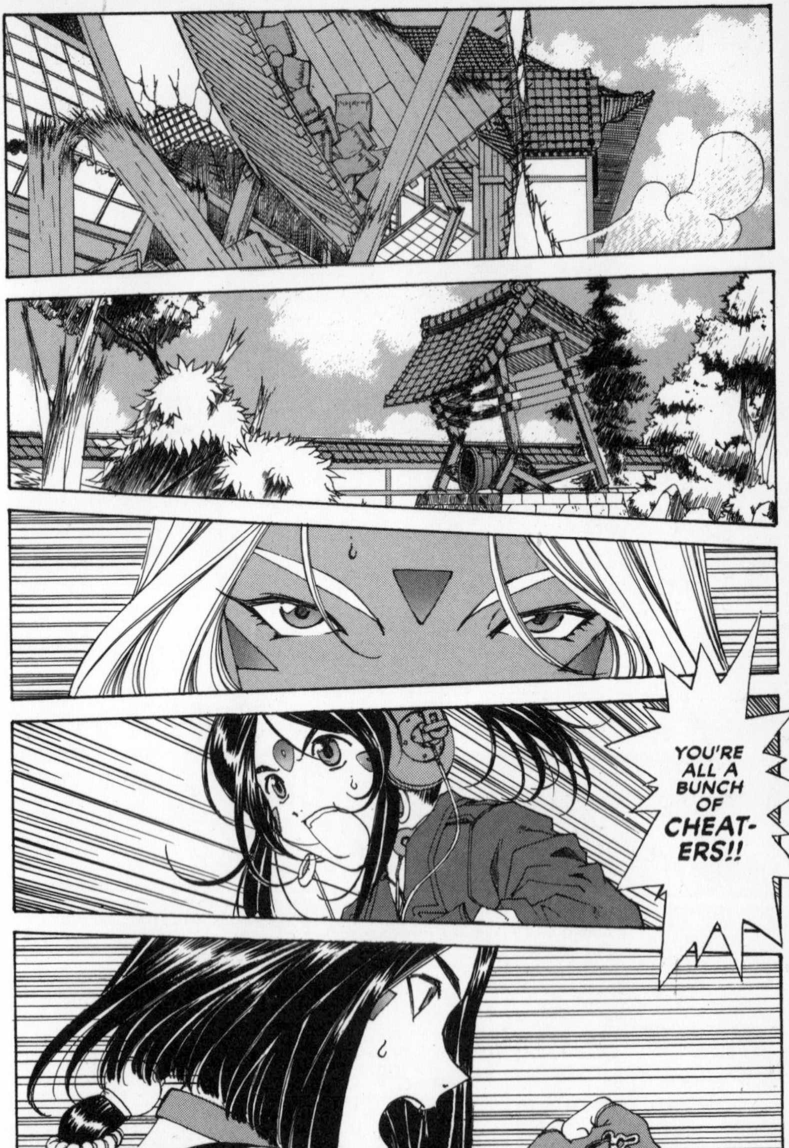
YOU'RE ALL A BUNCH OF CHEAT-ERS!!

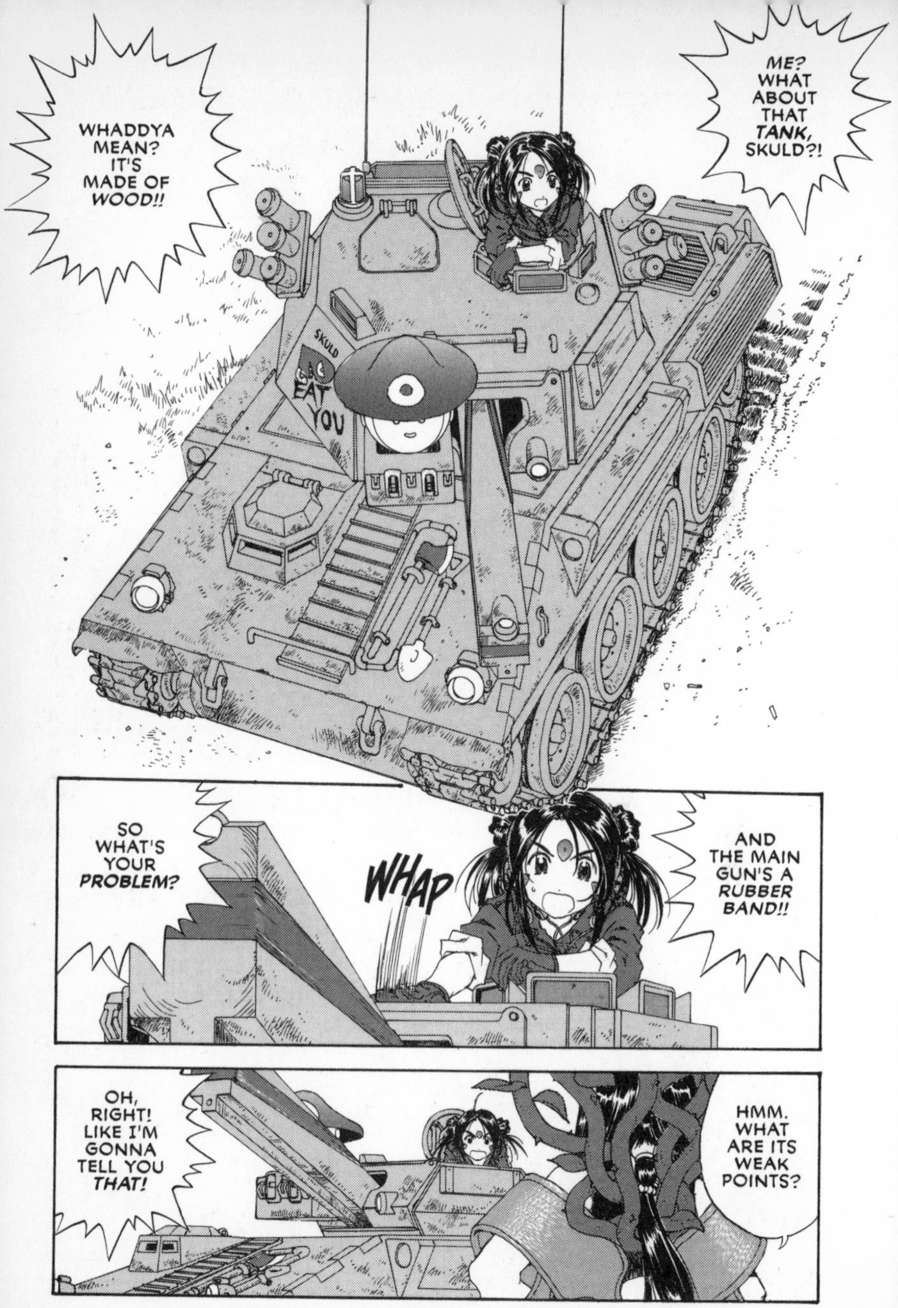
ME? WHAT ABOUT THAT TANK, SKULD?!
WHADDYA MEAN? IT'S MADE OF WOOD!!
SKULD
EAT YOU
AND THE MAIN GUN'S A RUBBER BAND!!
WHAP
SO WHAT'S YOUR PROBLEM?
HMM. WHAT ARE ITS WEAK POINTS?
OH, RIGHT! LIKE I'M GONNA TELL YOU THAT!

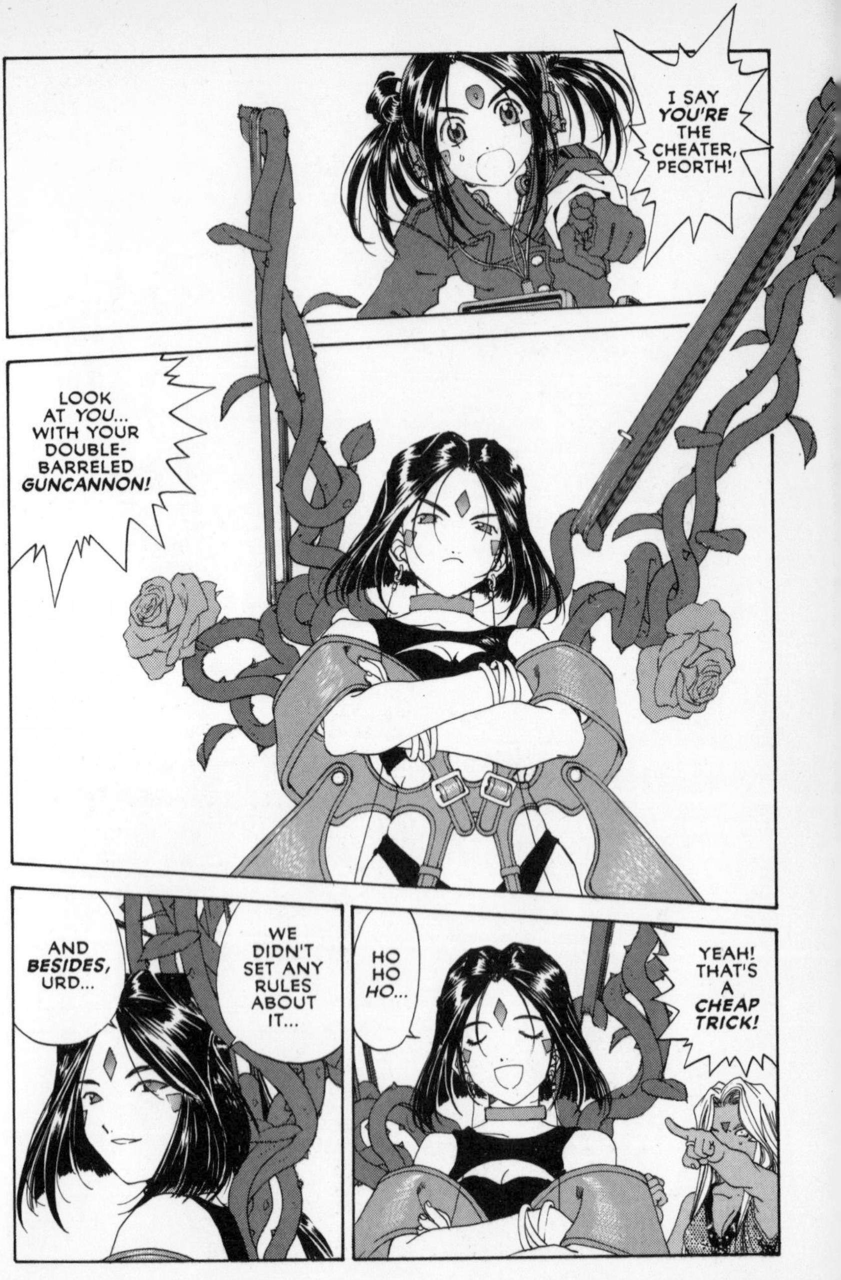
I SAY YOU'RE THE CHEATER, PEORTH!
LOOK AT YOU... WITH YOUR DOUBLE-BARRELED GUNCANNON!
YEAH! THAT'S A CHEAP TRICK!
HO HO HO...
WE DIDN'T SET ANY RULES ABOUT IT...
AND BESIDES, URD...

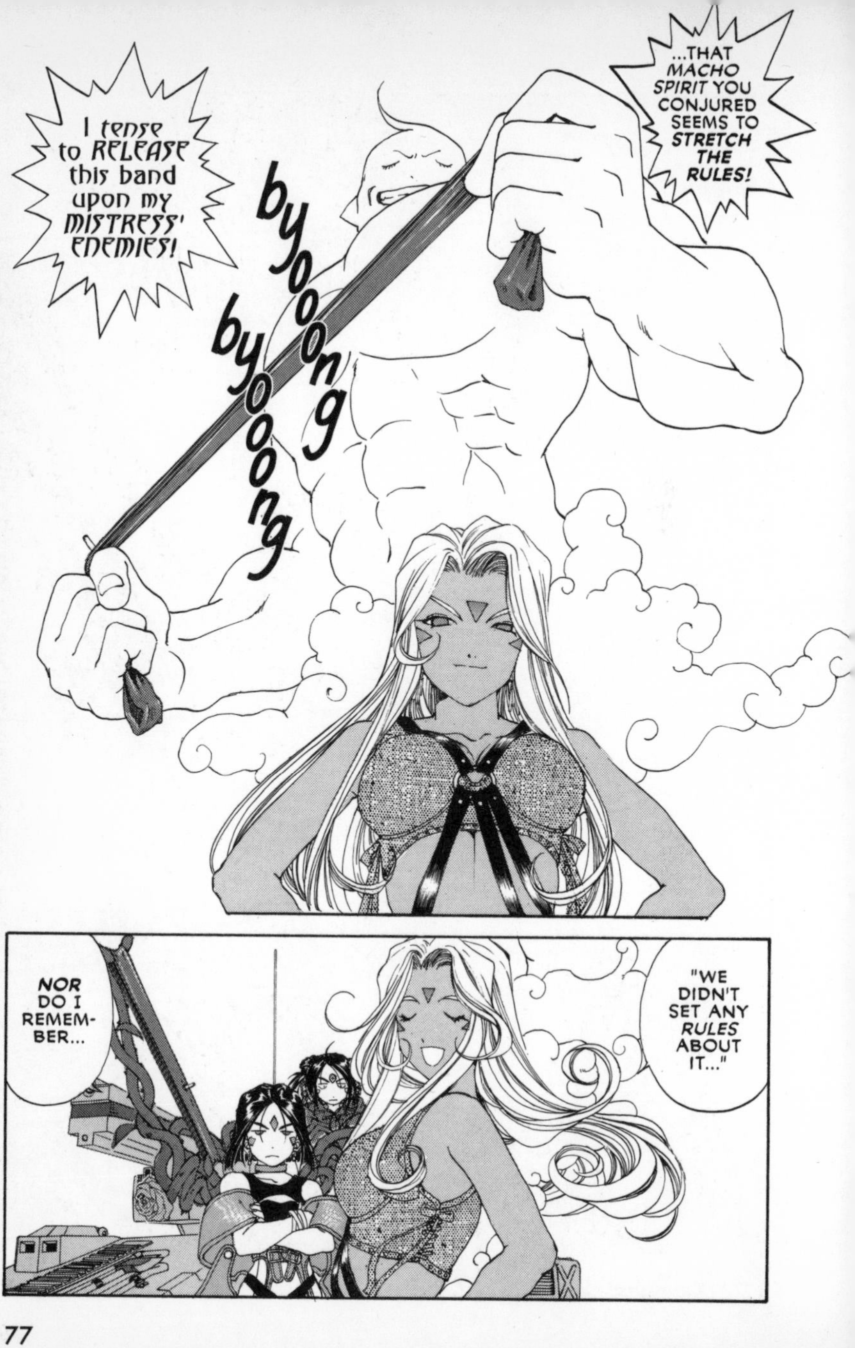
...THAT MACHO SPIRIT YOU CONJURED SEEMS TO STRETCH THE RULES!
I tense to RELEASE this band upon my MISTRESS' ENEMIES!
byoooong
byoooong
"WE DIDN'T SET ANY RULES ABOUT IT..."
NOR DO I REMEMBER...

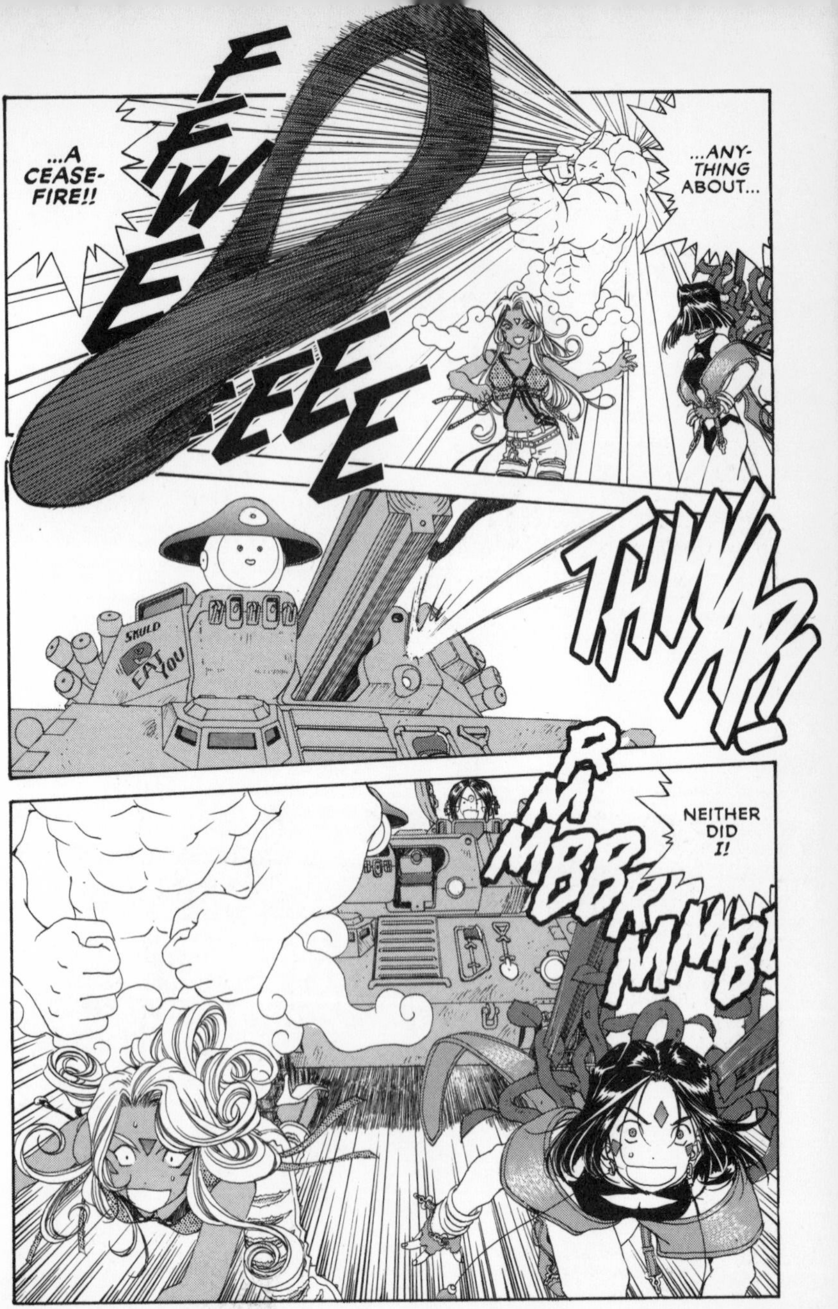
...ANY-THING ABOUT...
...A CEASE-FIRE!!
FFWEEEEE
THWAP!!
RMMBBRMMMB
NEITHER DID I!

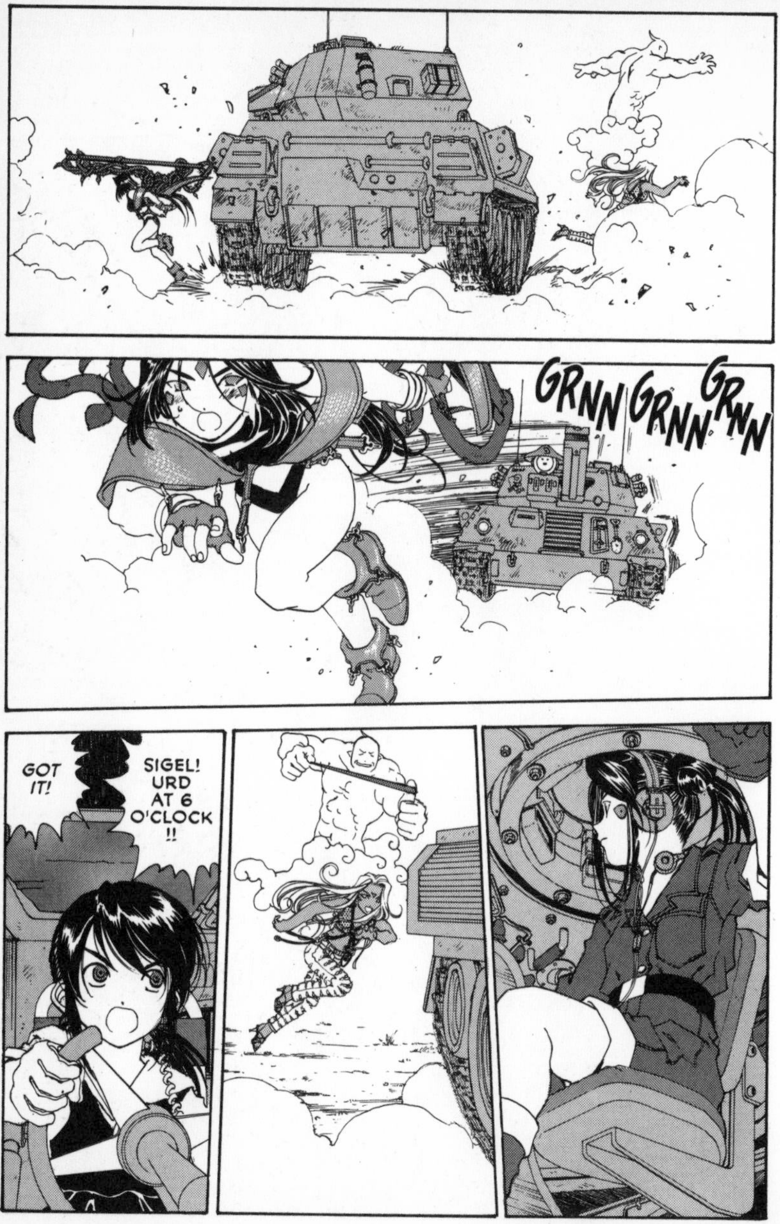
GRNN GRNN GRNN
SIGEL! URD AT 6 O'CLOCK !!
GOT IT!

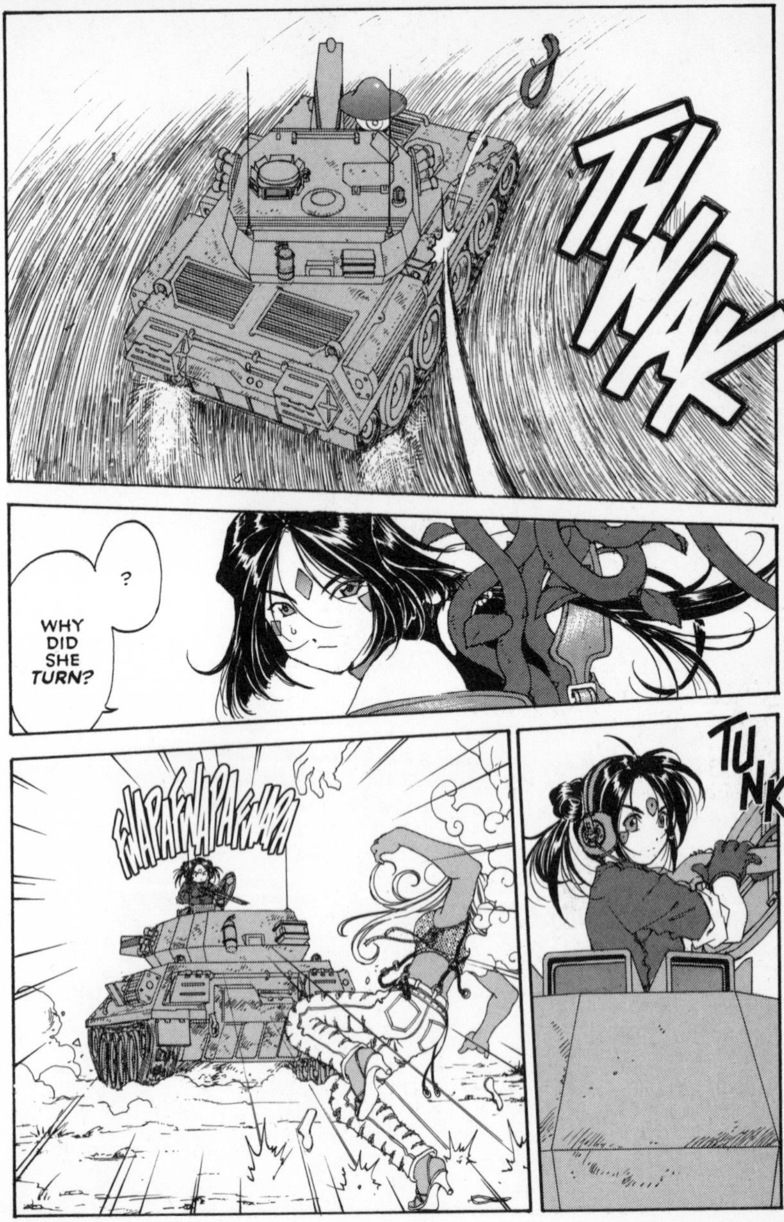
THWAK
?
WHY DID SHE TURN?
TUNK
FWAPAFWAPAFWAPA

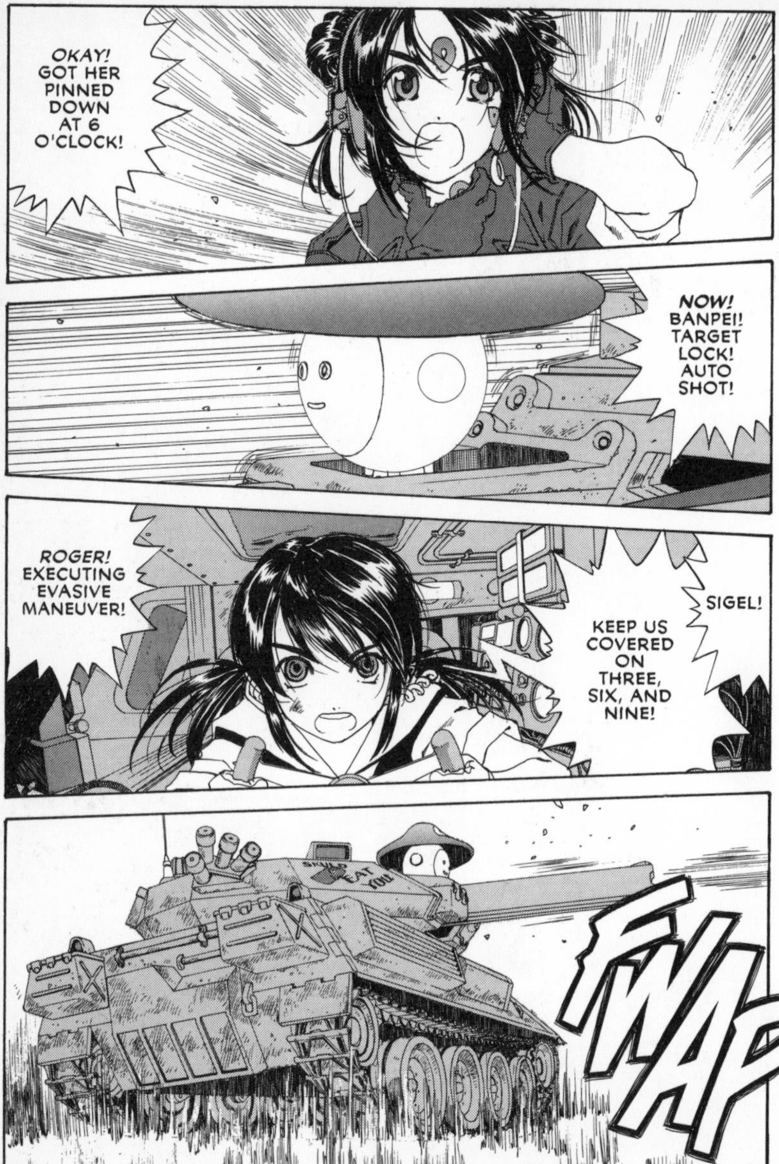
OKAY! GOT HER PINNED DOWN AT 6 O'CLOCK!
NOW! BANPEI! TARGET LOCK! AUTO SHOT!
SIGEL!
KEEP US COVERED ON THREE, SIX, AND NINE!
ROGER! EXECUTING EVASIVE MANEUVER!
FWAP

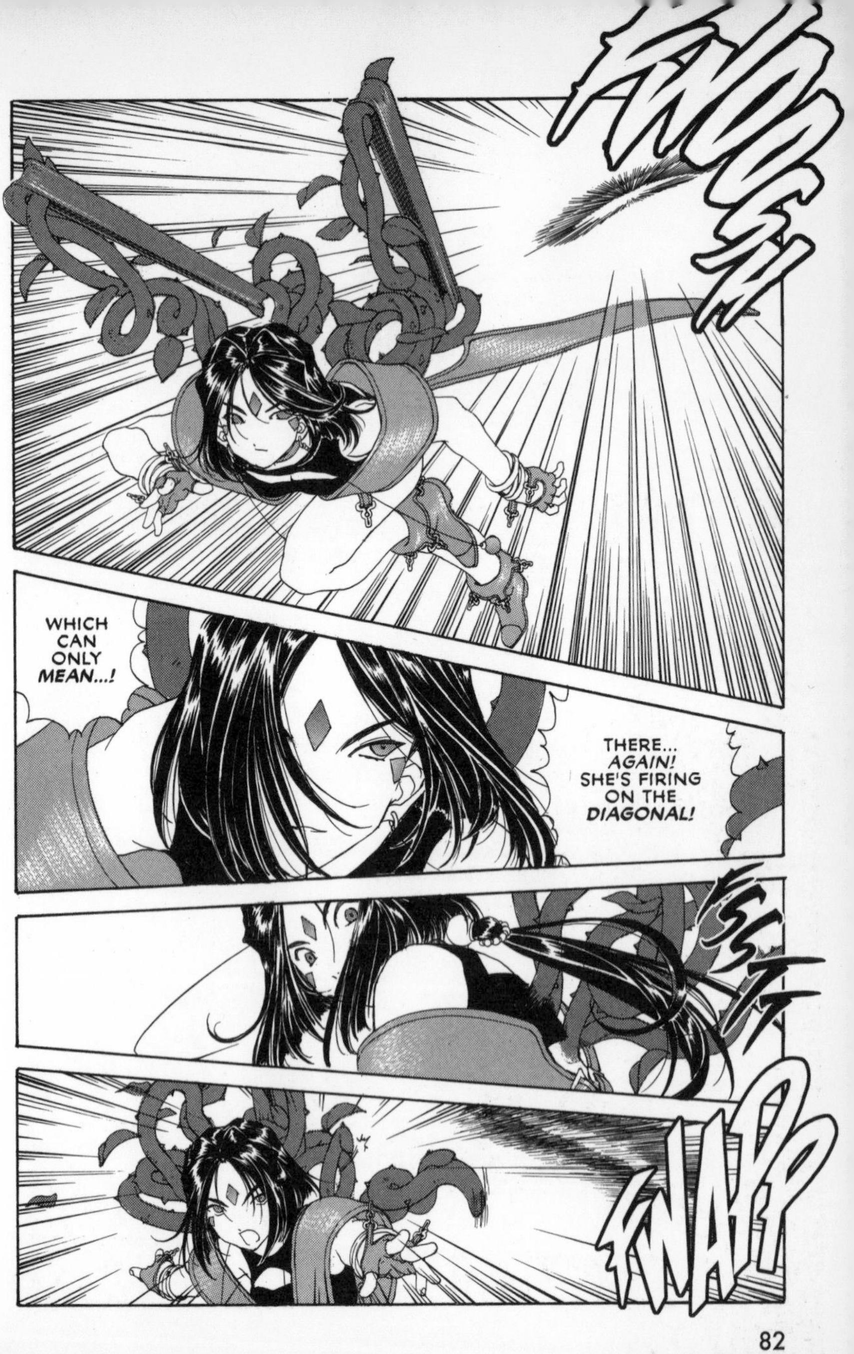
FWOOSH
THERE... AGAIN! SHE'S FIRING ON THE DIAGONAL!
WHICH CAN ONLY MEAN...!
FWAPP

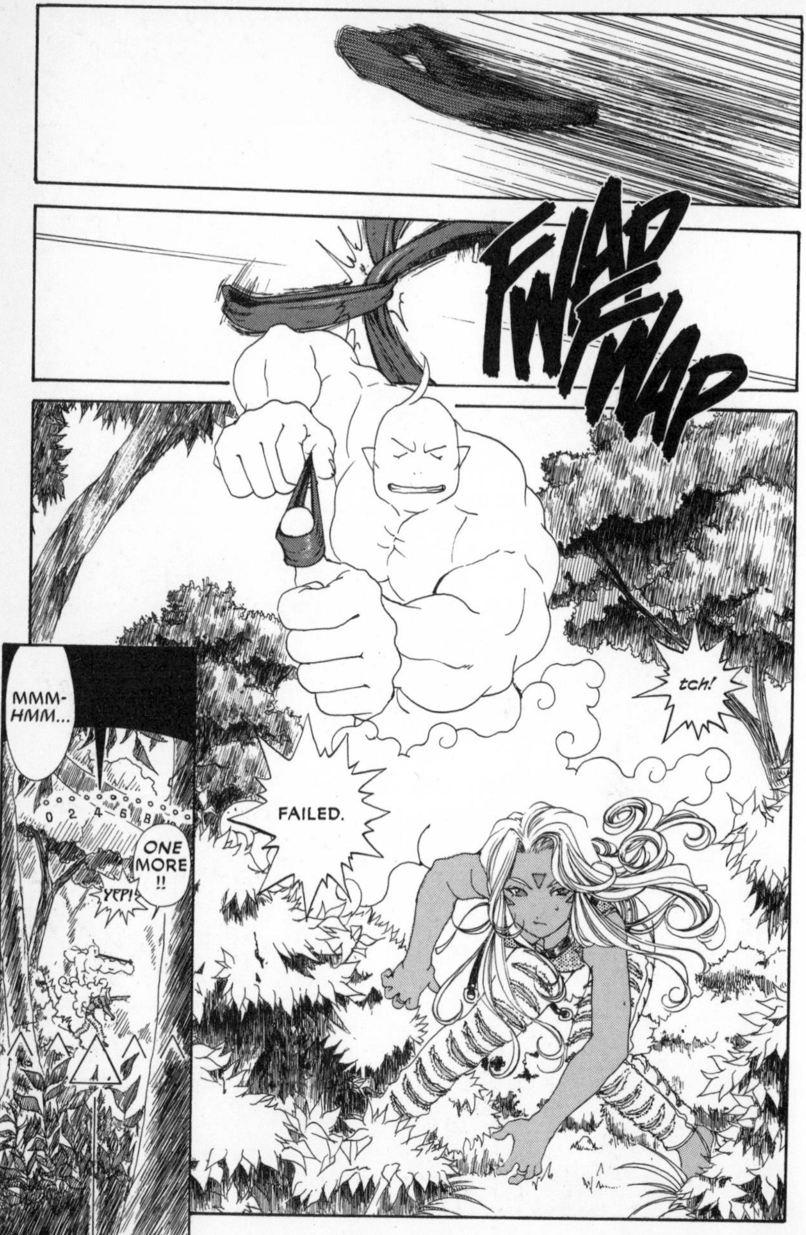
FWAP FWAP
tch!
FAILED.
MMM-HMM...
ONE MORE !!
YEP!

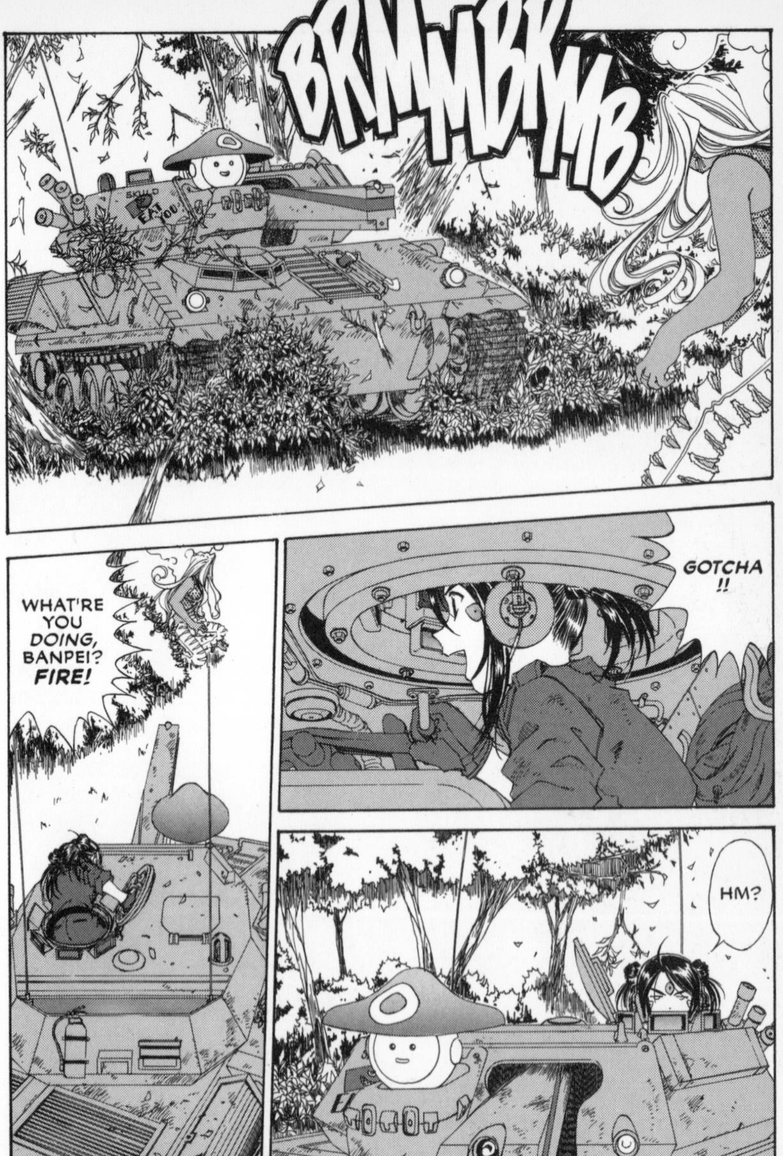
BRMMBRMMB
GOTCHA !!
HM?
WHAT'RE YOU *DOING,* BANPEI? *FIRE!*

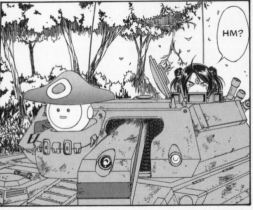

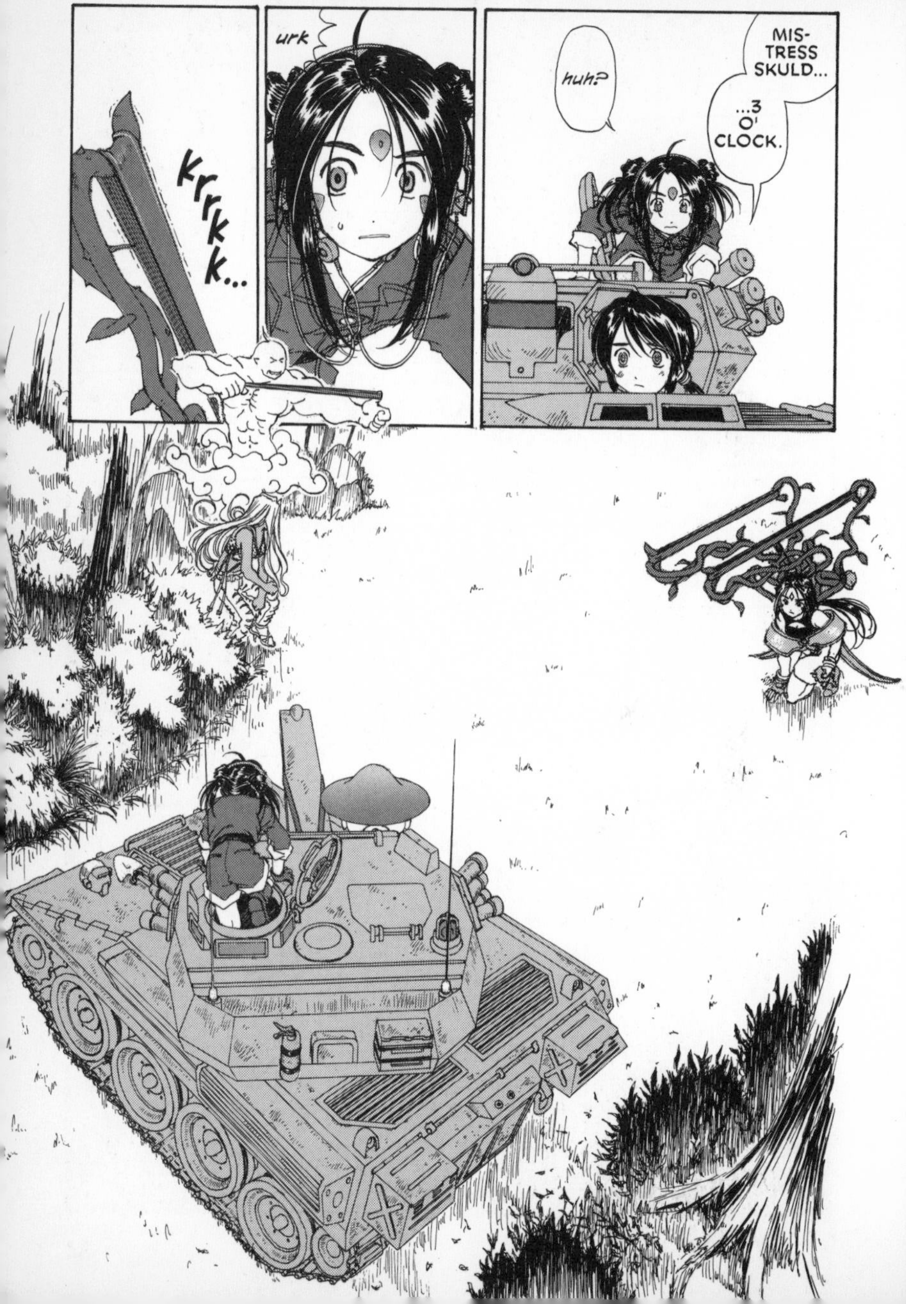
MIS-
TRESS
SKULD...
...3
O'
CLOCK.
huh?
urk
krrkk...

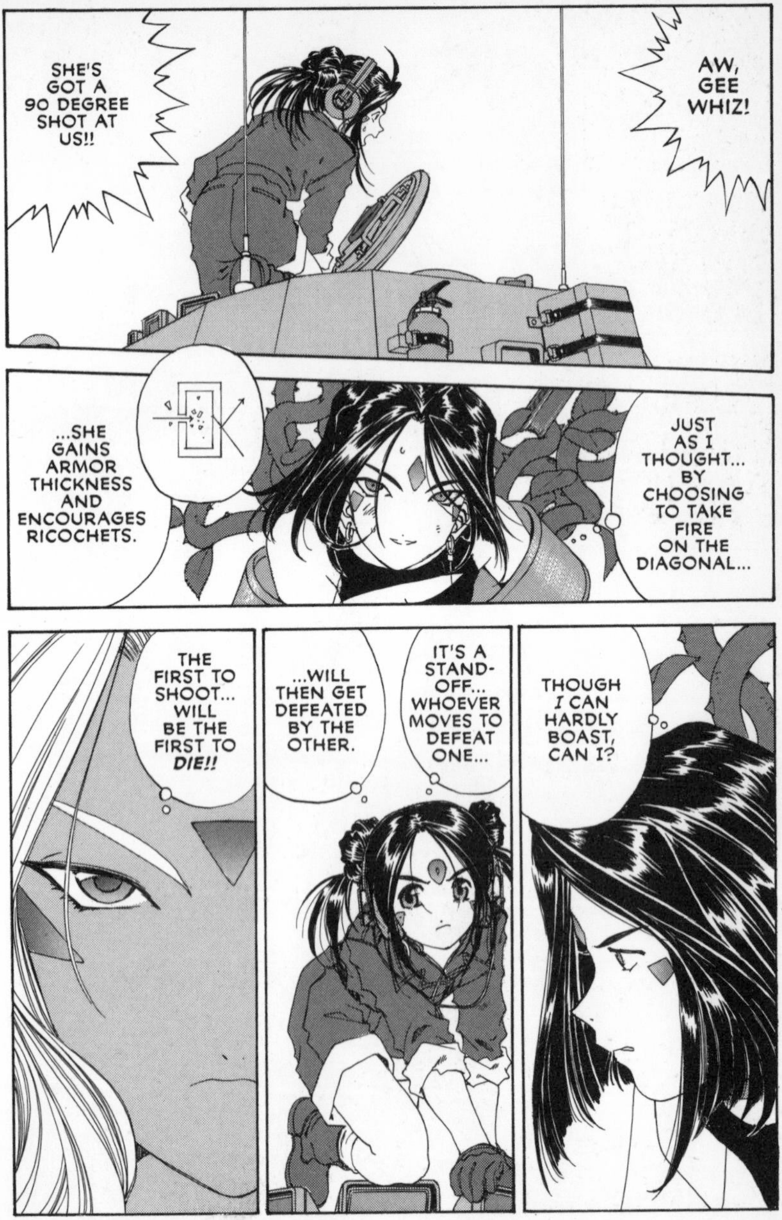
AW, GEE WHIZ!
SHE'S GOT A 90 DEGREE SHOT AT US!!
JUST AS I THOUGHT... BY CHOOSING TO TAKE FIRE ON THE DIAGONAL...
...SHE GAINS ARMOR THICKNESS AND ENCOURAGES RICOCHETS.
THOUGH *I* CAN HARDLY BOAST, CAN I?
IT'S A STAND-OFF... WHOEVER MOVES TO DEFEAT ONE...
...WILL THEN GET DEFEATED BY THE OTHER.
THE FIRST TO SHOOT... WILL BE THE FIRST TO *DIE!!*

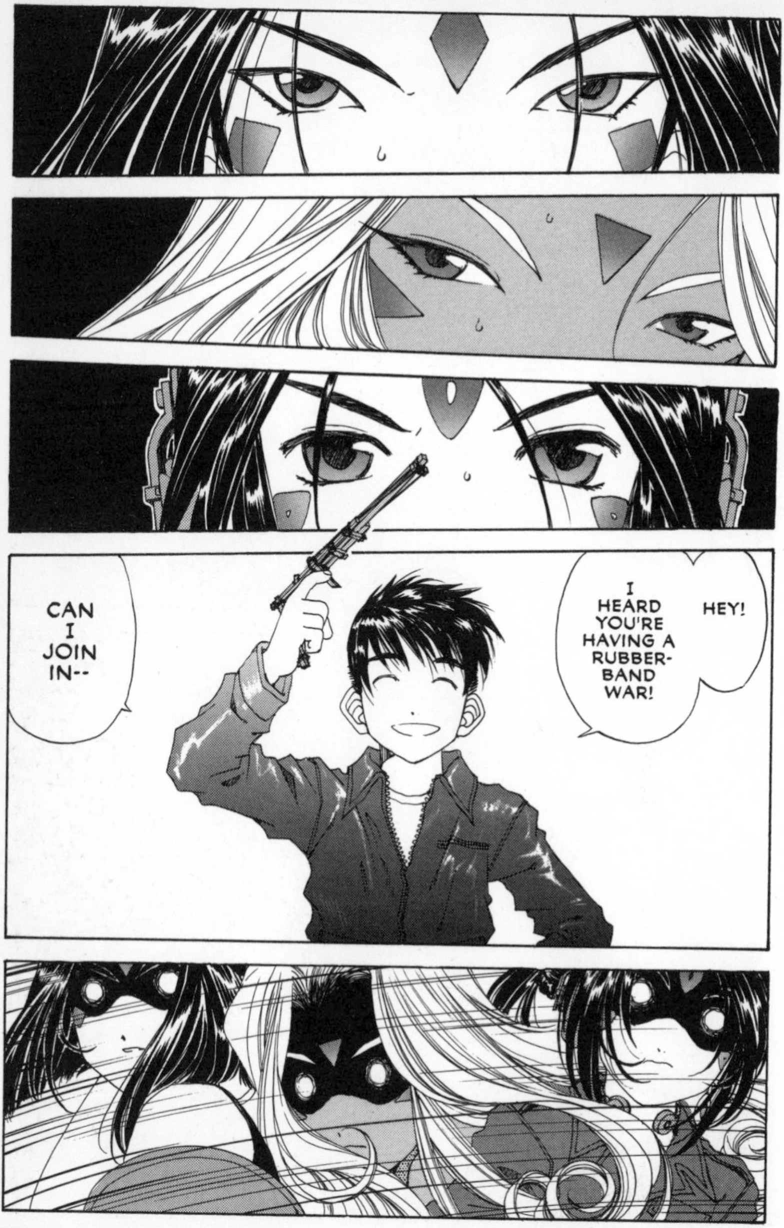
HEY!
I HEARD YOU'RE HAVING A RUBBER-BAND WAR!
CAN I JOIN IN--

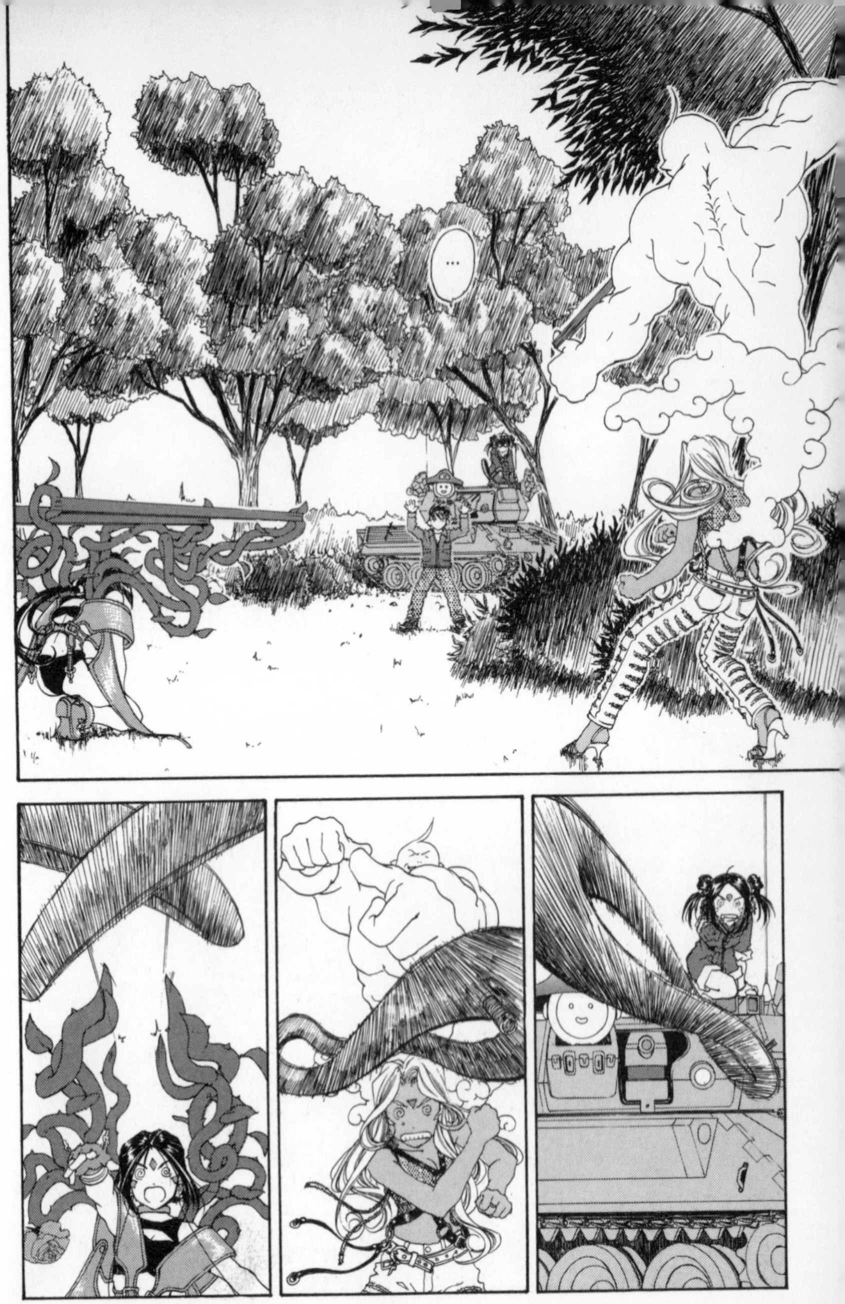
...

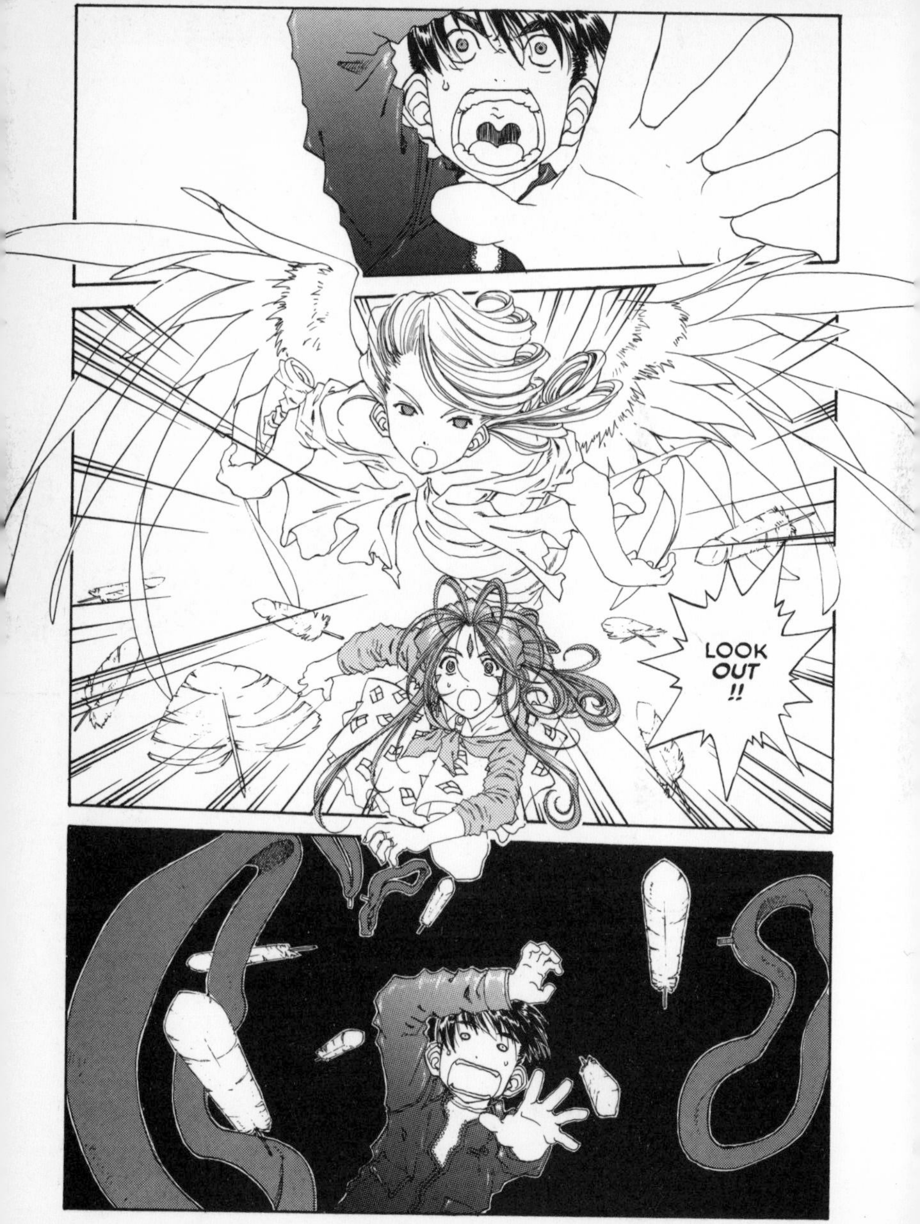
LOOK OUT !!

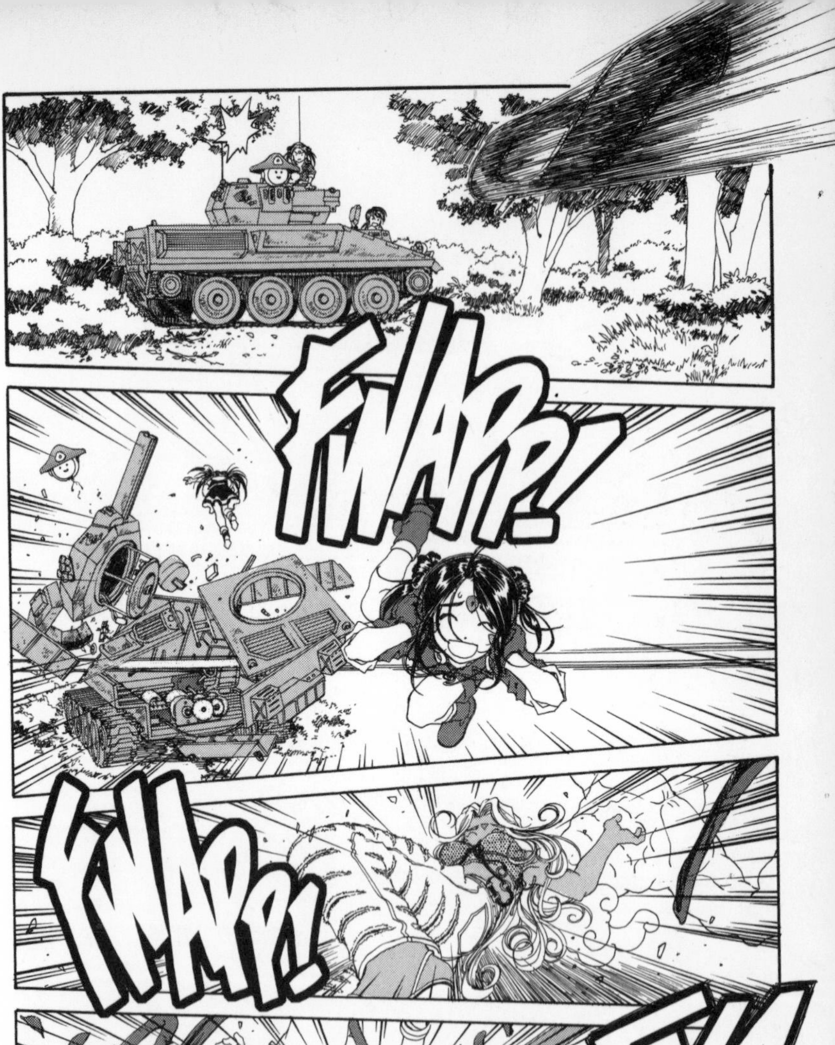
FWAPP!
FWAPP!
FWAPP!

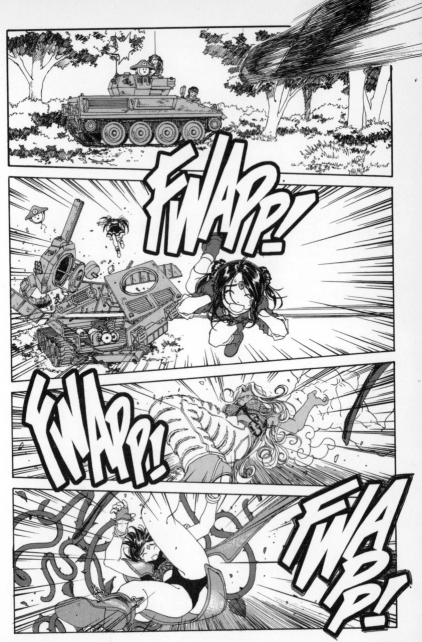

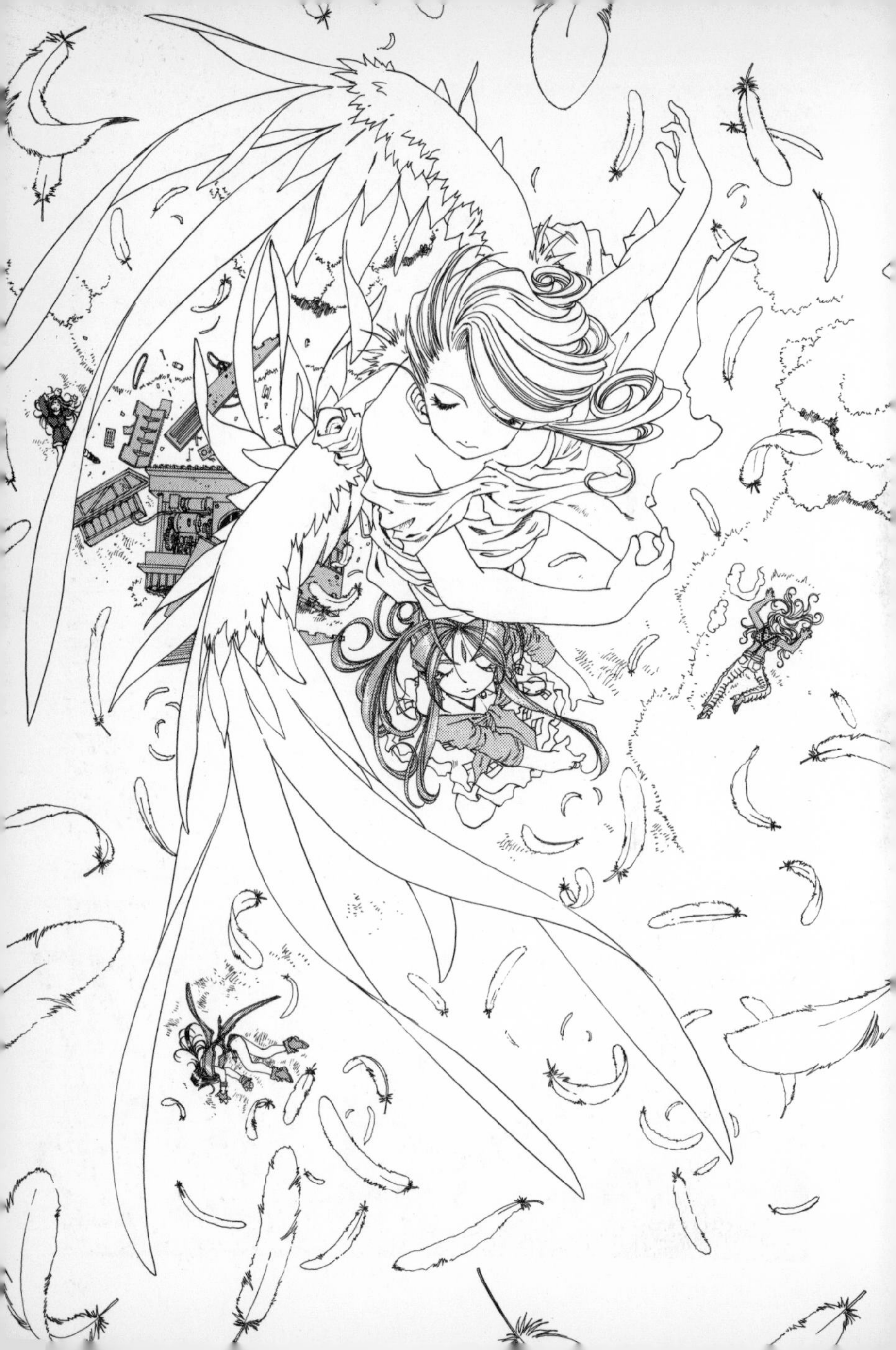

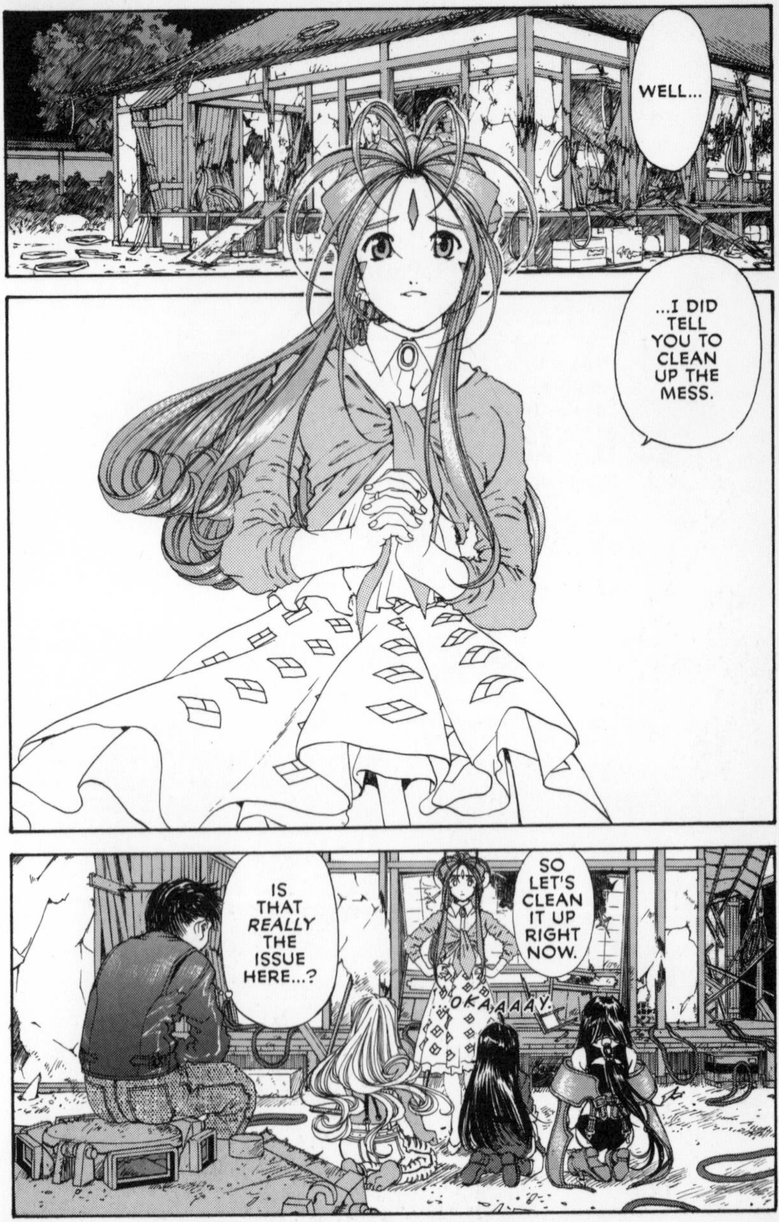
WELL...
...I DID TELL YOU TO CLEAN UP THE MESS.
SO LET'S CLEAN IT UP RIGHT NOW.
OKAAAAAY.
IS THAT *REALLY* THE ISSUE HERE...?

CHAPTER 174

Is Here She?

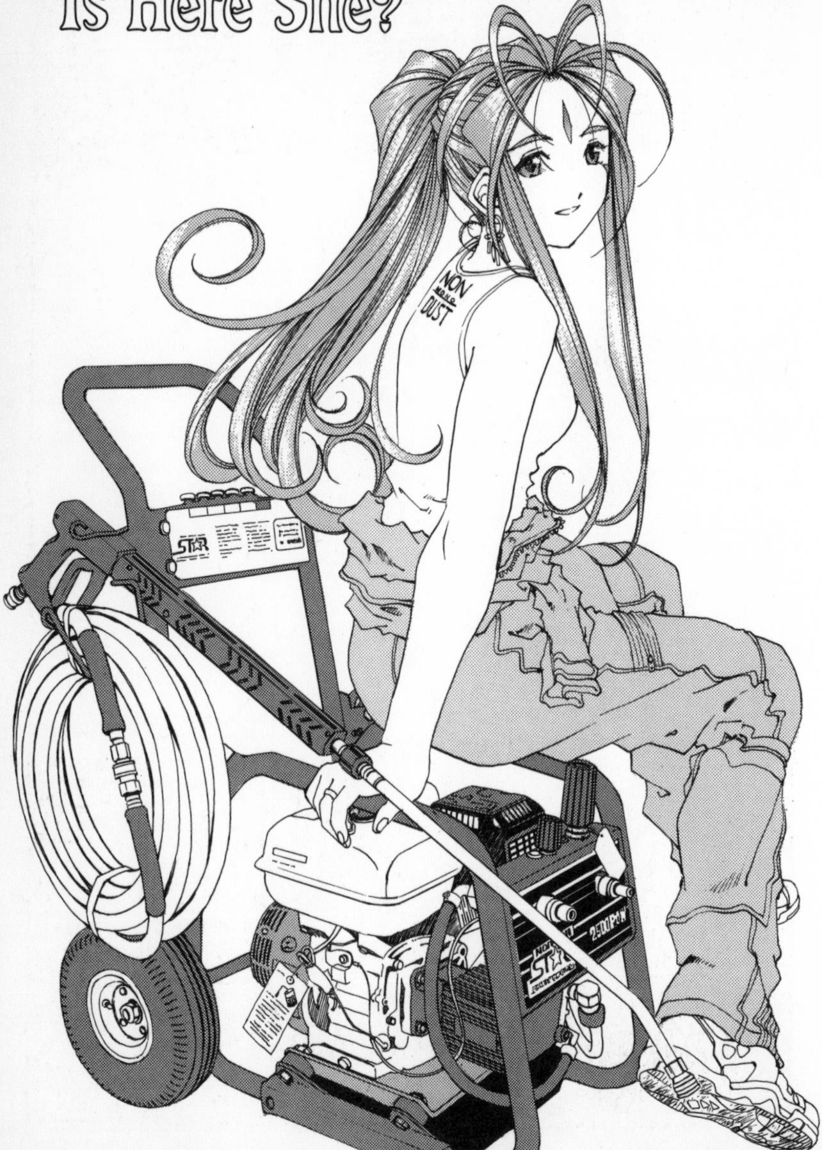
NON
DUST

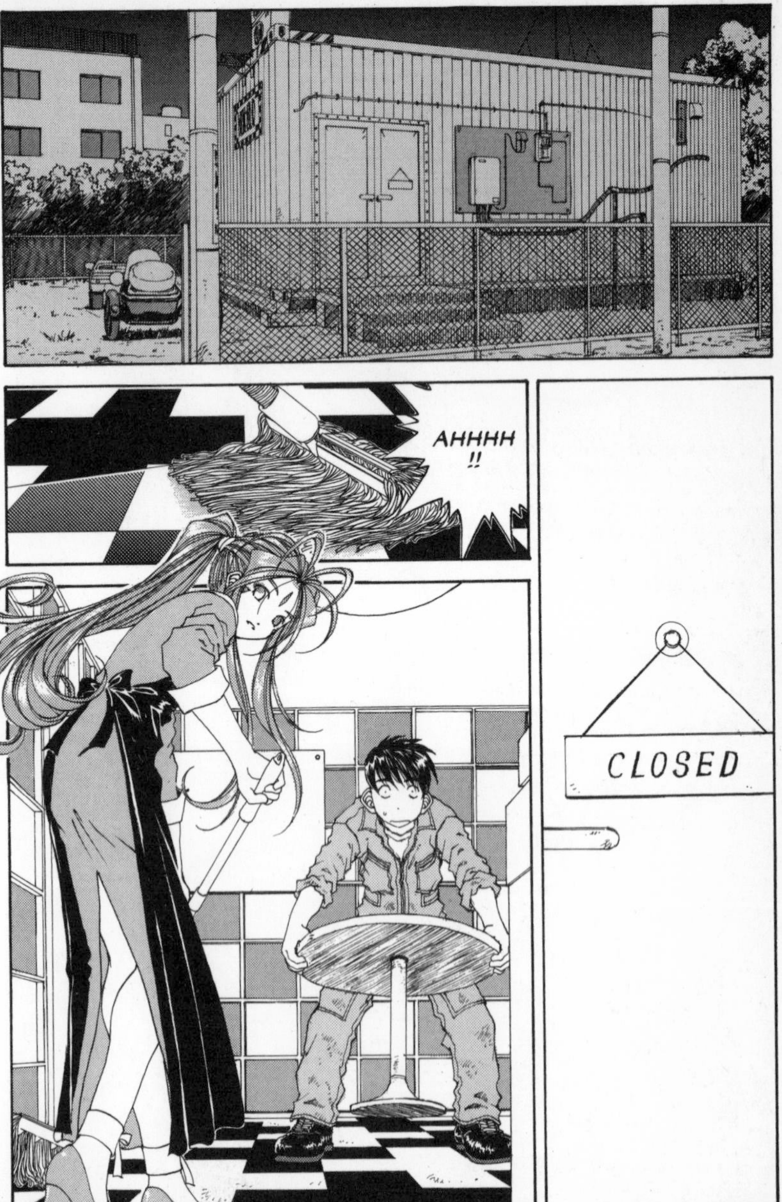
CLOSED
AHHHH !!

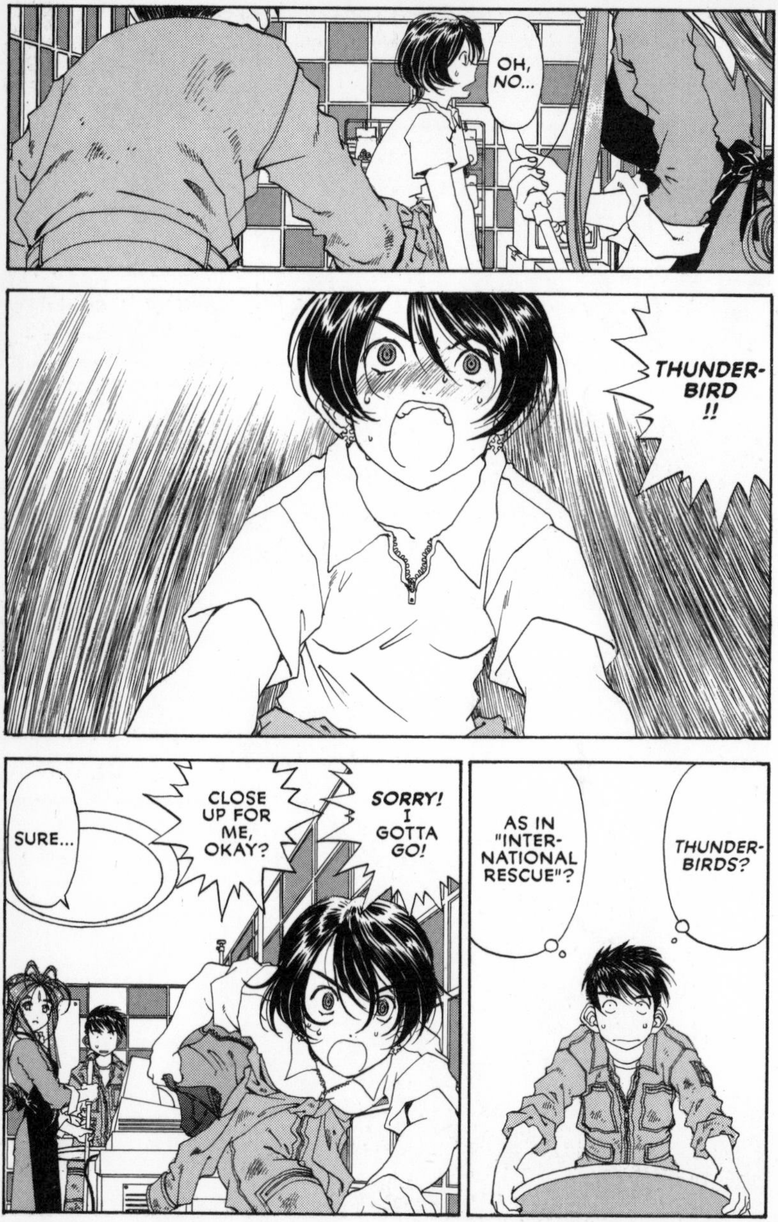
OH, NO...
THUNDER-BIRD !!
THUNDER-BIRDS?
AS IN "INTER-NATIONAL RESCUE"?
SORRY! I GOTTA GO!
CLOSE UP FOR ME, OKAY?
SURE...

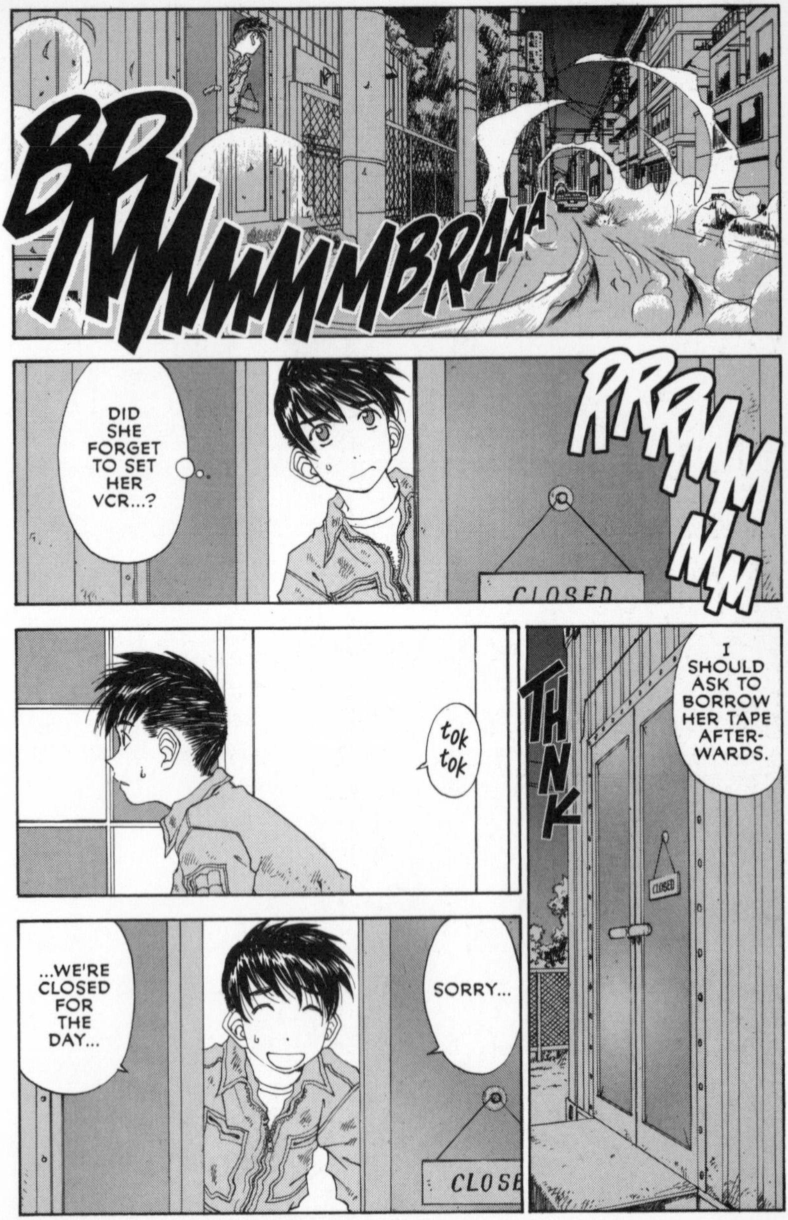
BRMMMMMBRAAA
RRRMMMMM
DID SHE FORGET TO SET HER VCR...?
CLOSED
I SHOULD ASK TO BORROW HER TAPE AFTERWARDS.
THNK
CLOSED
tok tok
SORRY...
...WE'RE CLOSED FOR THE DAY...
CLOSE

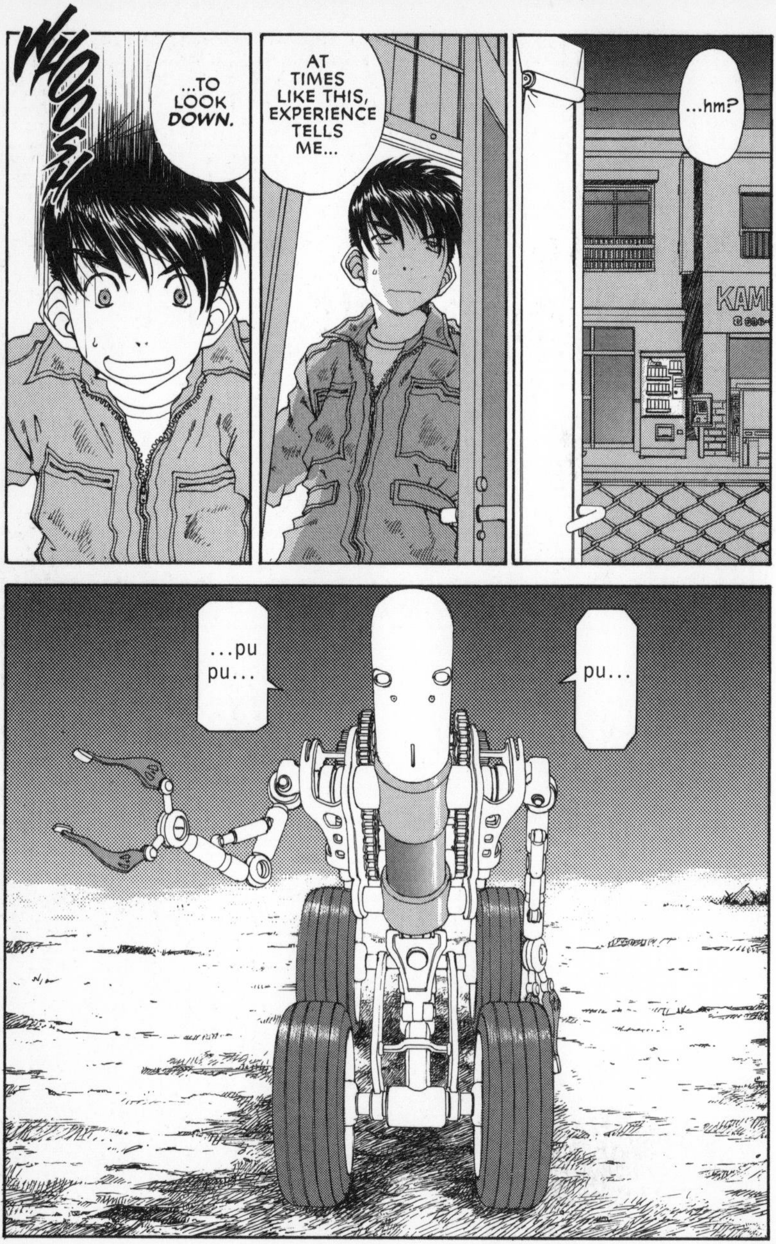
...hm?
AT TIMES LIKE THIS, EXPERIENCE TELLS ME...
...TO LOOK DOWN.
WHOOSH
pu...
...pu pu...

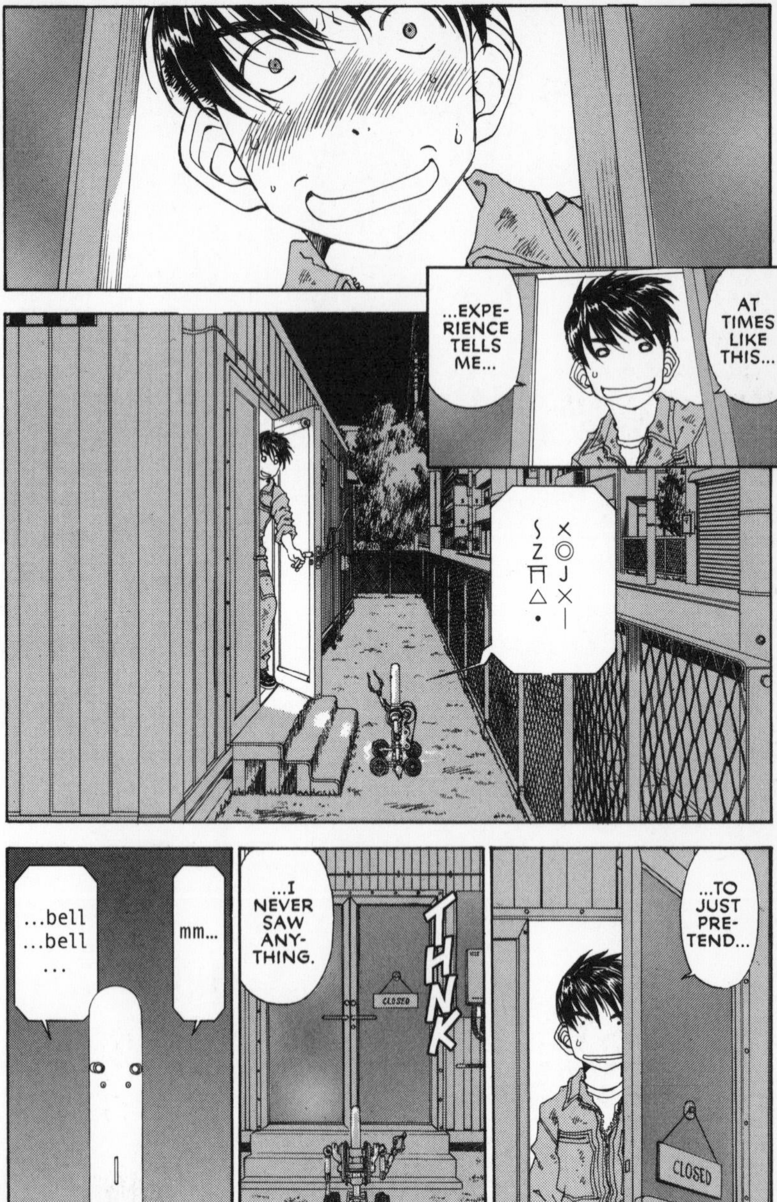
AT TIMES LIKE THIS...
...EXPERIENCE TELLS ME...
...TO JUST PRETEND...
CLOSED
...I NEVER SAW ANYTHING.
THNK
CLOSED
mm...
...bell ...bell ...

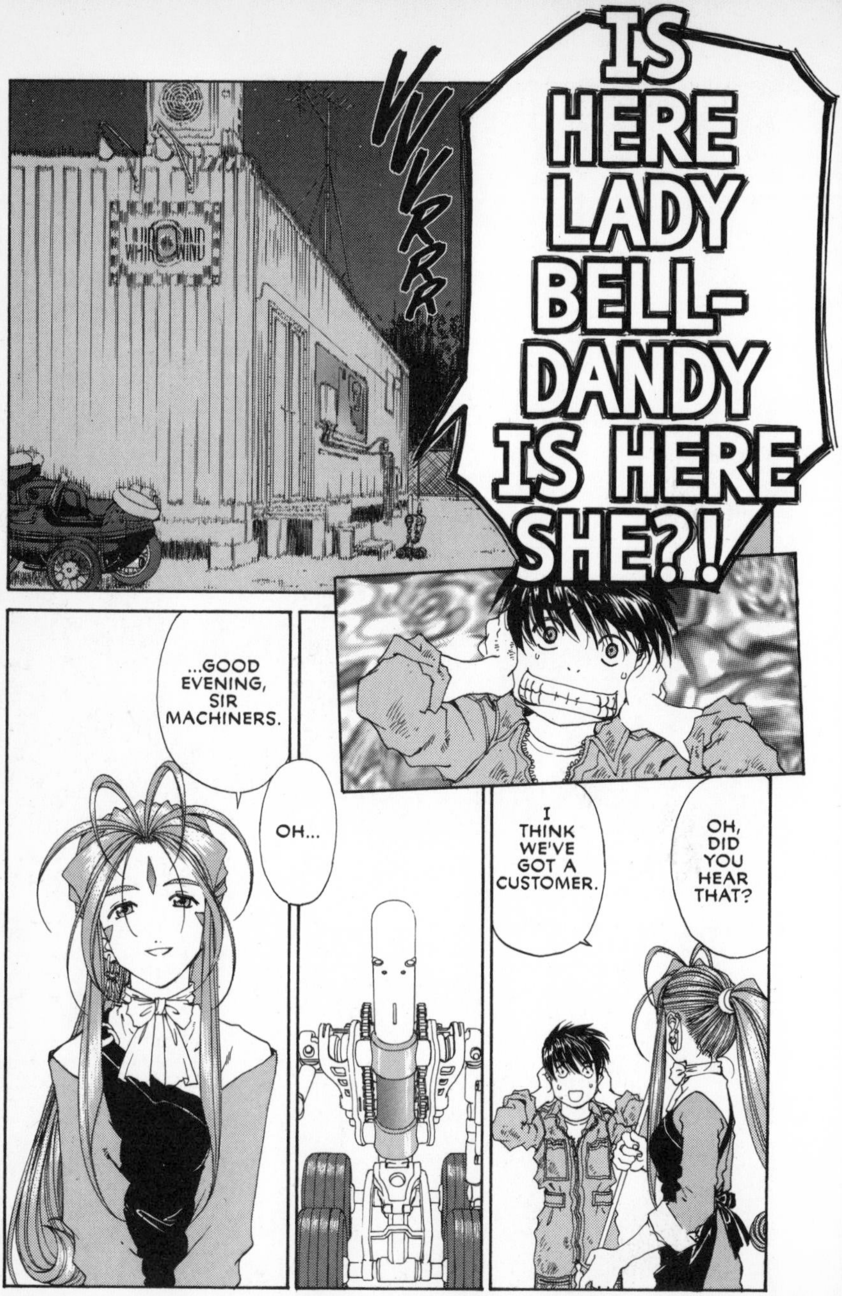

IS HERE LADY BELL-DANDY IS HERE SHE?!
VVVRRR
OH, DID YOU HEAR THAT?
I THINK WE'VE GOT A CUSTOMER.
OH...
...GOOD EVENING, SIR MACHINERS.

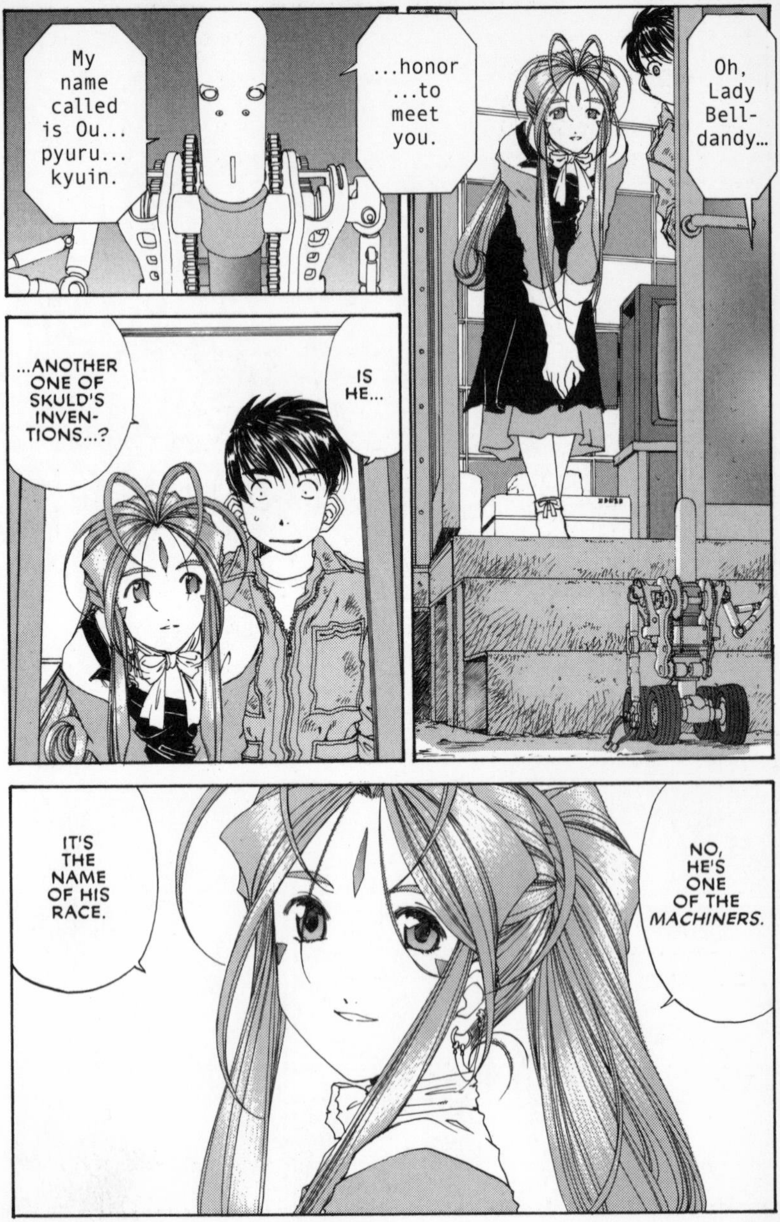
Oh, Lady Bell-dandy...
...honor ...to meet you.
My name called is Ou... pyuru... kyuin.
IS HE...
...ANOTHER ONE OF SKULD'S INVEN-TIONS...?
NO, HE'S ONE OF THE *MACHINERS.*
IT'S THE NAME OF HIS RACE.

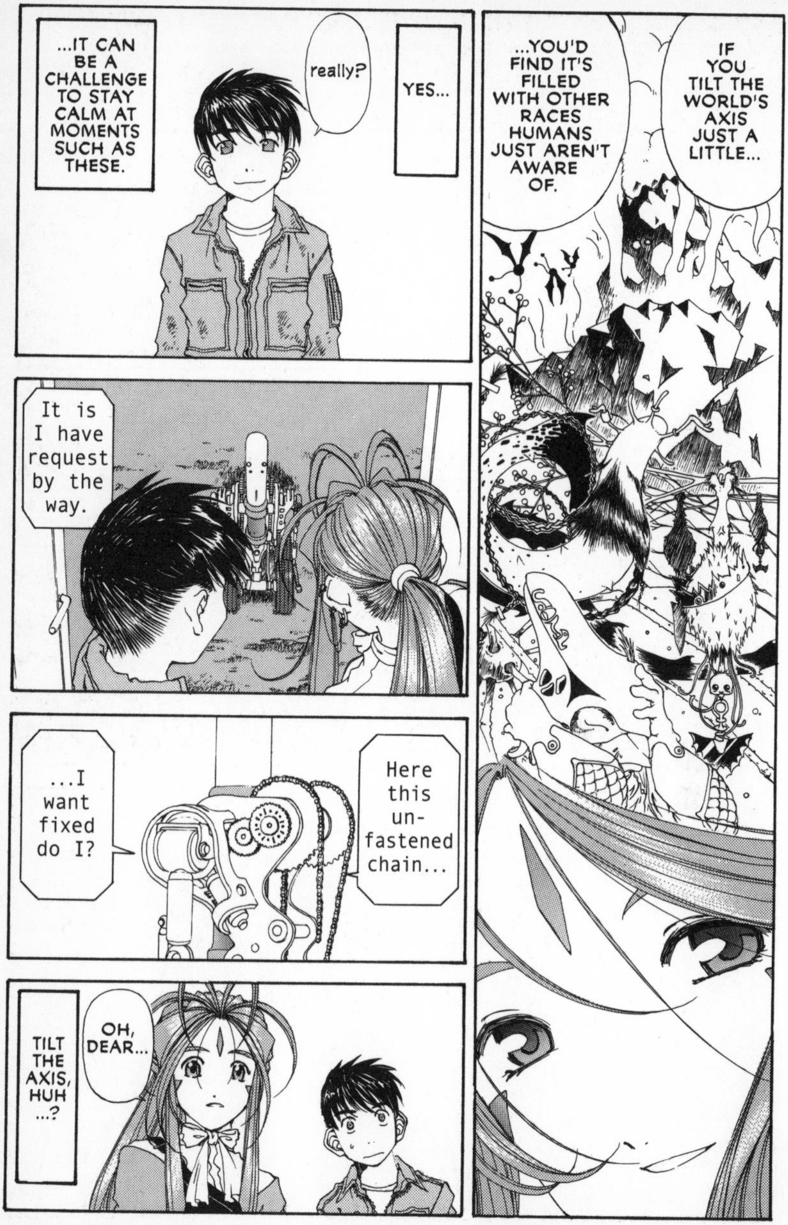
IF YOU TILT THE WORLD'S AXIS JUST A LITTLE...
...YOU'D FIND IT'S FILLED WITH OTHER RACES HUMANS JUST AREN'T AWARE OF.
YES...
really?
...IT CAN BE A CHALLENGE TO STAY CALM AT MOMENTS SUCH AS THESE.
It is I have request by the way.
Here this un-fastened chain...
...I want fixed do I?
OH, DEAR...
TILT THE AXIS, HUH ...?

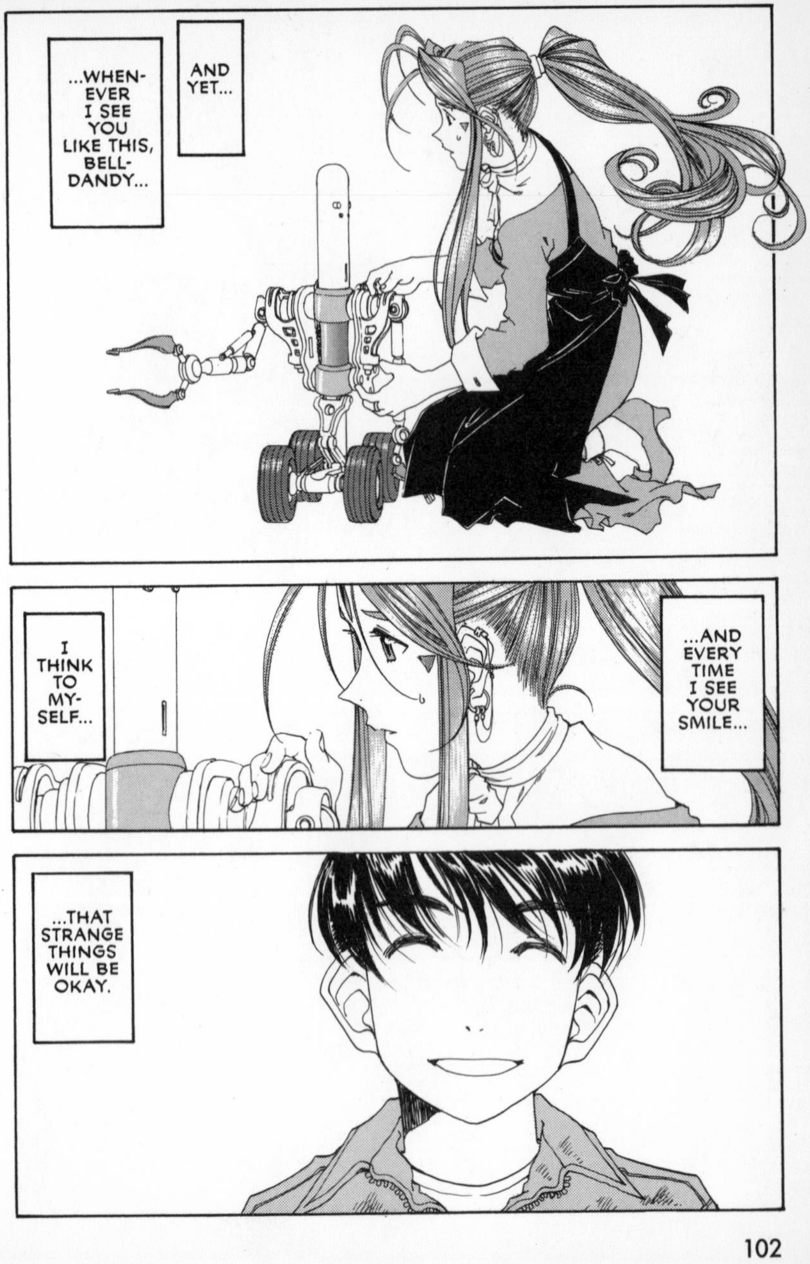
AND YET...
...WHENEVER I SEE YOU LIKE THIS, BELLDANDY...
...AND EVERY TIME I SEE YOUR SMILE...
I THINK TO MYSELF...
...THAT STRANGE THINGS WILL BE OKAY.

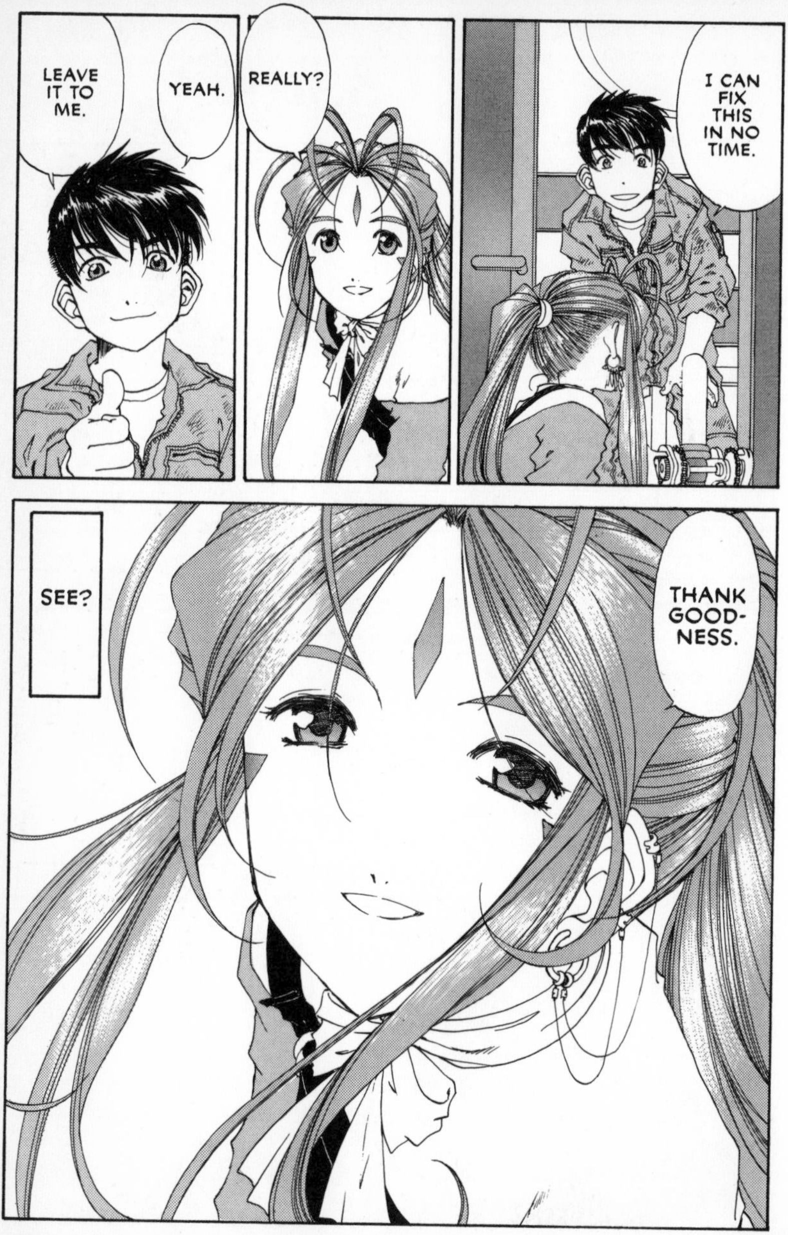
I CAN FIX THIS IN NO TIME.
REALLY?
YEAH.
LEAVE IT TO ME.
THANK GOOD-NESS.
SEE?

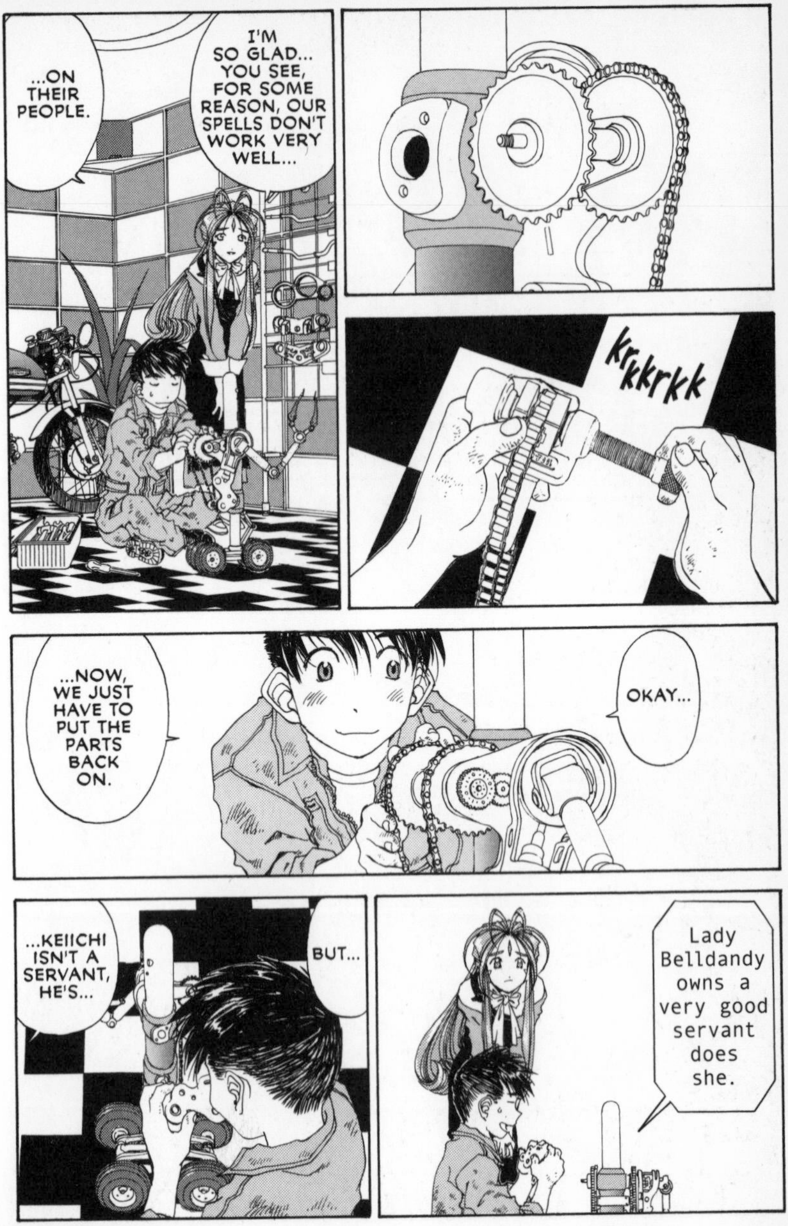
KRKKRKK
I'M SO GLAD... YOU SEE, FOR SOME REASON, OUR SPELLS DON'T WORK VERY WELL...
...ON THEIR PEOPLE.
OKAY...
...NOW, WE JUST HAVE TO PUT THE PARTS BACK ON.
Lady Belldandy owns a very good servant does she.
BUT...
...KEIICHI ISN'T A SERVANT, HE'S...

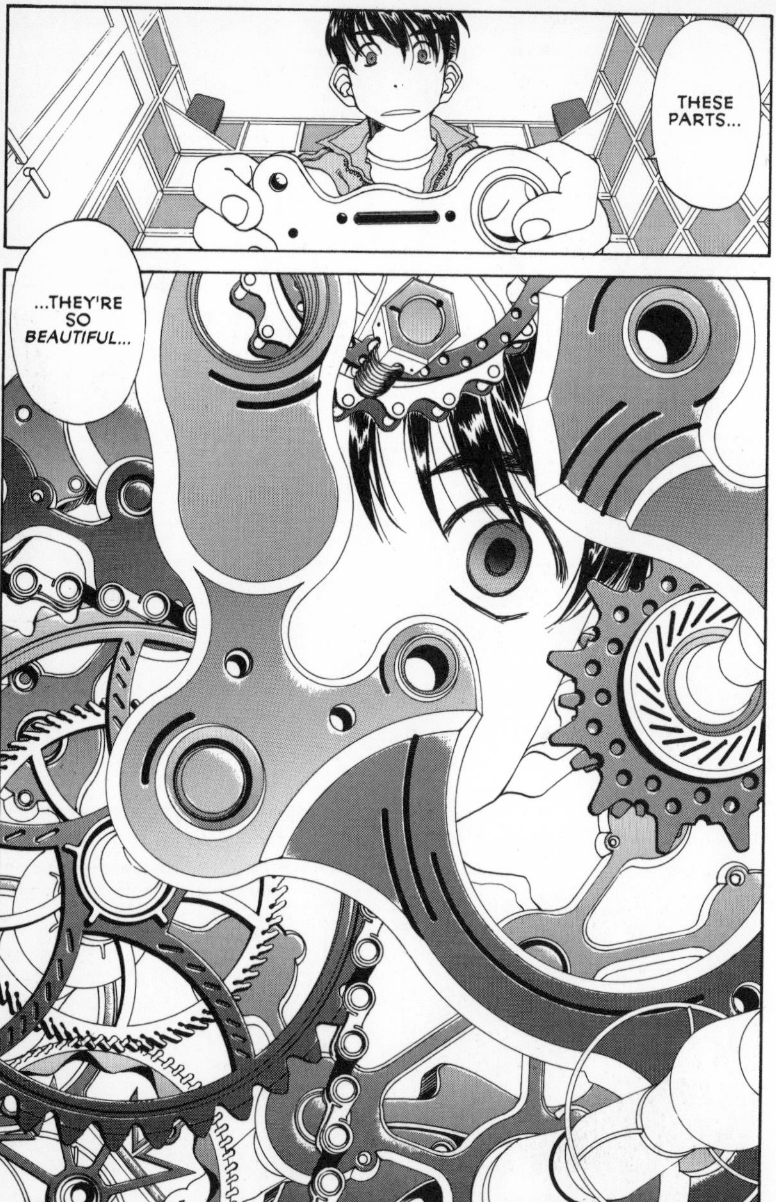
THESE PARTS...
...THEY'RE SO BEAUTIFUL...

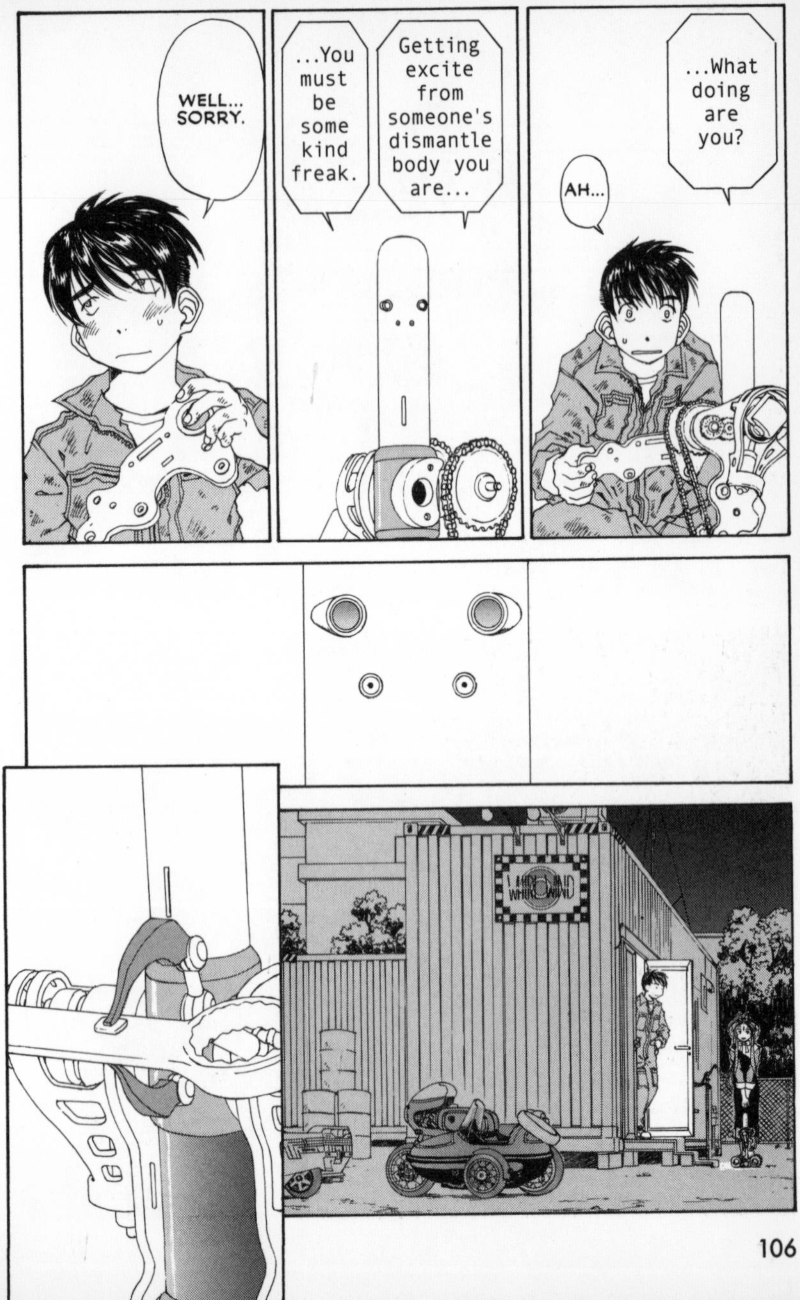
...What doing are you?
AH...
Getting excite from someone's dismantle body you are...
...You must be some kind freak.
WELL... SORRY.

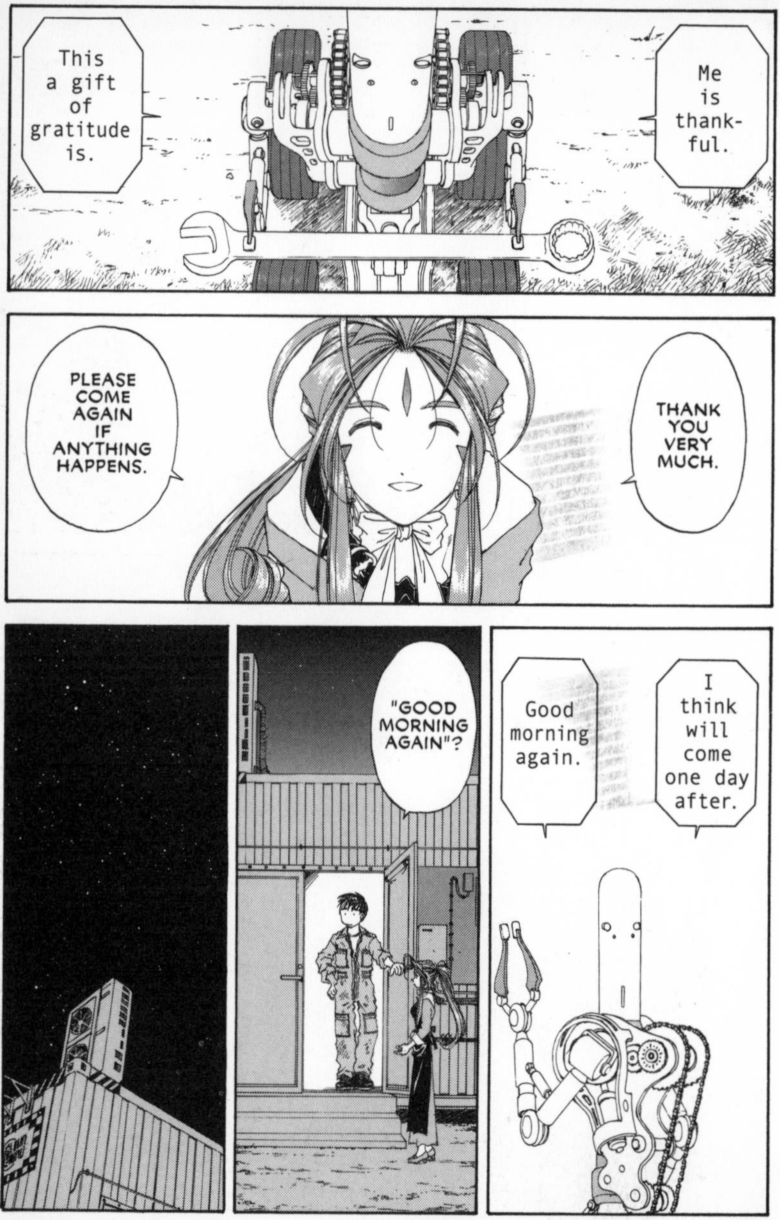
Me is thank-ful.
This a gift of gratitude is.
THANK YOU VERY MUCH.
PLEASE COME AGAIN IF ANYTHING HAPPENS.
I think will come one day after.
Good morning again.
"GOOD MORNING AGAIN"?

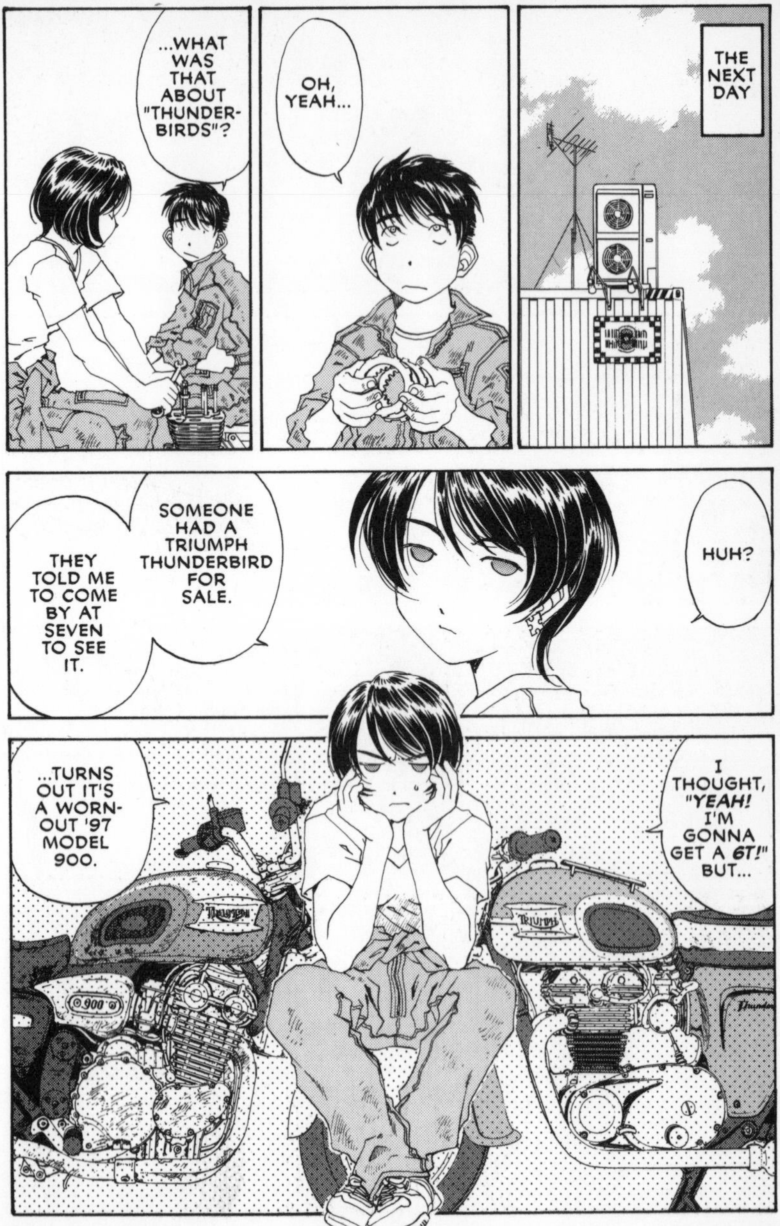
THE NEXT DAY
OH, YEAH...
...WHAT WAS THAT ABOUT "THUNDER-BIRDS"?
HUH?
SOMEONE HAD A TRIUMPH THUNDERBIRD FOR SALE.
THEY TOLD ME TO COME BY AT SEVEN TO SEE IT.
I THOUGHT, "*YEAH!* I'M GONNA GET A *6T!*" BUT...
...TURNS OUT IT'S A WORN-OUT '97 MODEL 900.

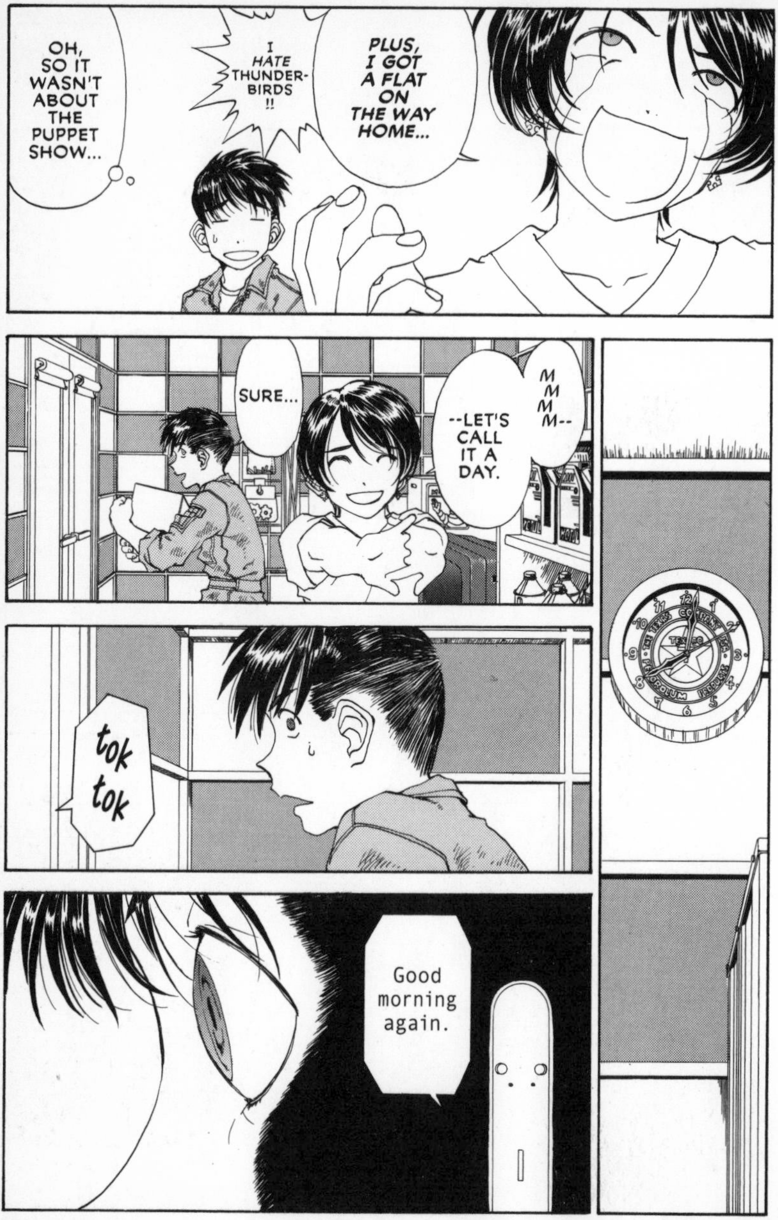
PLUS, I GOT A FLAT ON THE WAY HOME...
I HATE THUNDERBIRDS !!
OH, SO IT WASN'T ABOUT THE PUPPET SHOW...
MMMM-- --LET'S CALL IT A DAY.
SURE...
tok tok
Good morning again.

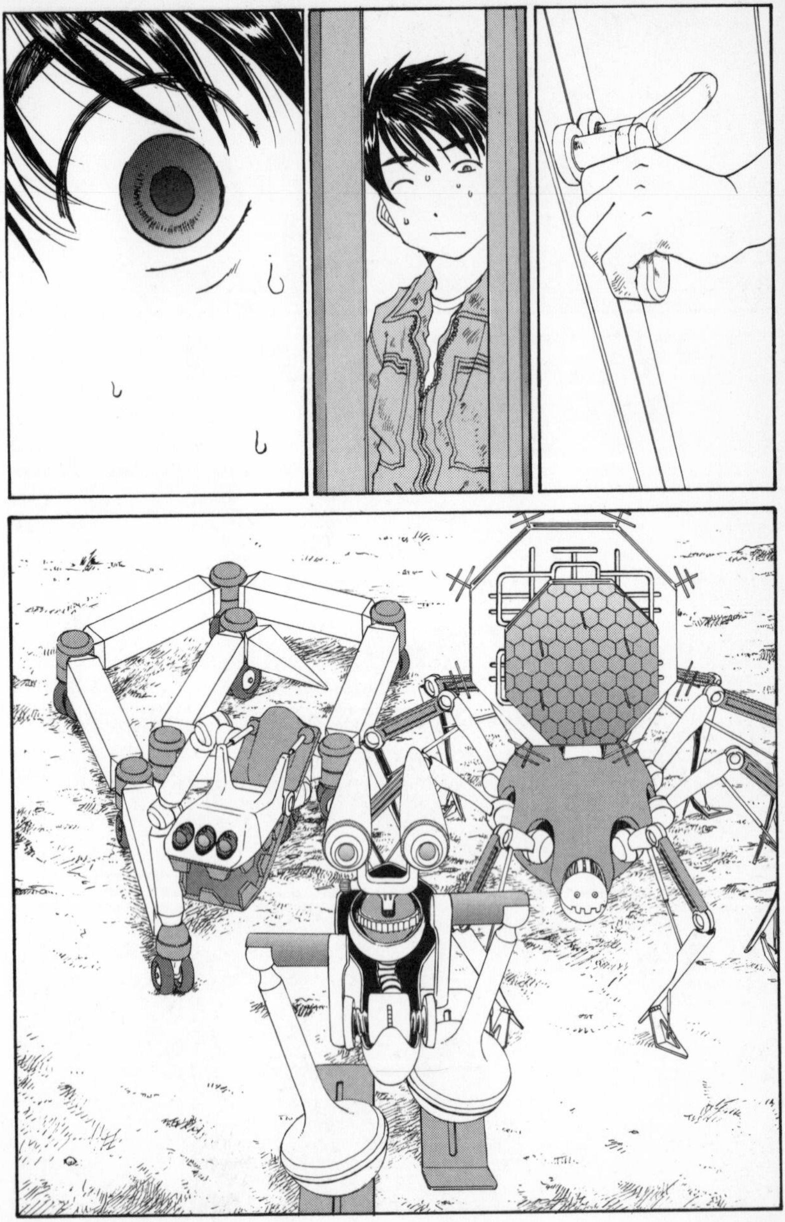

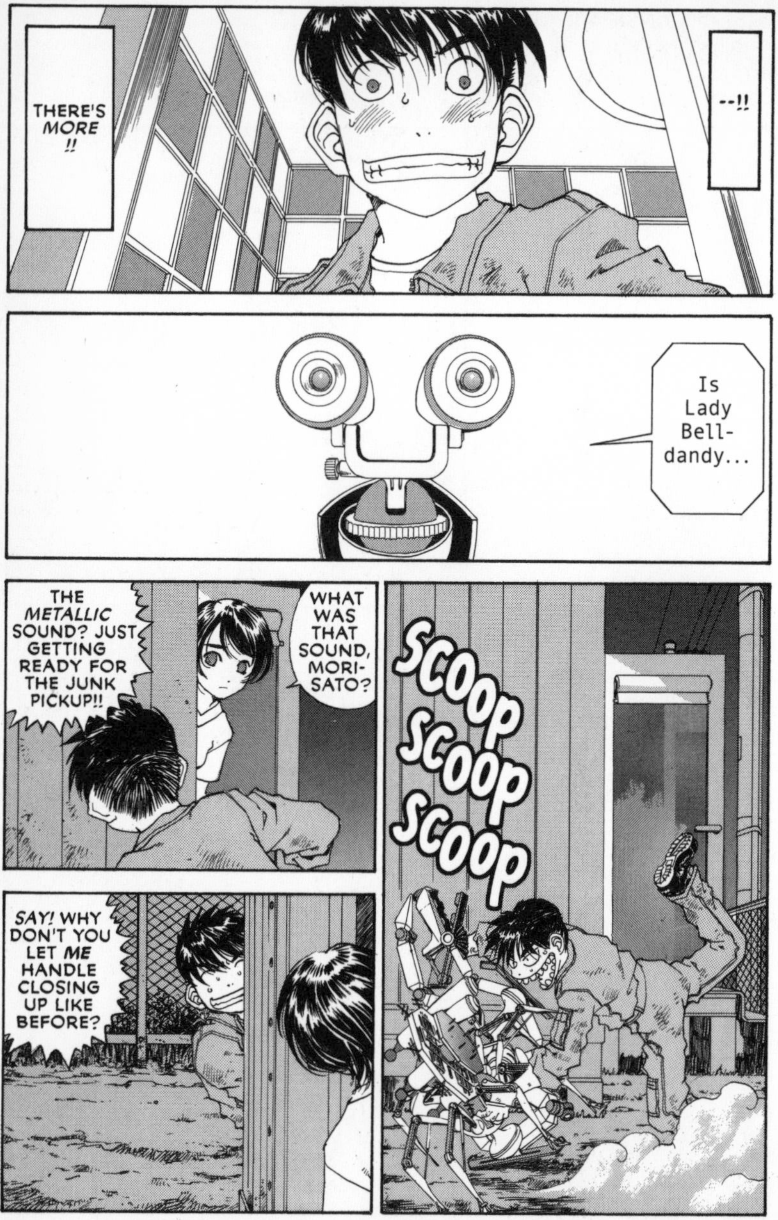
--!!
THERE'S *MORE* !!
Is Lady Bell-dandy...
SCOOP SCOOP SCOOP
WHAT WAS THAT SOUND, MORI-SATO?
THE *METALLIC* SOUND? JUST GETTING READY FOR THE JUNK PICKUP!!
SAY! WHY DON'T YOU LET *ME* HANDLE CLOSING UP LIKE BEFORE?

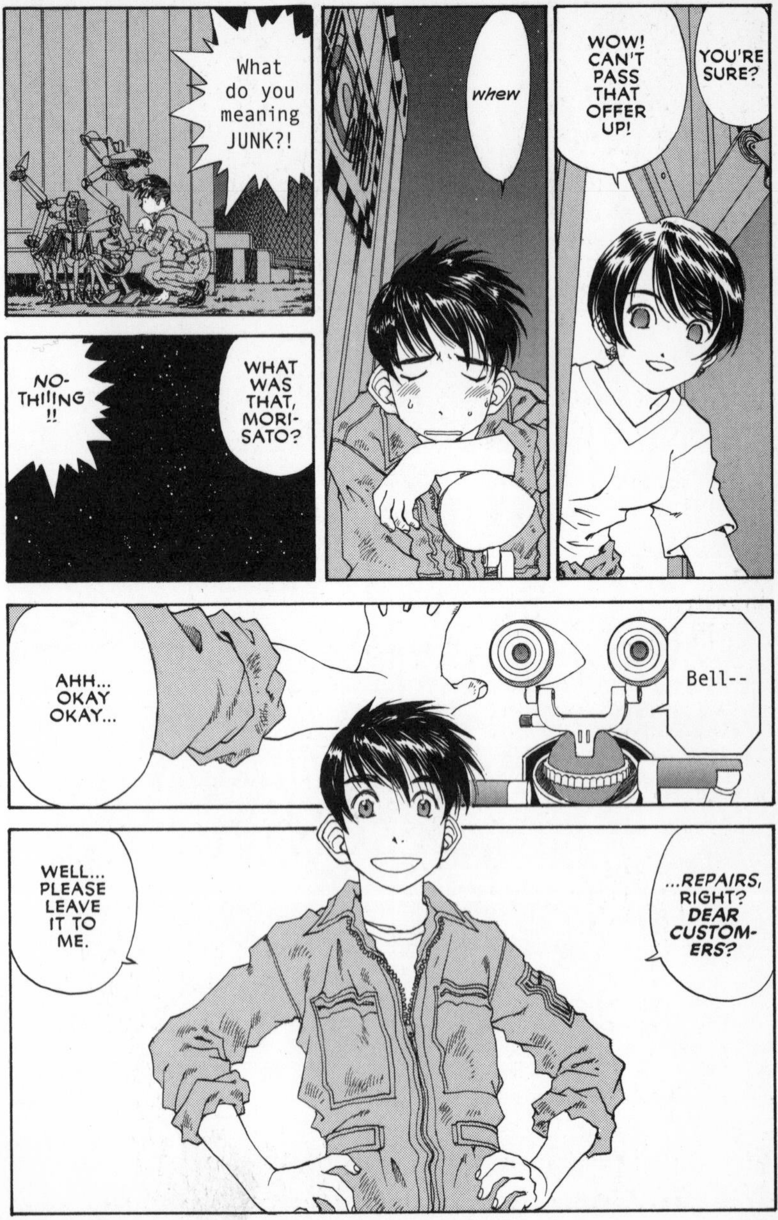
YOU'RE SURE?
WOW! CAN'T PASS THAT OFFER UP!
whew
What do you meaning JUNK?!
WHAT WAS THAT, MORI-SATO?
NO-THIIING!!
Bell--
AHH... OKAY OKAY...
...REPAIRS, RIGHT? DEAR CUSTOM-ERS?
WELL... PLEASE LEAVE IT TO ME.

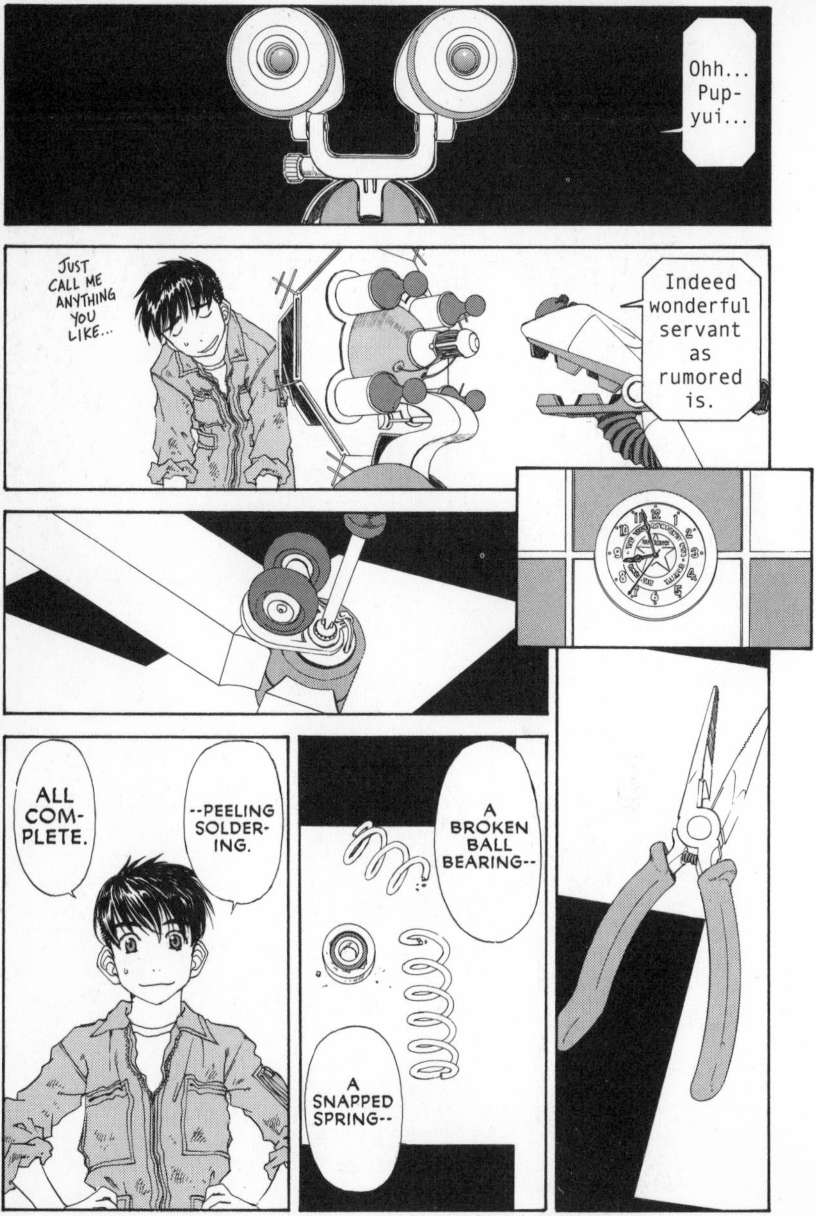
Ohh... Pup-yui...
Indeed wonderful servant as rumored is.
JUST CALL ME ANYTHING YOU LIKE...
A BROKEN BALL BEARING--
A SNAPPED SPRING--
--PEELING SOLDER-ING.
ALL COM-PLETE.

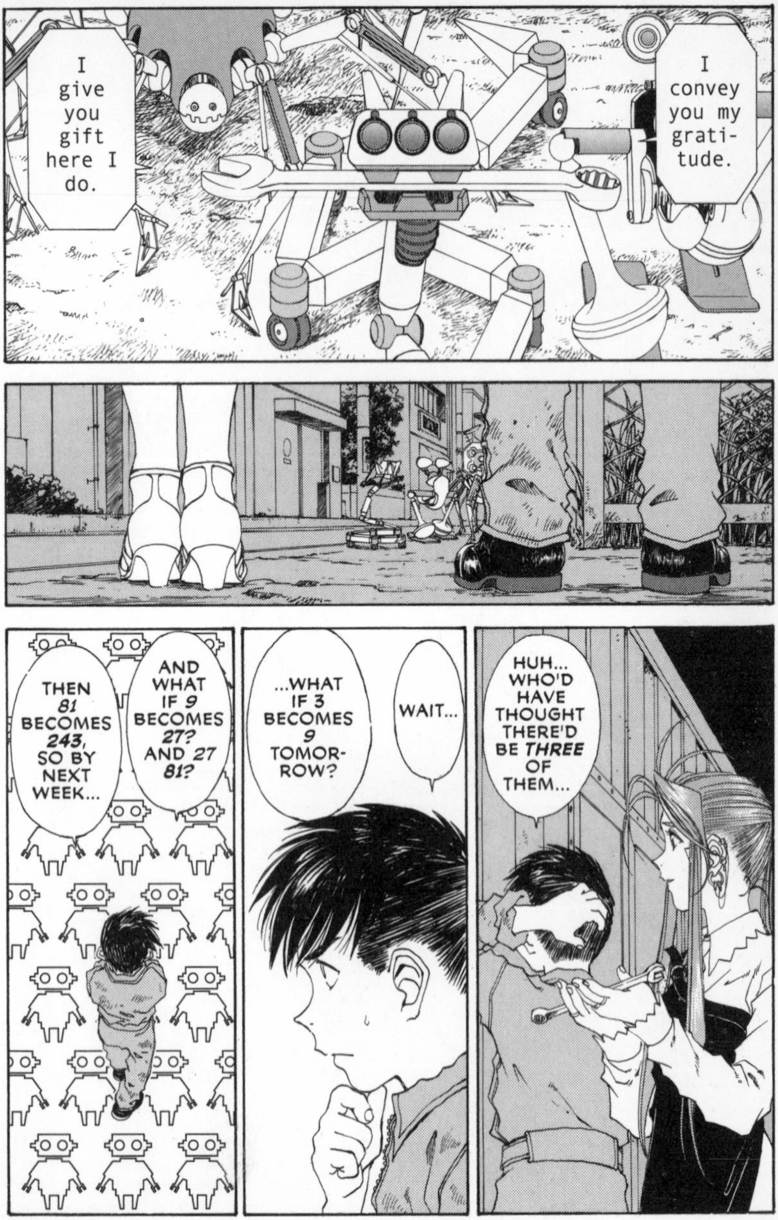
I convey you my gratitude.
I give you gift here I do.
HUH... WHO'D HAVE THOUGHT THERE'D BE *THREE* OF THEM...
WAIT...
...WHAT IF 3 BECOMES *9* TOMORROW?
AND WHAT IF *9* BECOMES *27?* AND *27 81?*
THEN *81* BECOMES ***243***, SO BY NEXT WEEK...

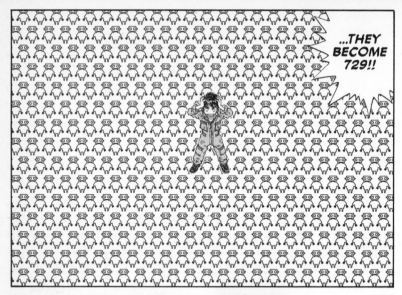

...THEY BECOME 729!!

...YOU *DO* WANT THEM TO COME AGAIN TOMORROW, RIGHT?

BUT...

...YOU CAN TELL?

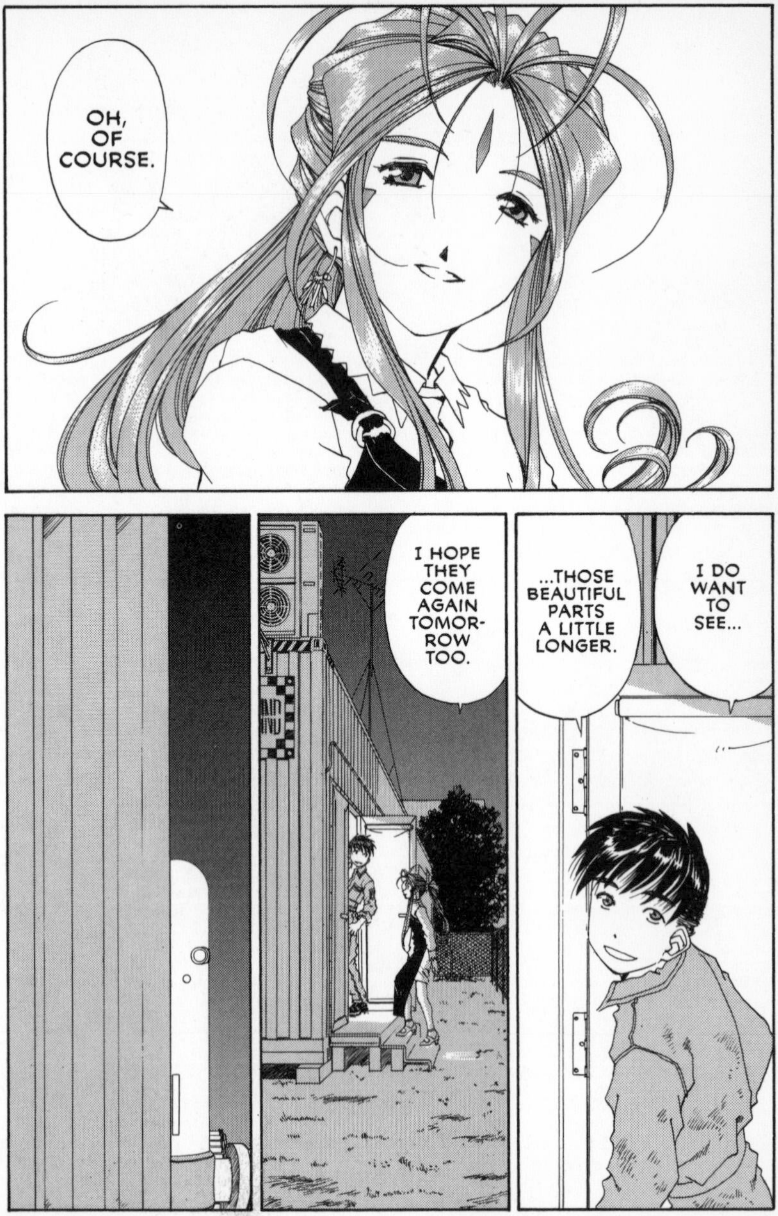
OH, OF COURSE.
I DO WANT TO SEE...
...THOSE BEAUTIFUL PARTS A LITTLE LONGER.
I HOPE THEY COME AGAIN TOMORROW TOO.

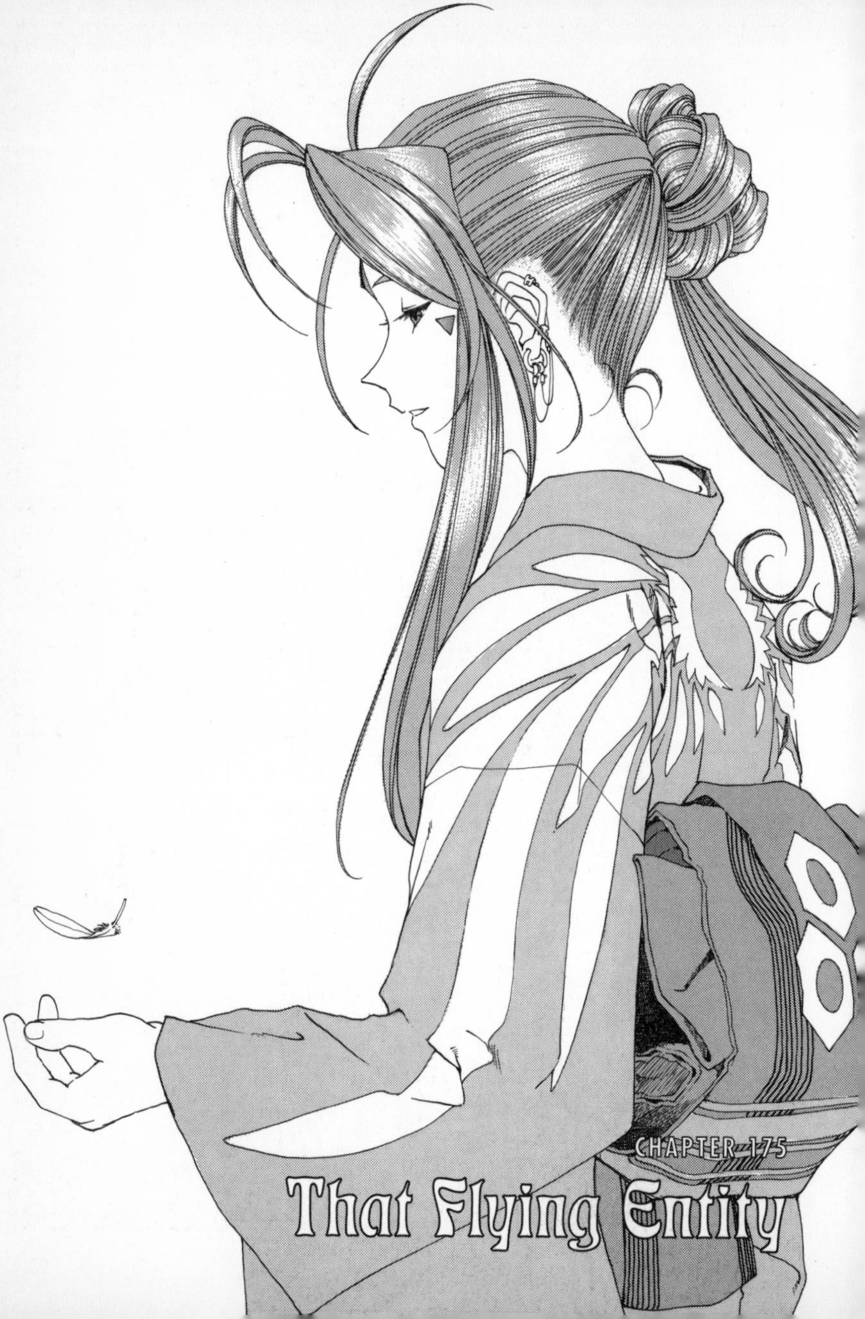

CHAPTER 175

That Flying Entity

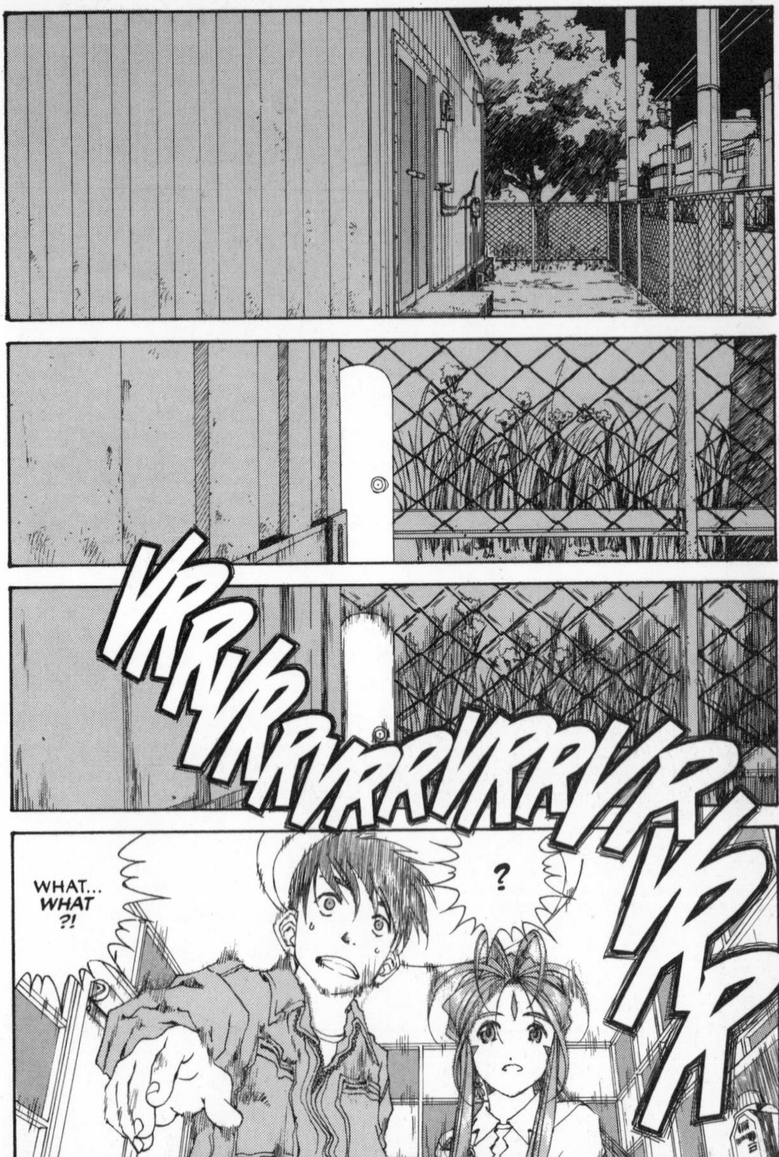
?
WHAT... WHAT ?!

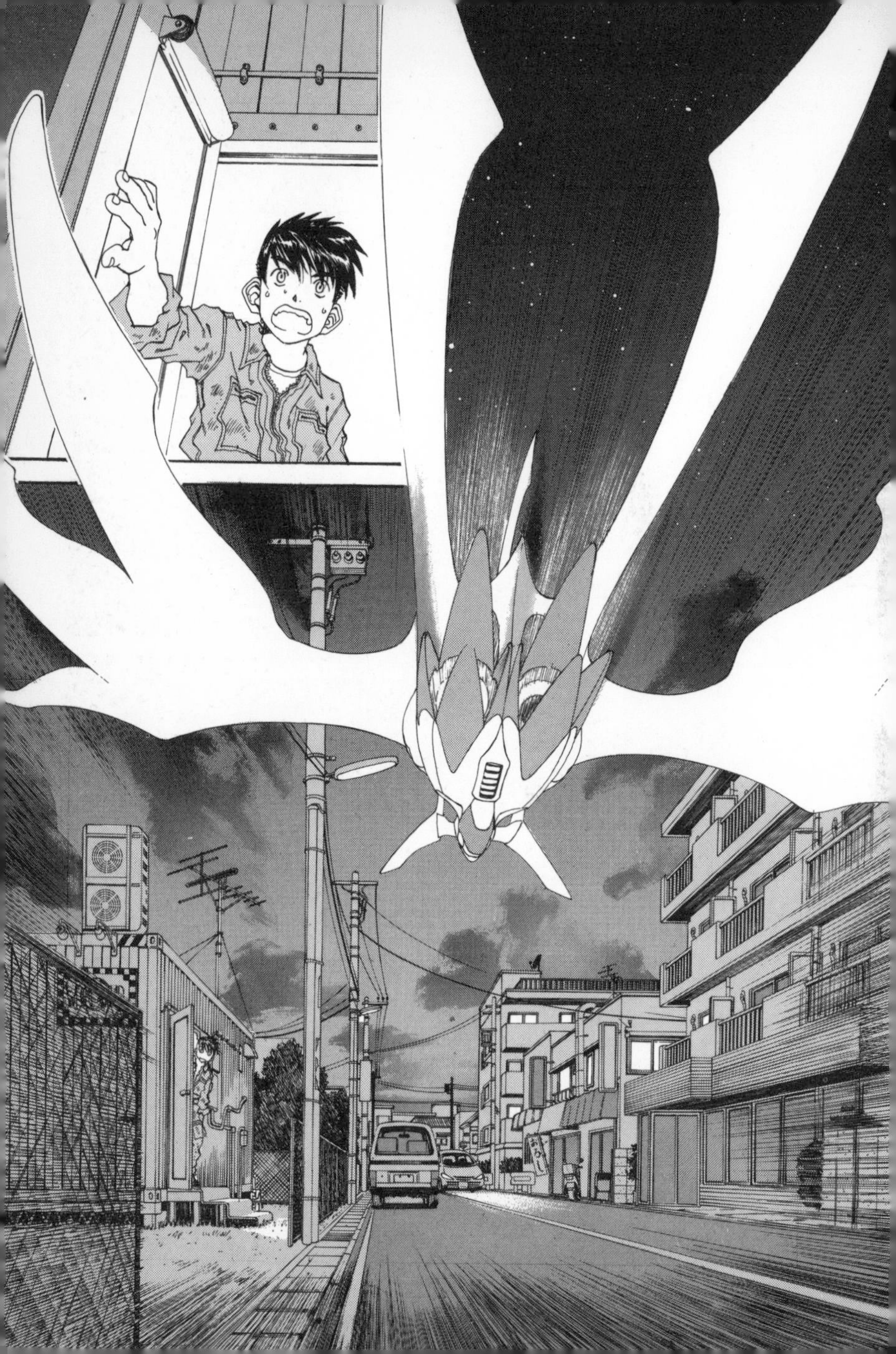

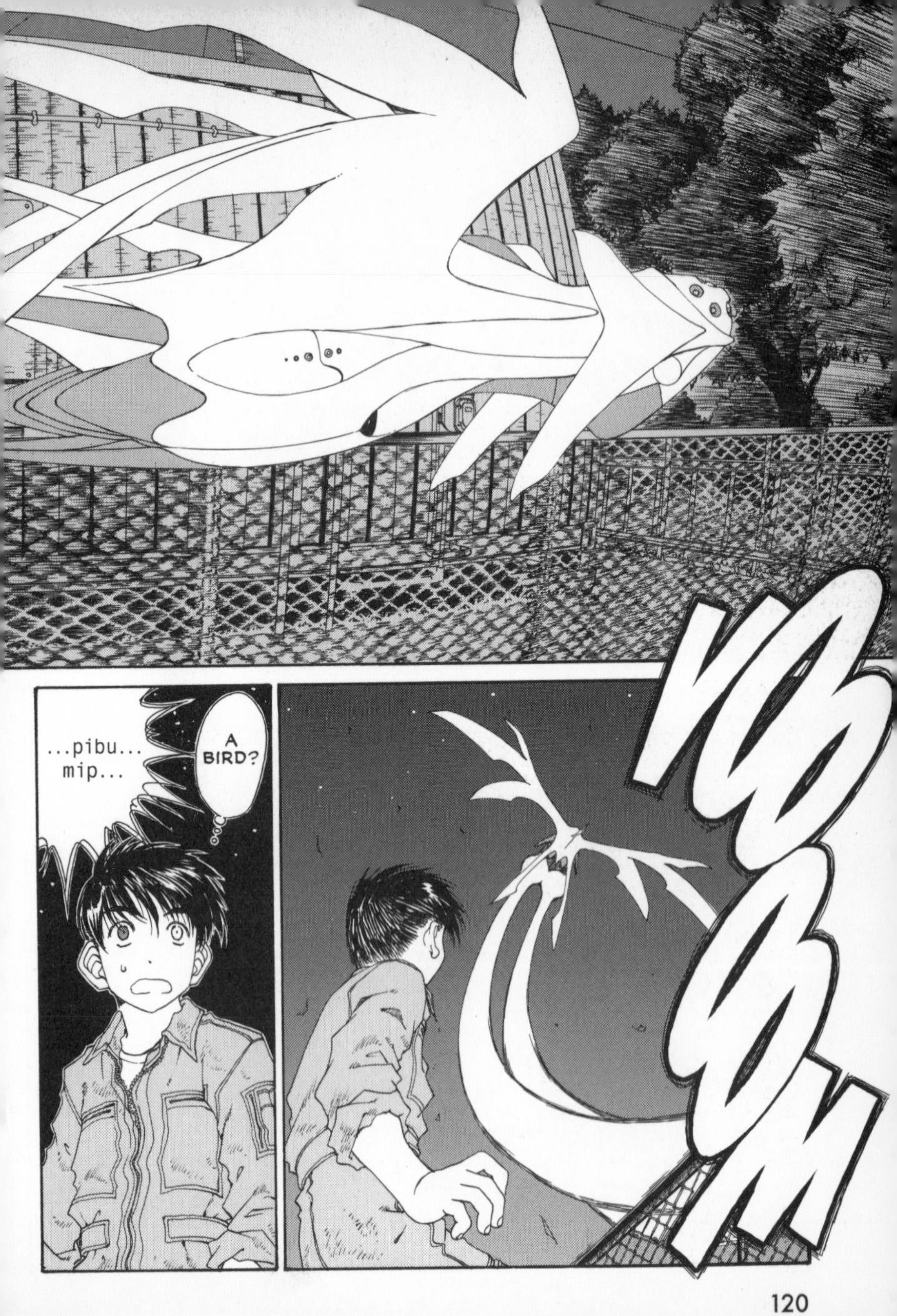
WOOSH
A BIRD?
...pibu... mip...

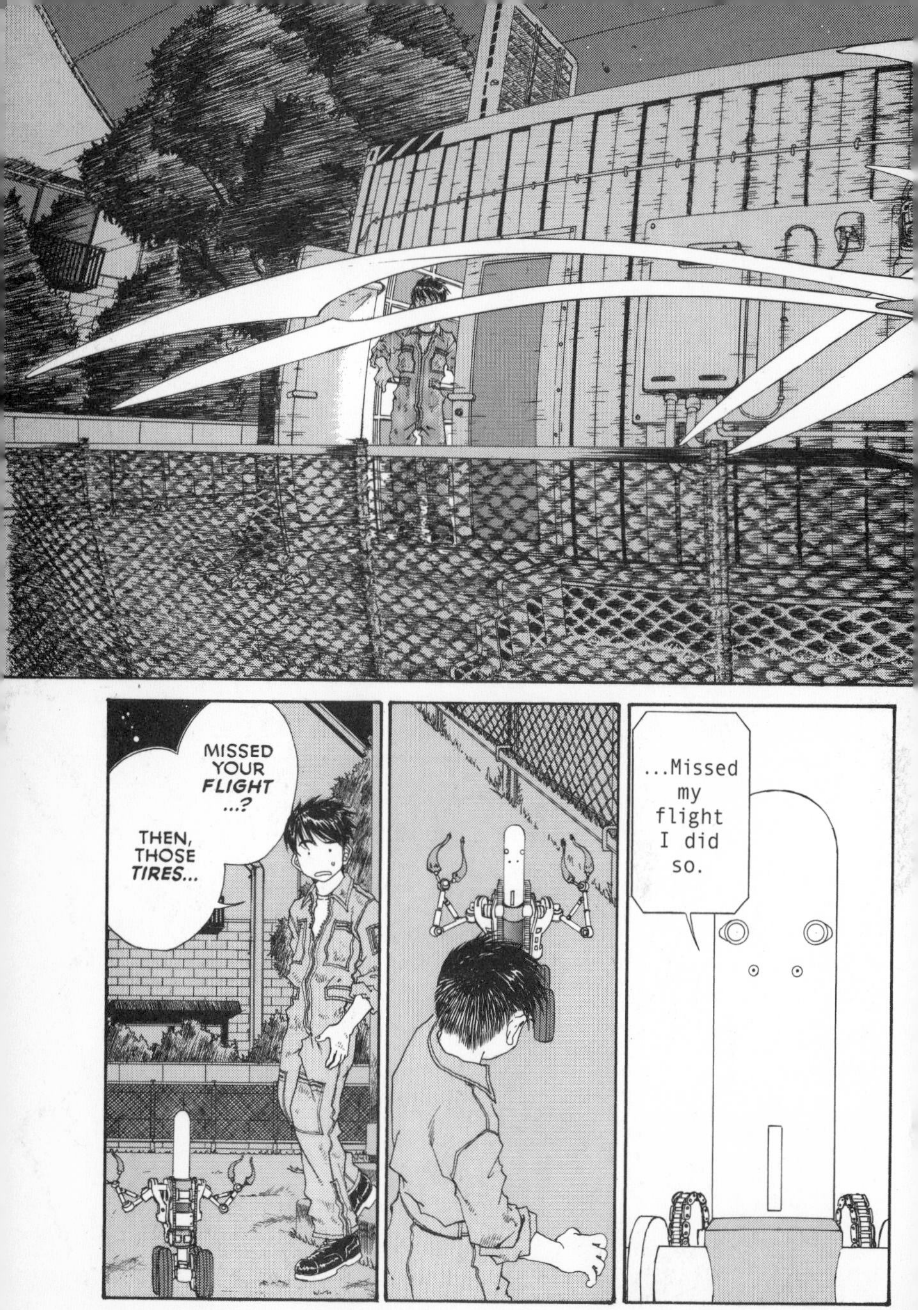
...Missed my flight I did so.
MISSED YOUR FLIGHT ...?
THEN, THOSE TIRES...

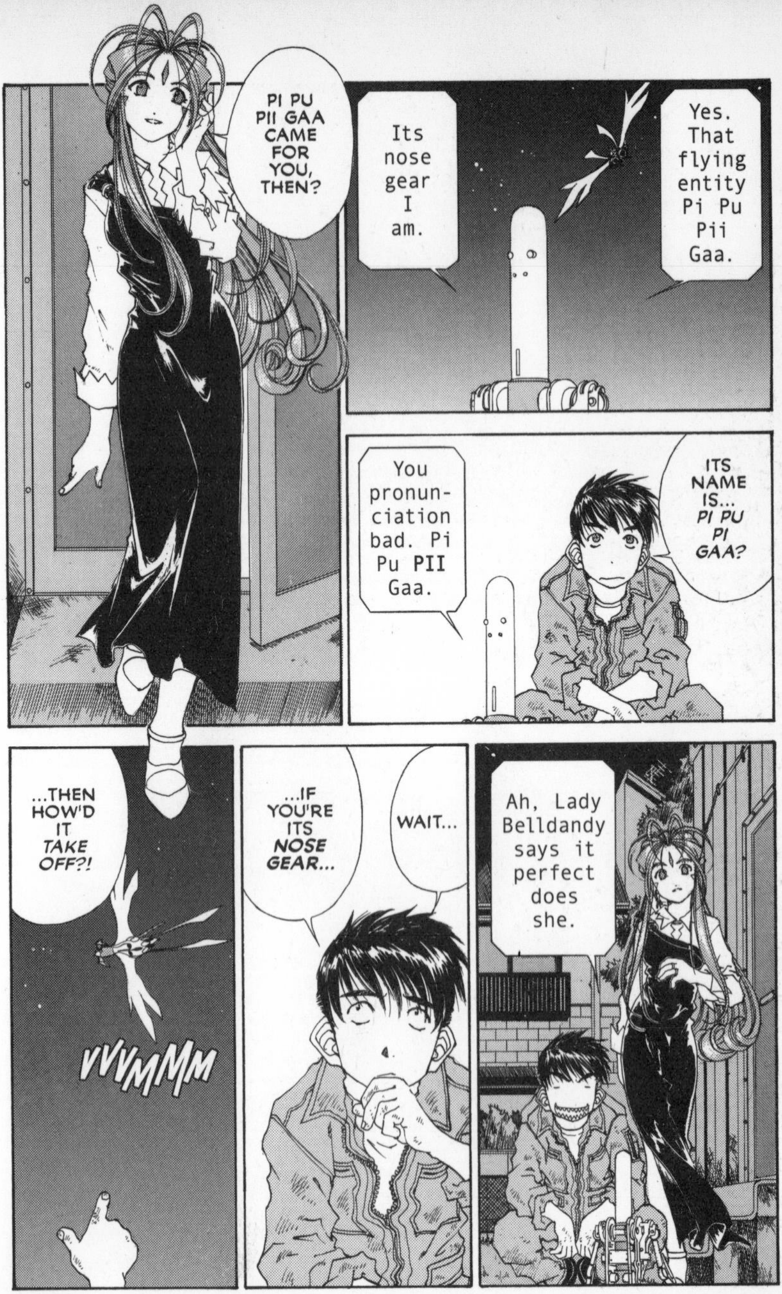

Yes. That flying entity Pi Pu Pii Gaa.
Its nose gear I am.
ITS NAME IS... *PI PU PI GAA?*
You pronunciation bad. Pi Pu **PII** Gaa.
PI PU PII GAA CAME FOR YOU, THEN?
Ah, Lady Belldandy says it perfect does she.
WAIT...
...IF YOU'RE ITS ***NOSE GEAR...***
...THEN HOW'D IT *TAKE OFF?!*
VVVMMM

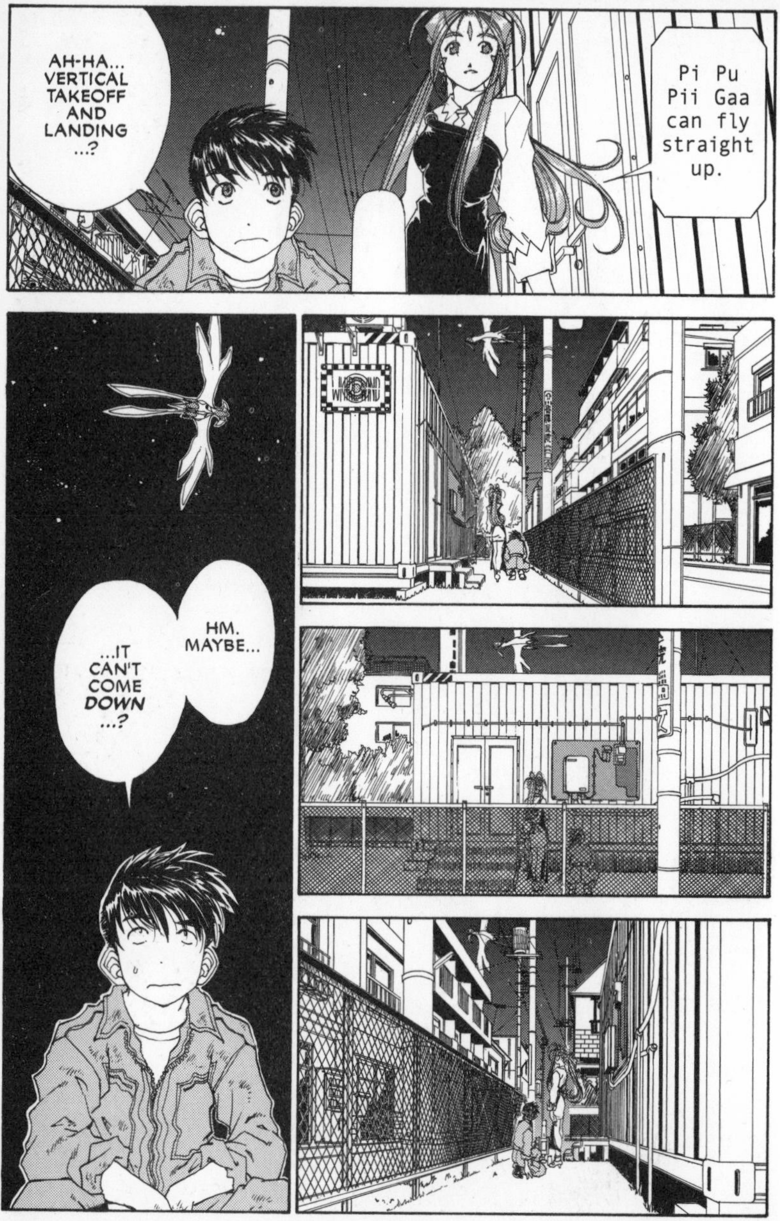
Pi Pu Pii Gaa can fly straight up.
AH-HA... VERTICAL TAKEOFF AND LANDING ...?
HM. MAYBE...
...IT CAN'T COME DOWN ...?

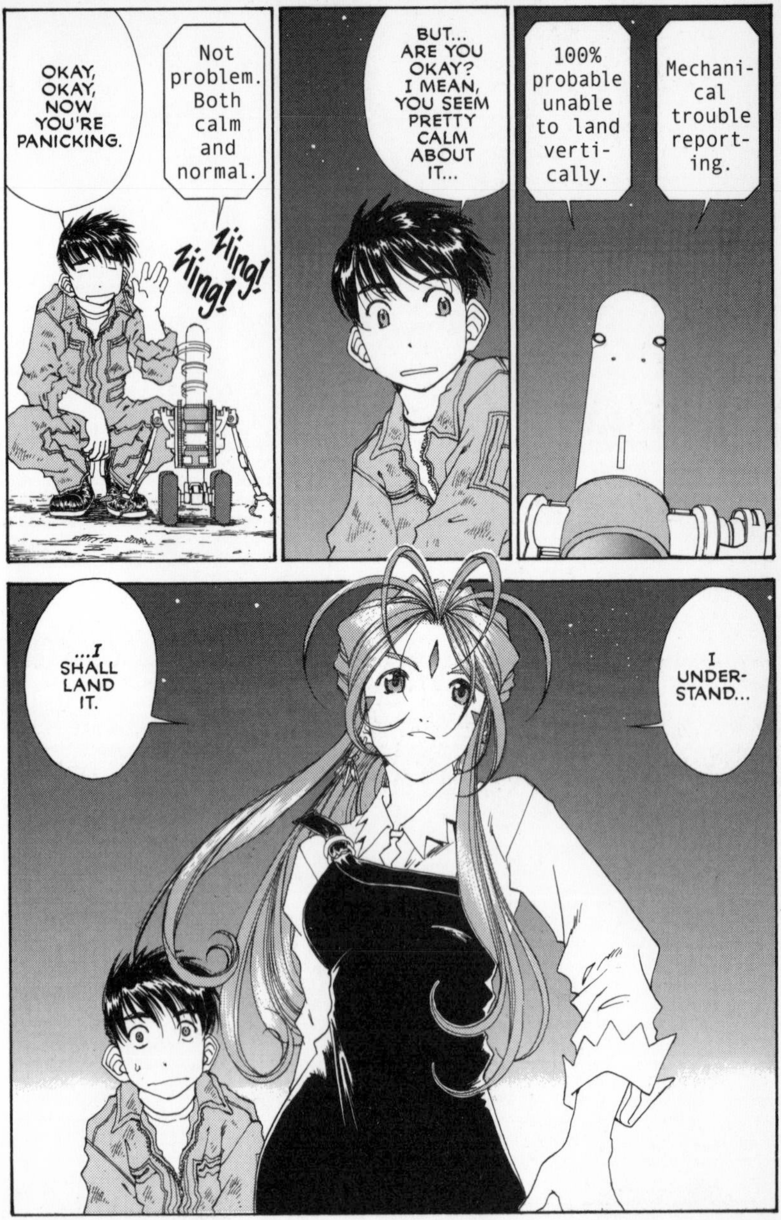
Mechanical trouble reporting.
100% probable unable to land vertically.
BUT... ARE YOU OKAY? I MEAN, YOU SEEM PRETTY CALM ABOUT IT...
Not problem. Both calm and normal.
OKAY, OKAY, NOW YOU'RE PANICKING.
Ziing! Ziing!
I UNDERSTAND...
...I SHALL LAND IT.

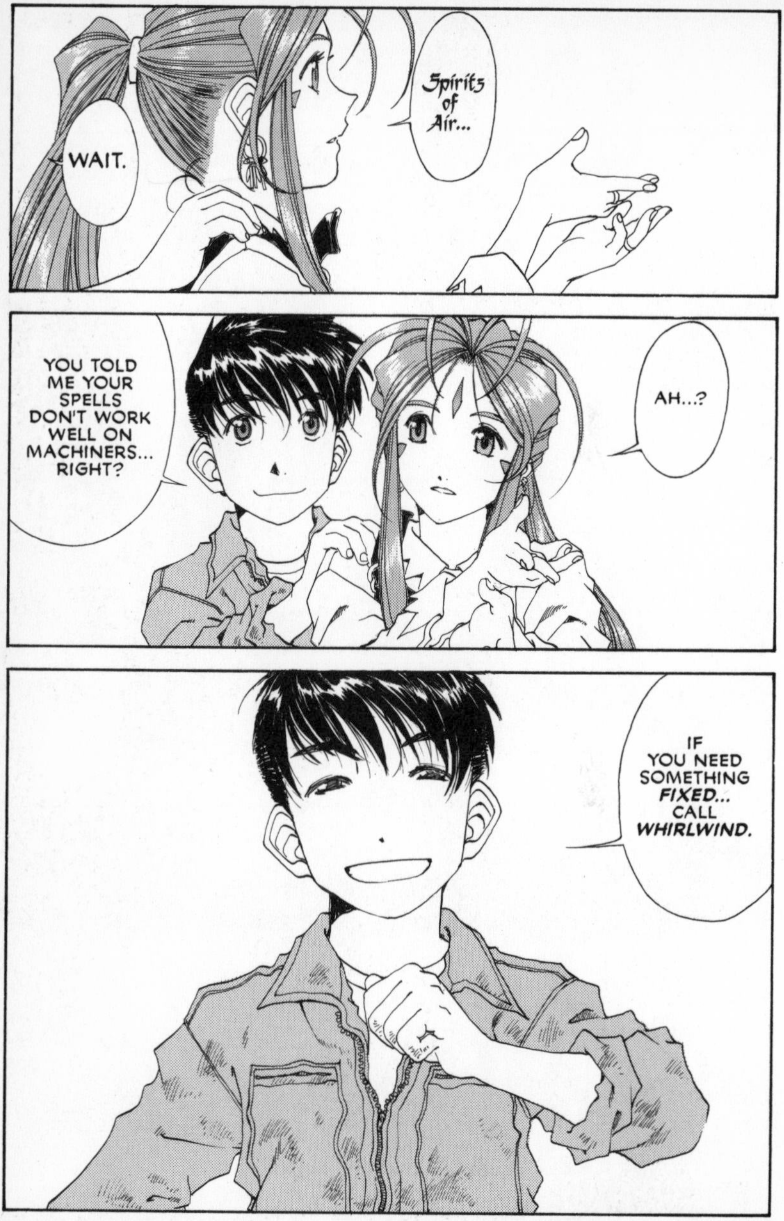
Spirits of Air...
WAIT.
AH...?
YOU TOLD ME YOUR SPELLS DON'T WORK WELL ON MACHINERS... RIGHT?
IF YOU NEED SOMETHING FIXED... CALL WHIRLWIND.

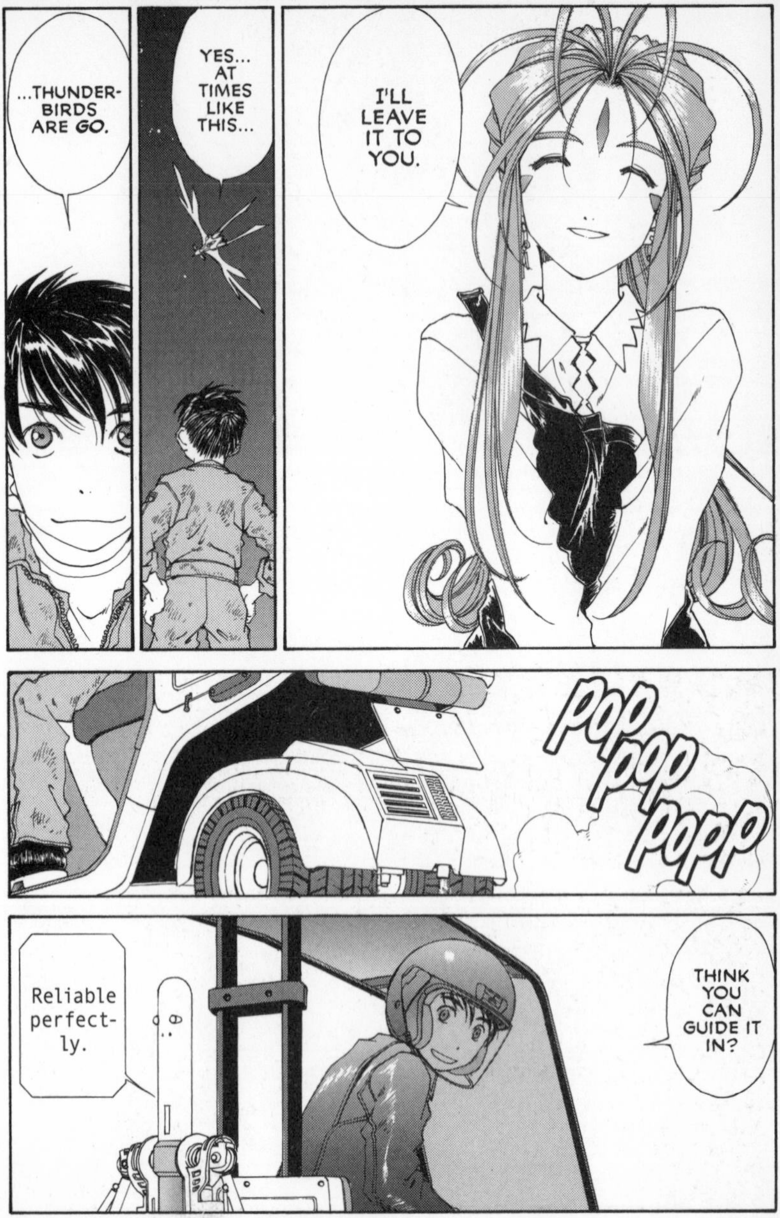
I'LL LEAVE IT TO YOU.
YES... AT TIMES LIKE THIS...
...THUNDER-BIRDS ARE GO.
POP POP POPP
THINK YOU CAN GUIDE IT IN?
Reliable perfect-ly.

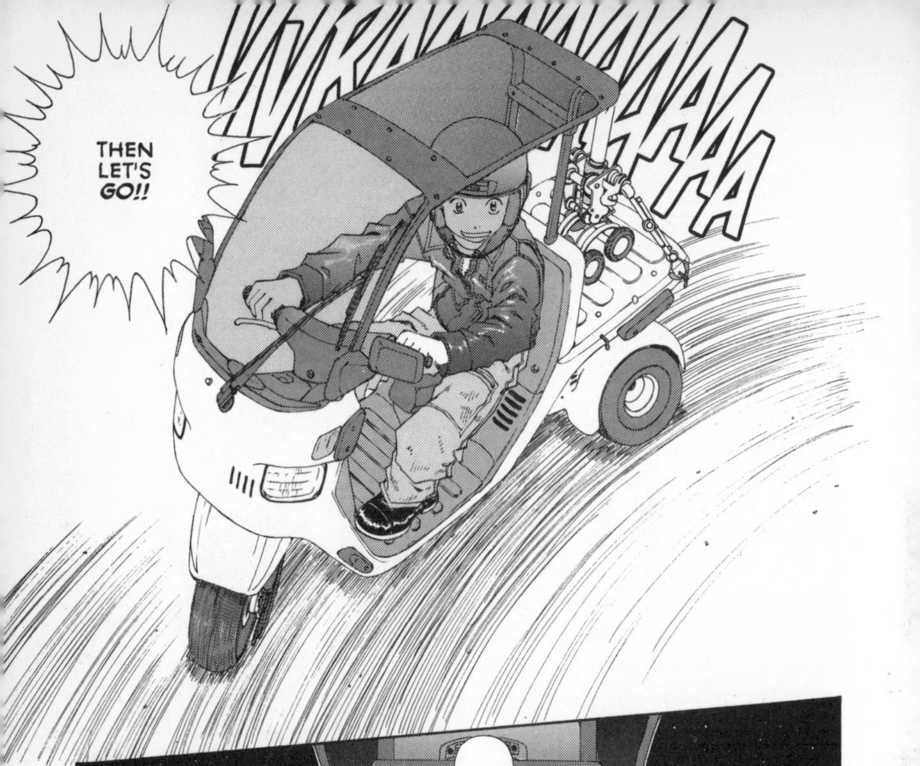
THEN LET'S GO!!
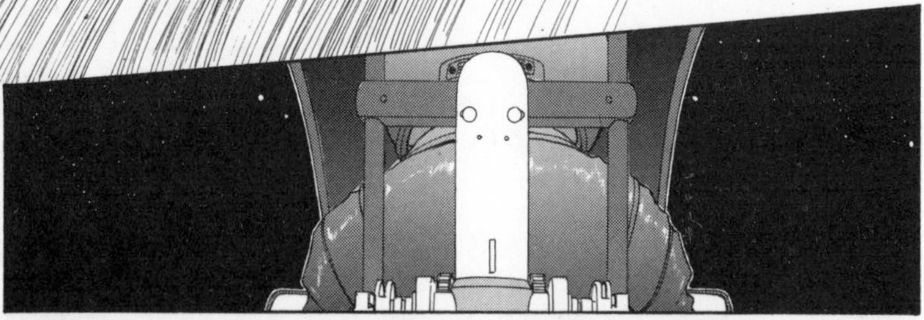
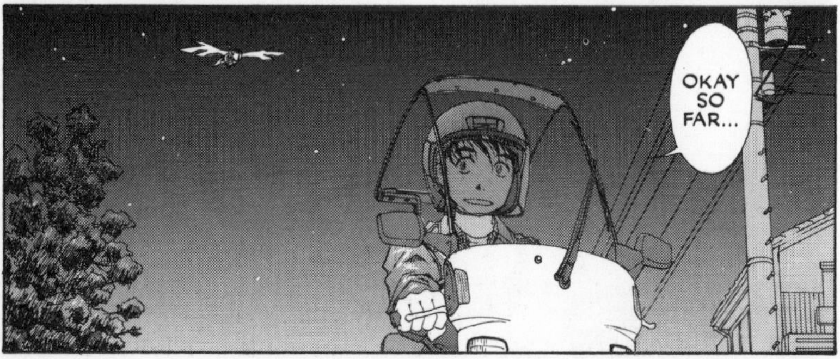
OKAY SO FAR...

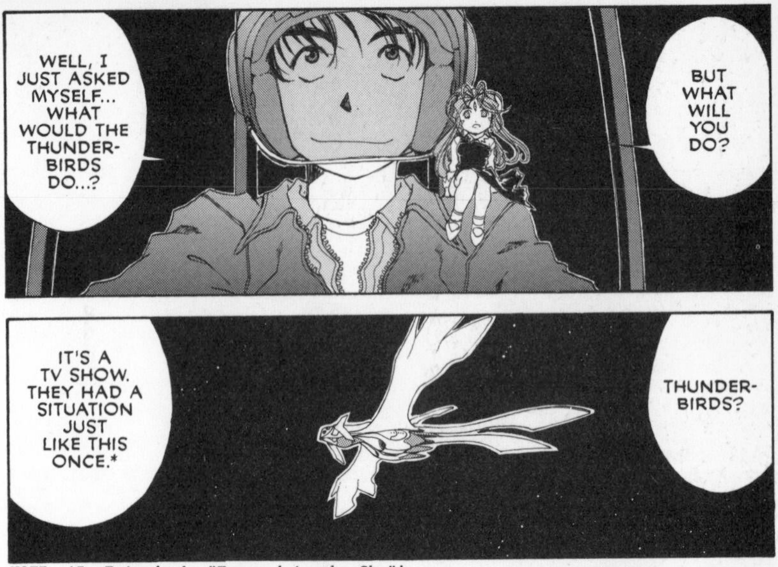
BUT WHAT WILL YOU DO?
WELL, I JUST ASKED MYSELF... WHAT WOULD THE THUNDER-BIRDS DO...?
THUNDER-BIRDS?
IT'S A TV SHOW. THEY HAD A SITUATION JUST LIKE THIS ONCE.*

NOTE: *In Episode 1, "Trapped in the Sky"!

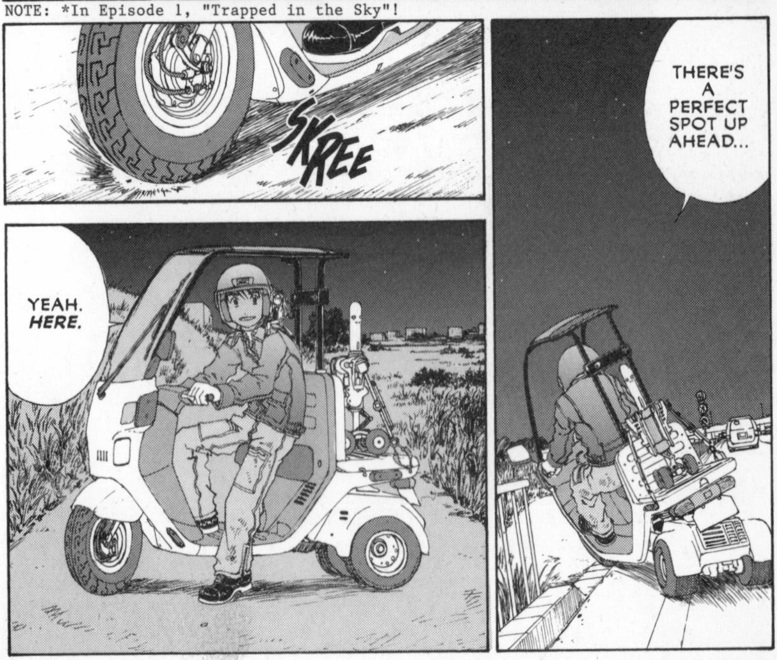
THERE'S A PERFECT SPOT UP AHEAD...
SKREE
YEAH. *HERE.*

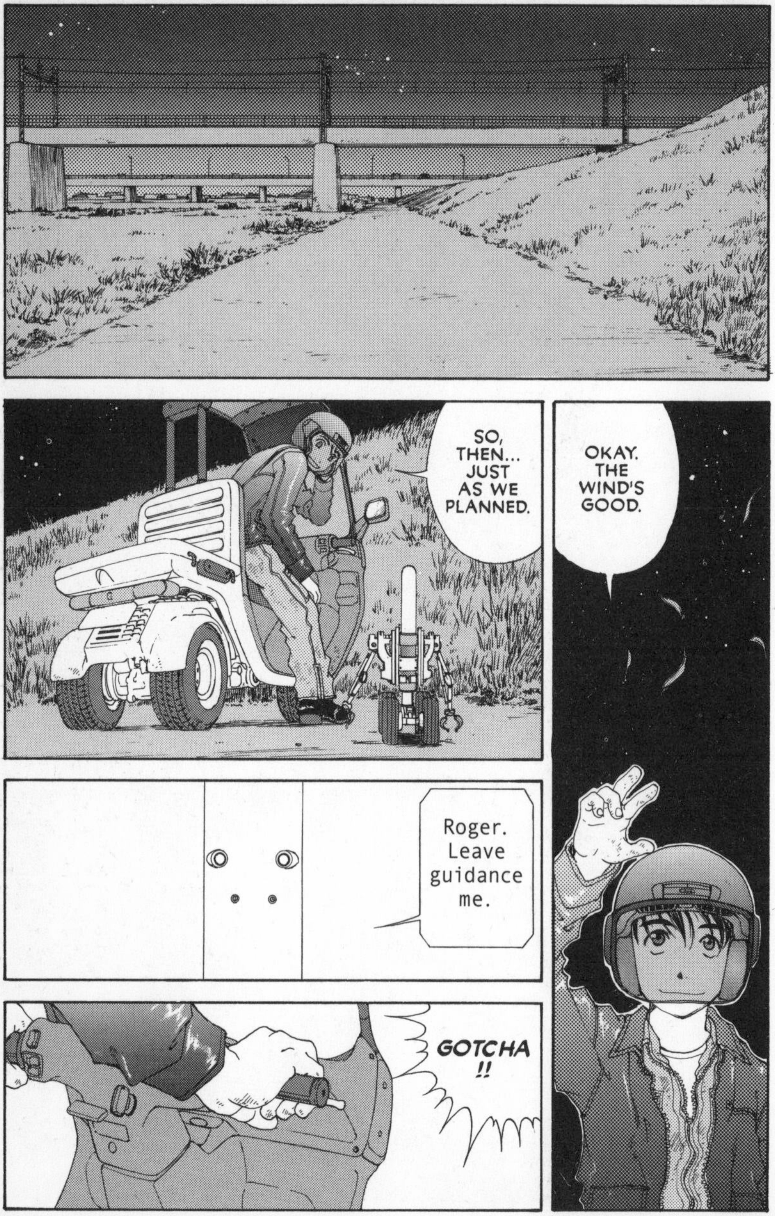
OKAY. THE WIND'S GOOD.
SO, THEN... JUST AS WE PLANNED.
Roger. Leave guidance me.
GOTCHA !!

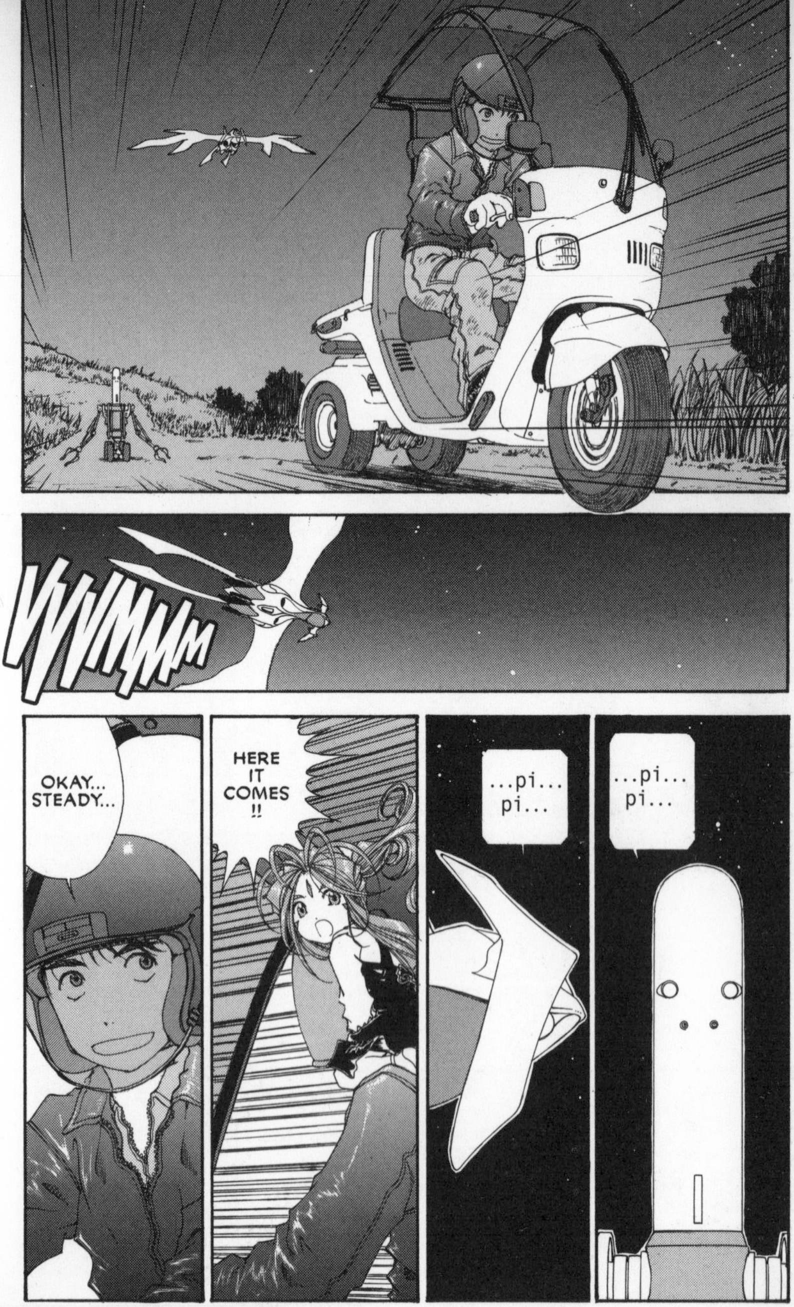
VVVMMMM
...pi... pi...
...pi... pi...
HERE IT COMES !!
OKAY... STEADY...

VWEEEEEN
CHNKK

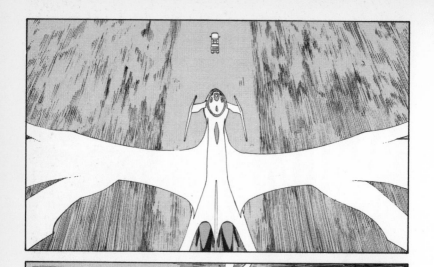

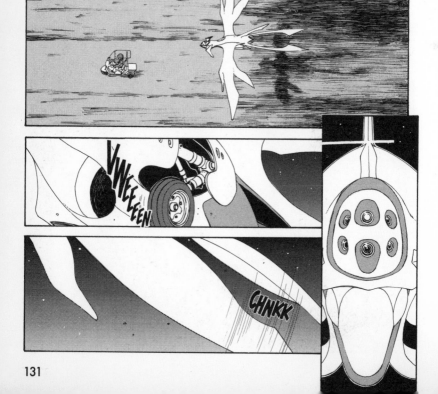

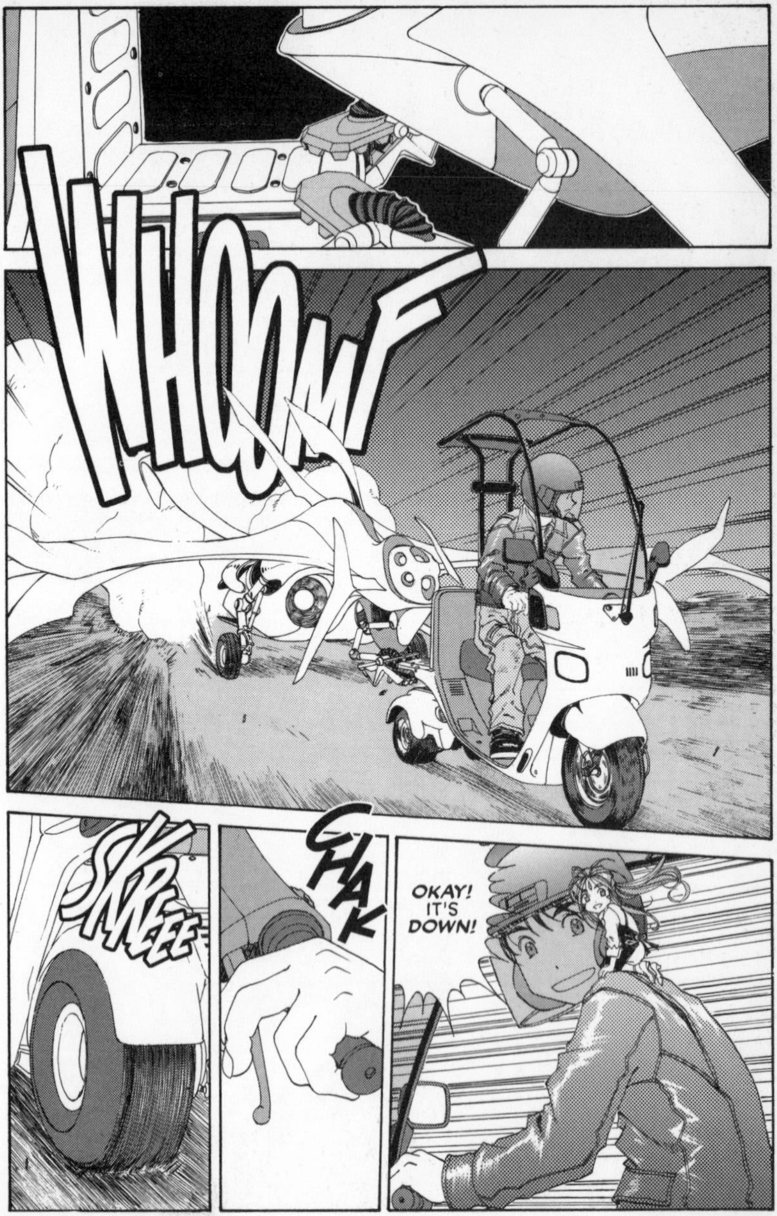
WHOOMF
OKAY! IT'S DOWN!
CHAK
SKREEE

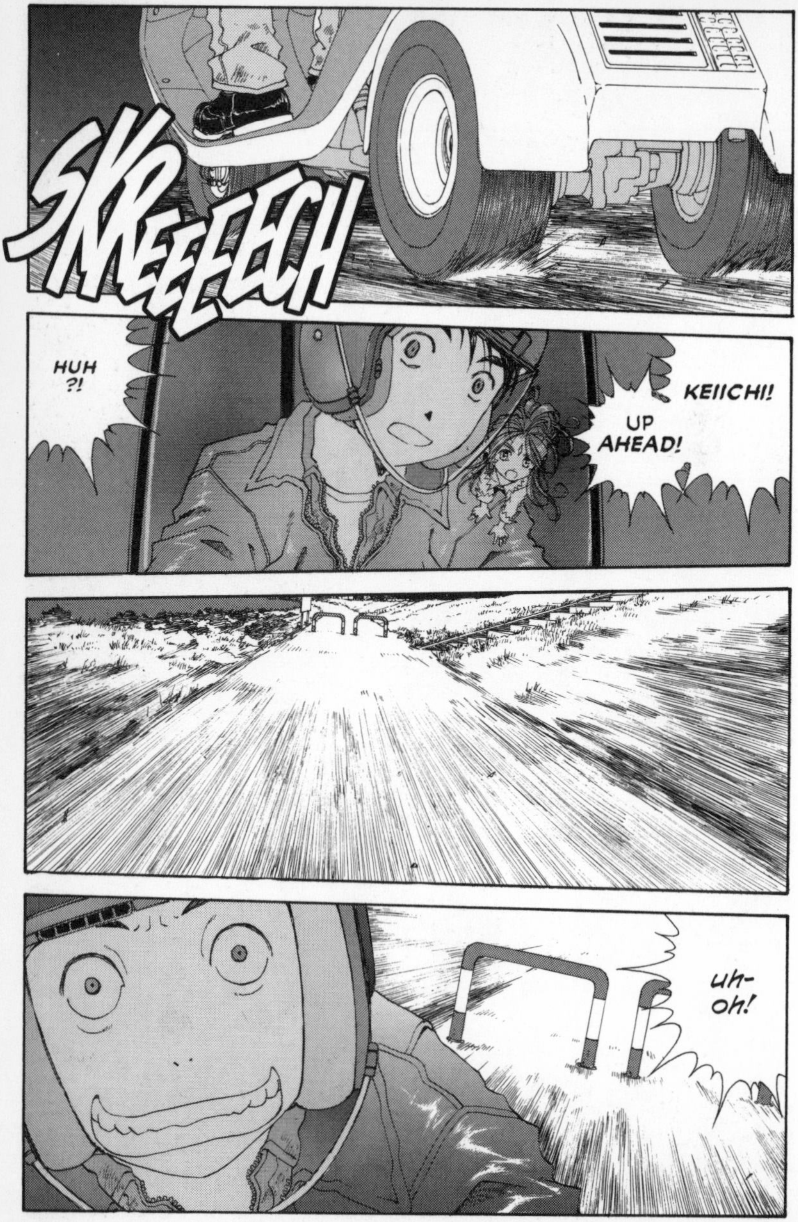
SKREEEECH
KEIICHI! UP AHEAD!
HUH ?!
uh-oh!

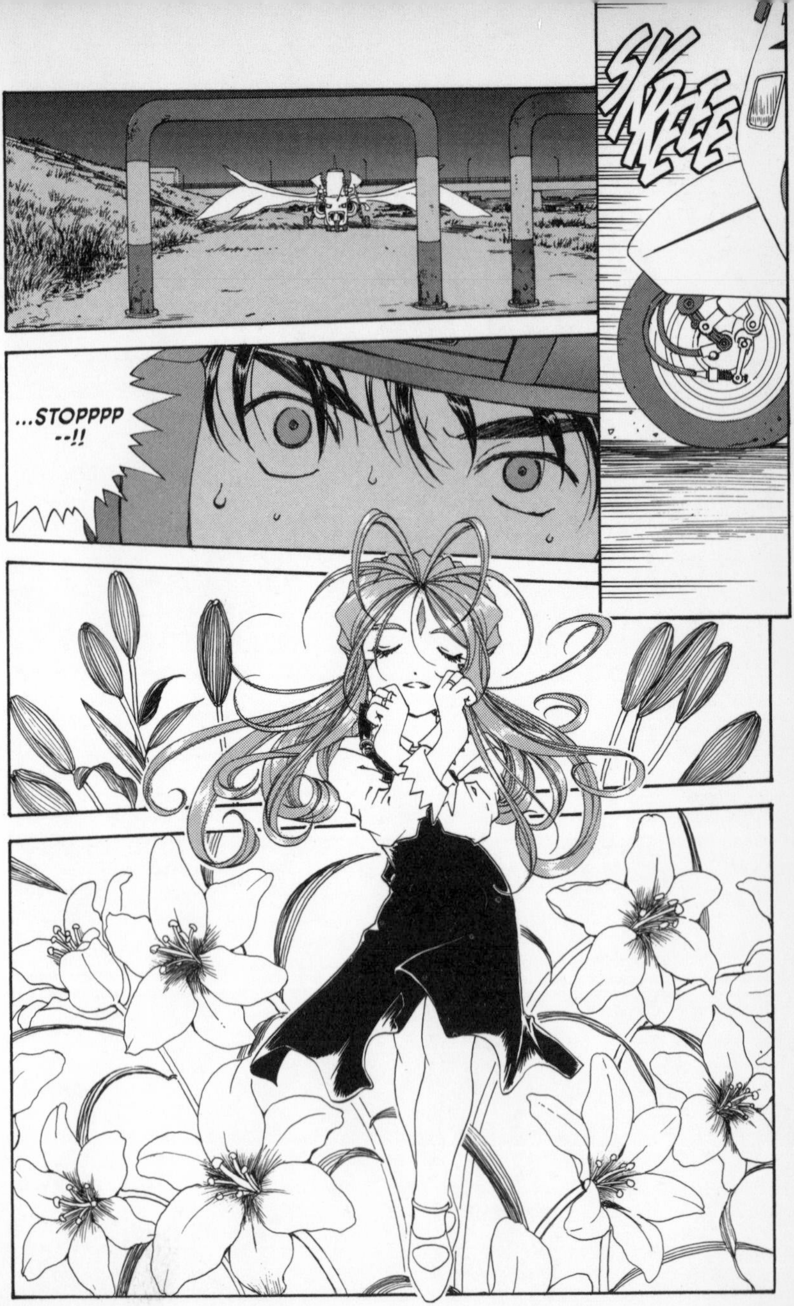
SKREEE
...STOPPPP
--!!

CHAPTER 176

Sign of Gratitude

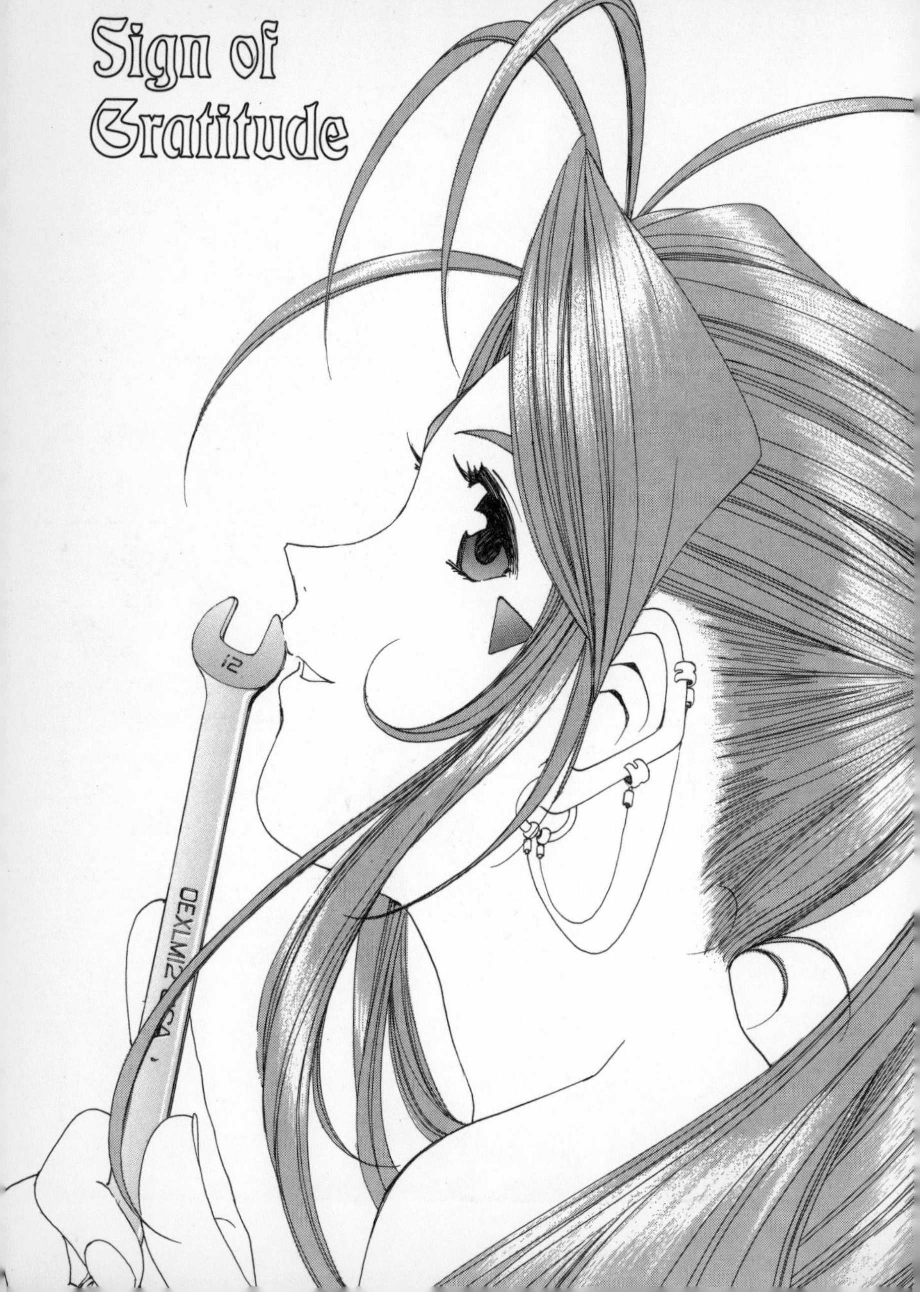

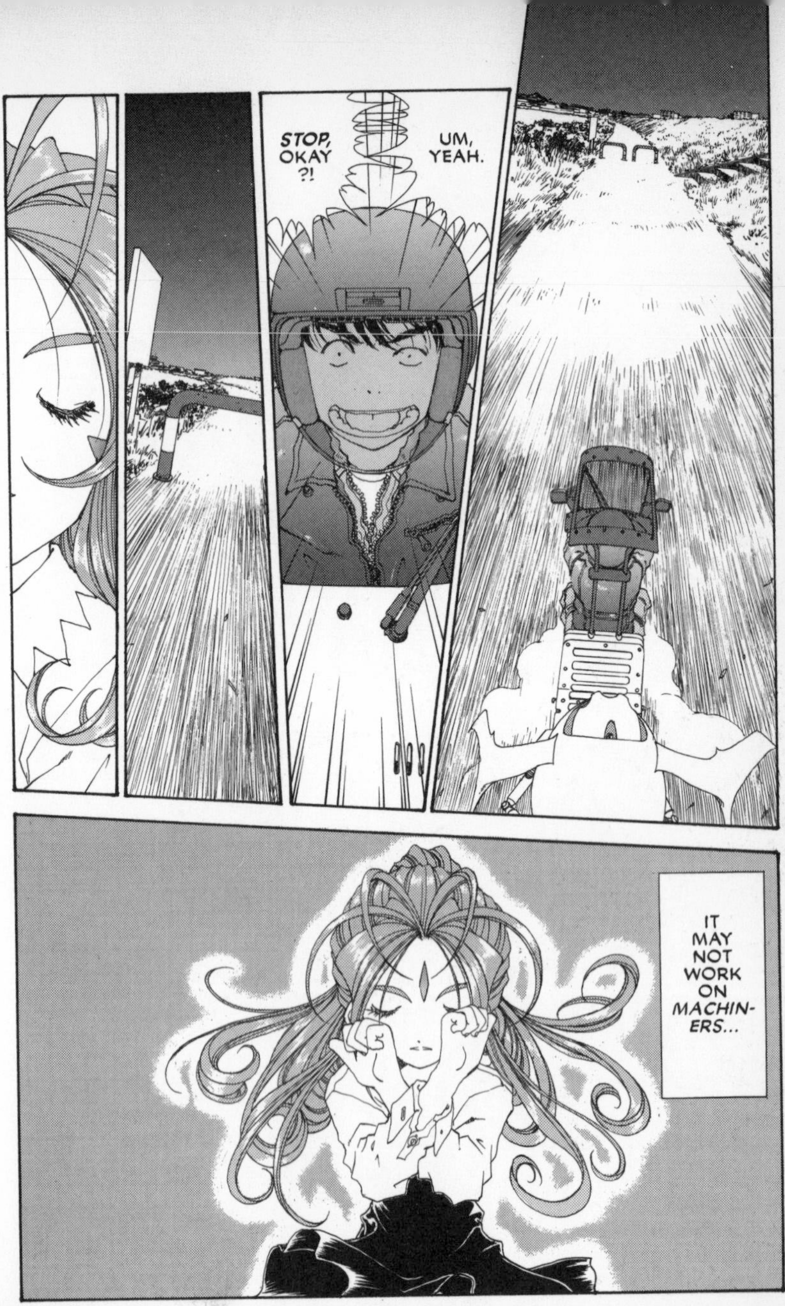
UM, YEAH.
STOP, OKAY?!
IT MAY NOT WORK ON *MACHINERS*...

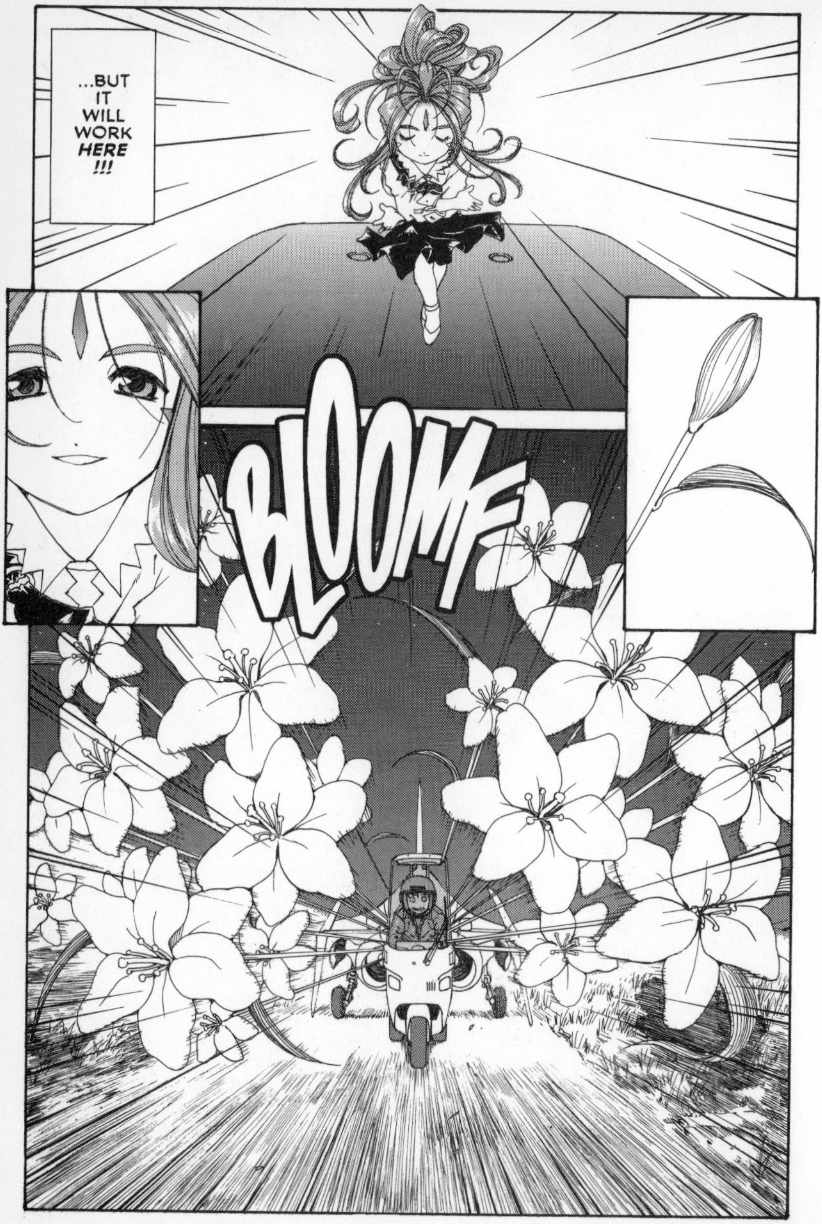
...BUT IT WILL WORK HERE!!!
BLOOMF

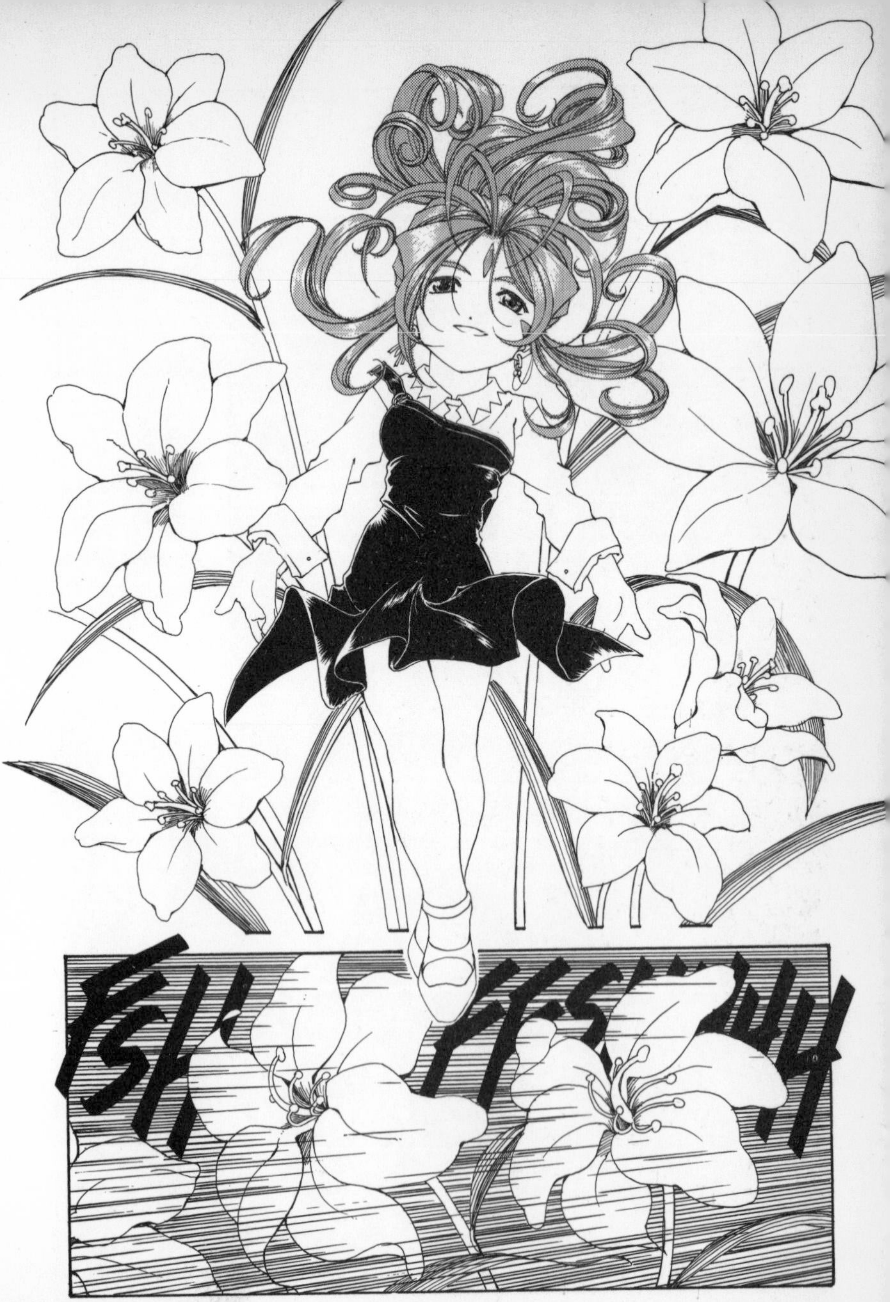

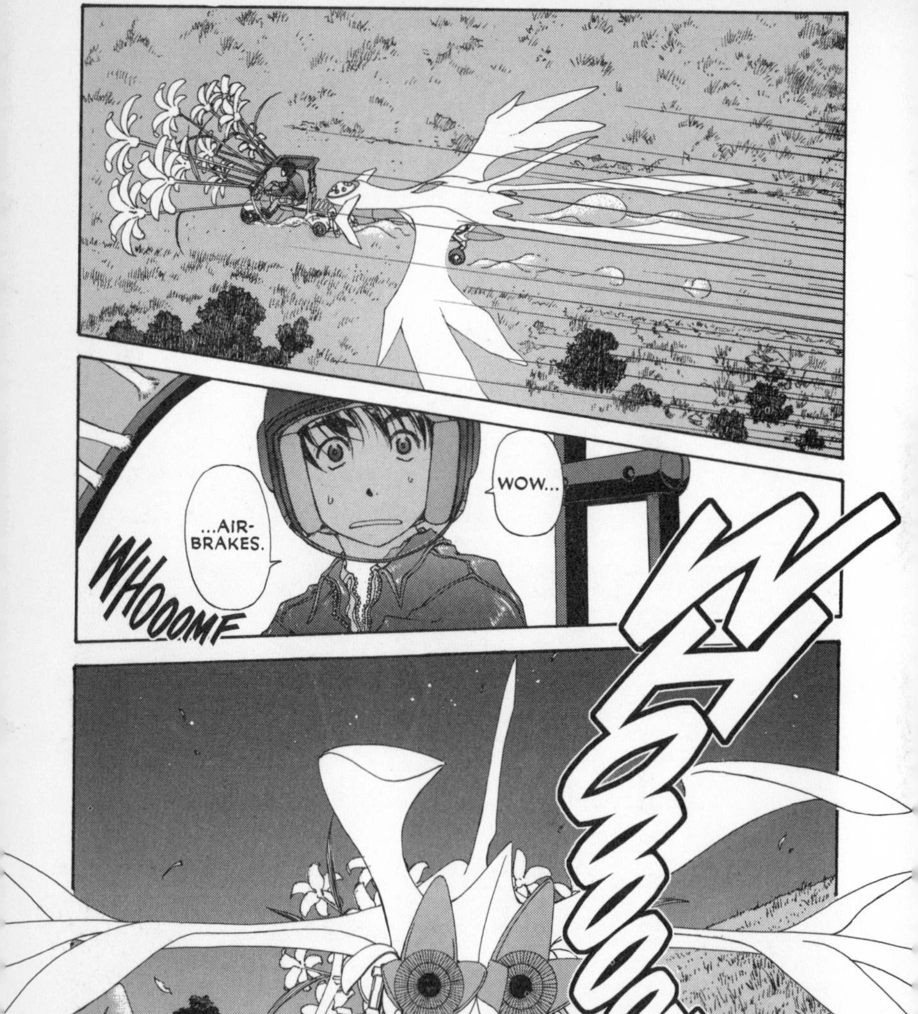
WOW...
...AIR-BRAKES.
WHOOOMF
WHOOOOOOMMFF

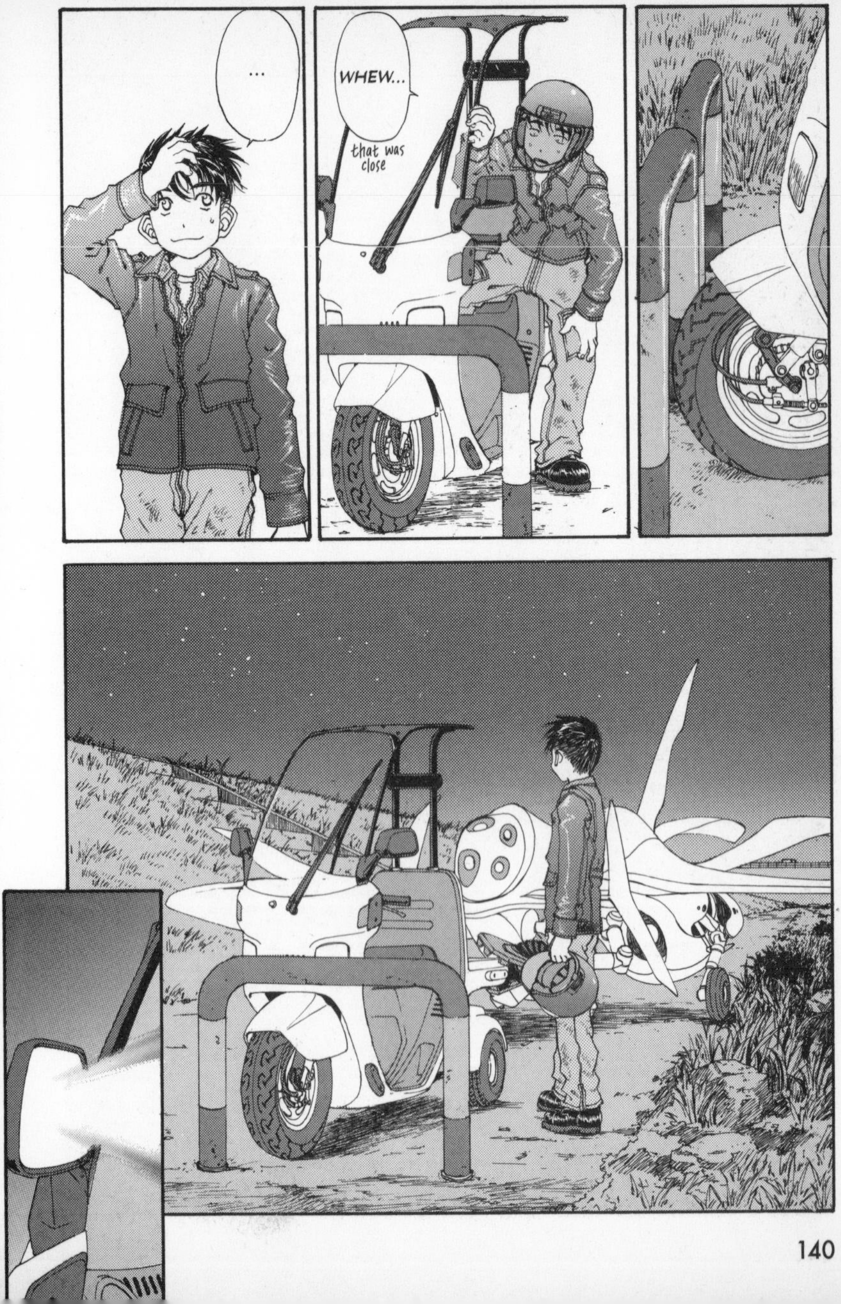
WHEW...
that was close
...

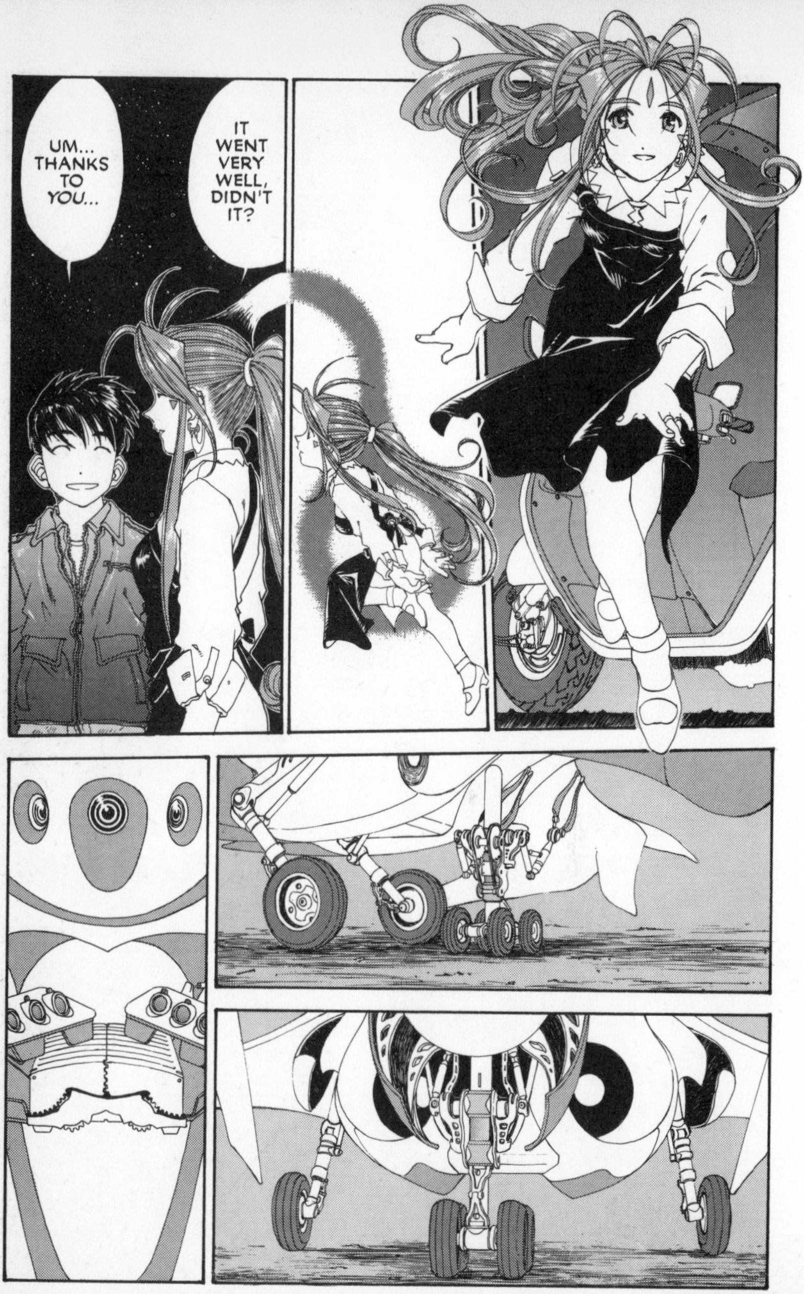
IT WENT VERY WELL, DIDN'T IT?
UM... THANKS TO *YOU*...

This sign of gratitude is.

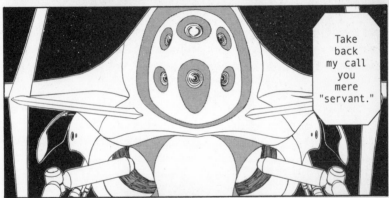

Take back my call you mere "servant."

WHRRRN

You HIGH GRADE of servant are.

OH... THAT'S ALL...

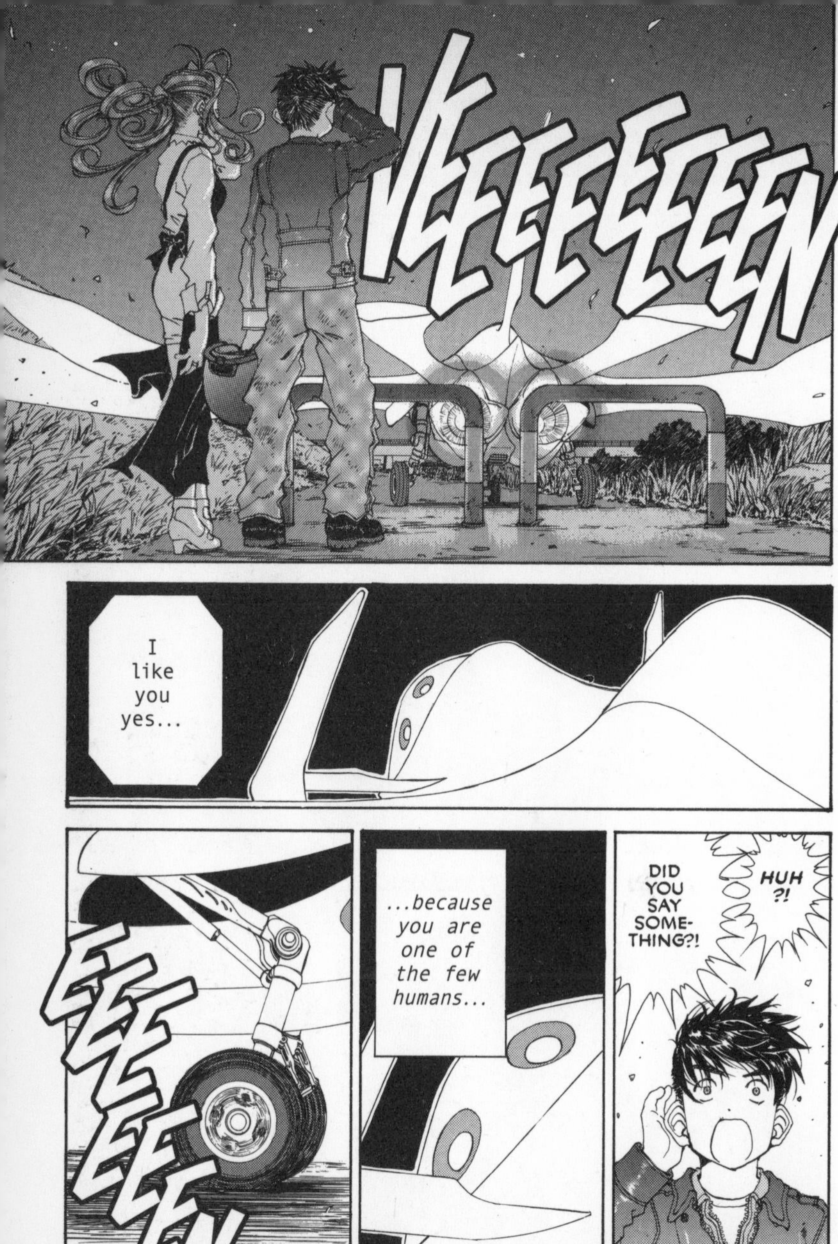
VEEEEEEEEN
I like you yes...
HUH?!
DID YOU SAY SOME-THING?!
...because you are one of the few humans...
EEEEEEN

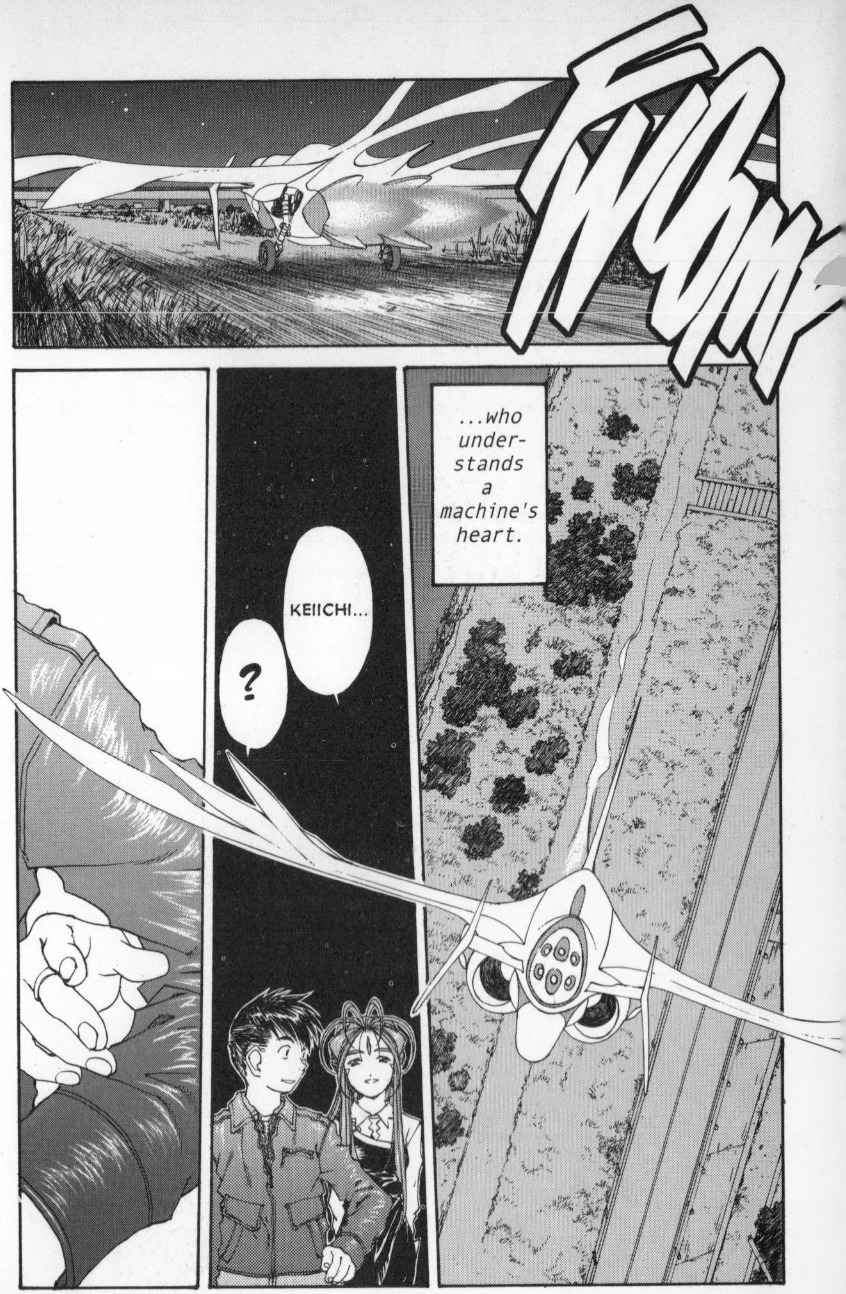
...who understands a machine's heart.
KEIICHI...
?

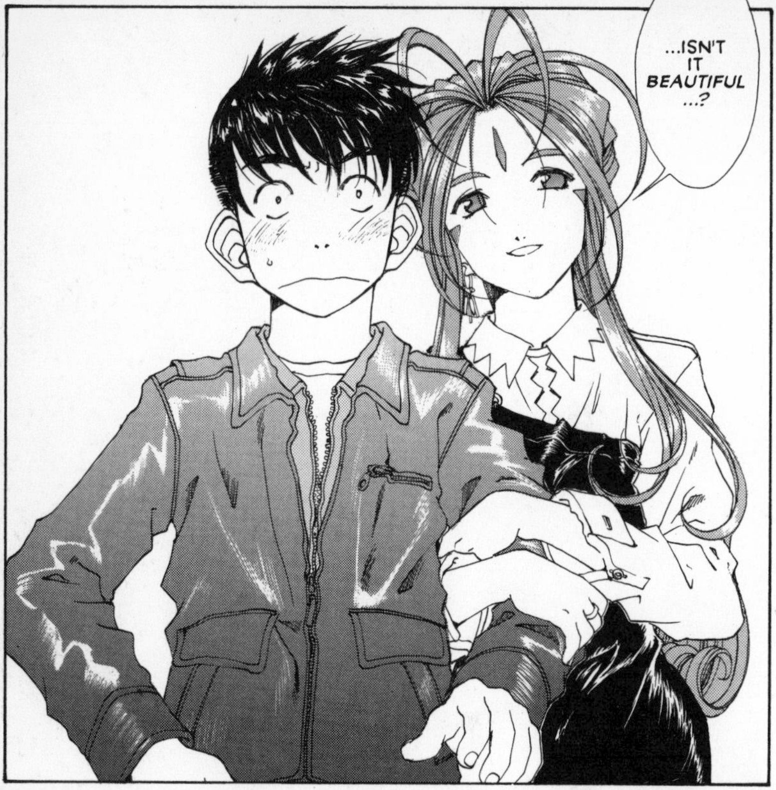
...ISN'T IT BEAUTIFUL ...?

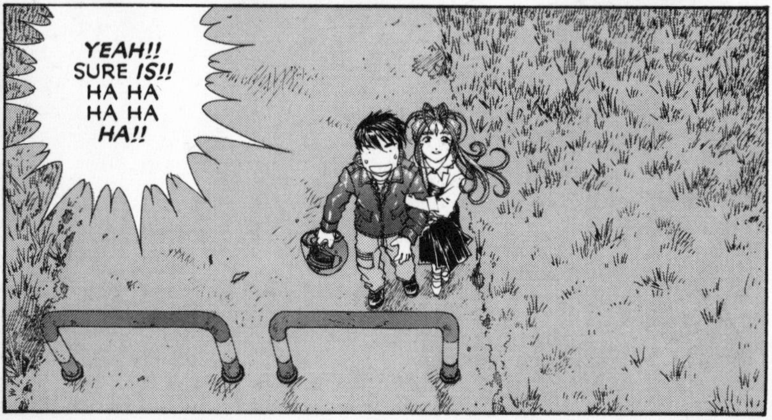
YEAH!! SURE IS!! HA HA HA HA HA!!

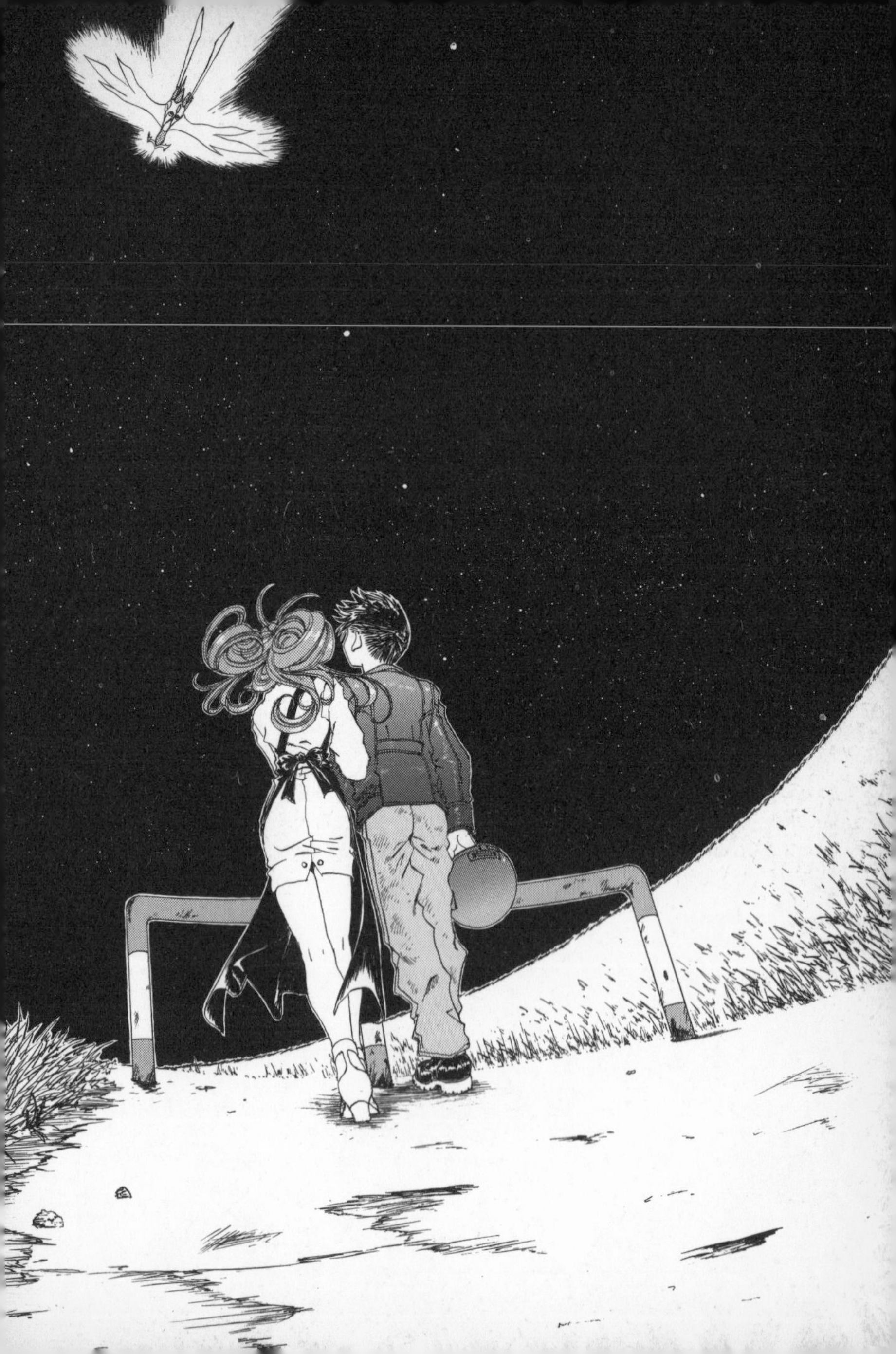

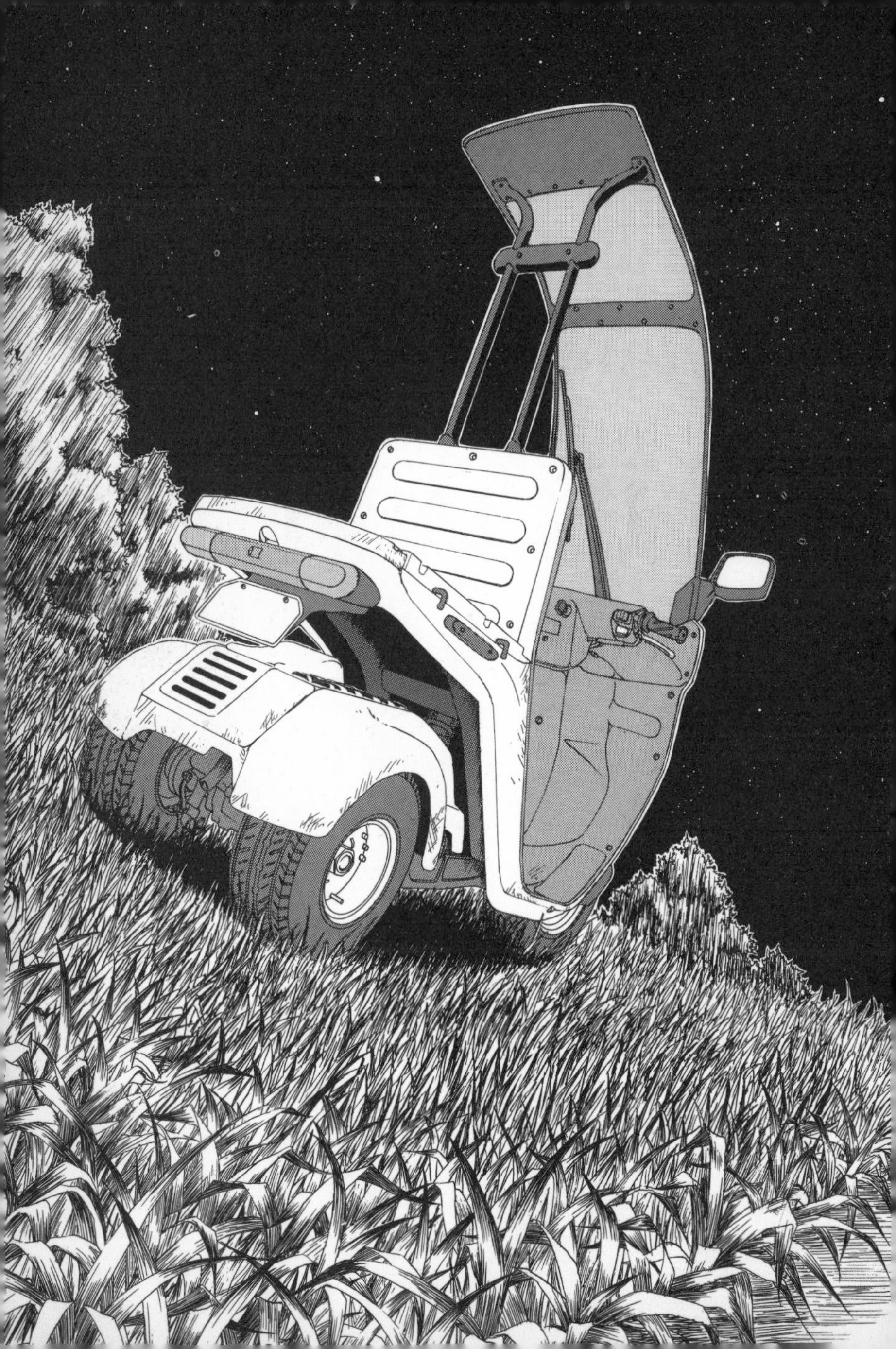

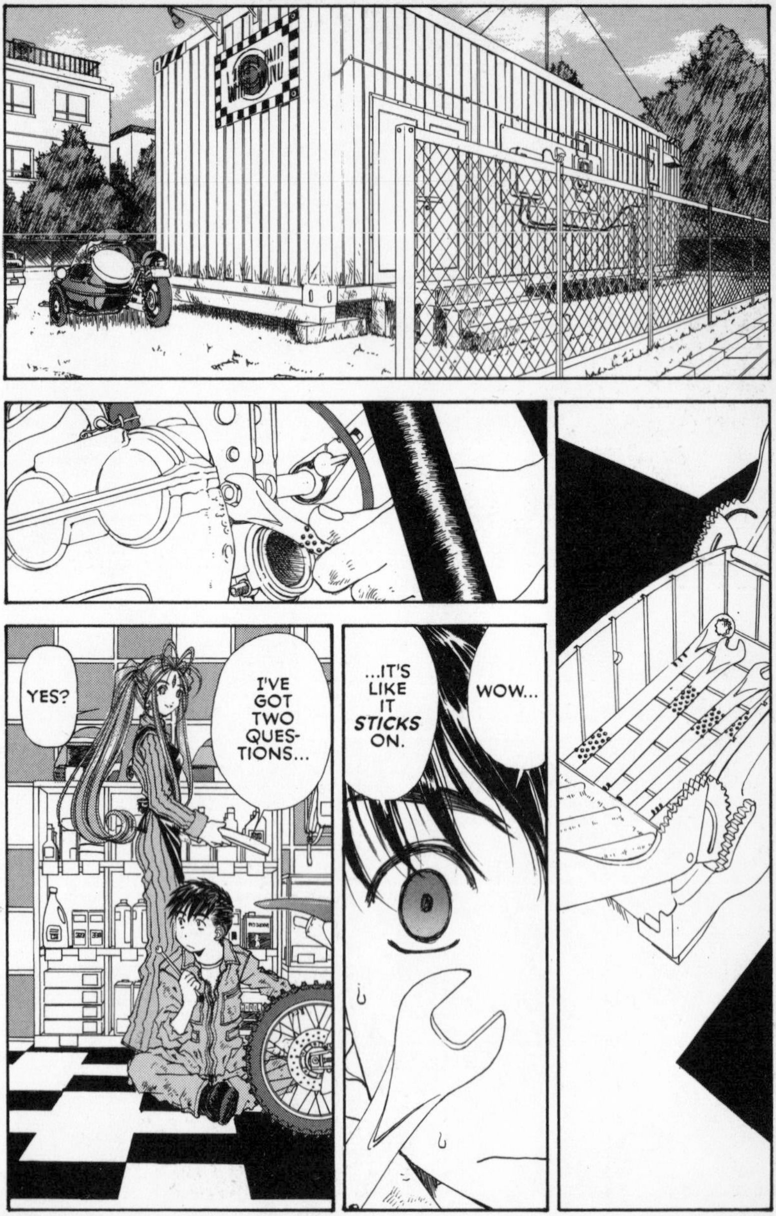
WOW...
...IT'S LIKE IT STICKS ON.
I'VE GOT TWO QUES-TIONS...
YES?

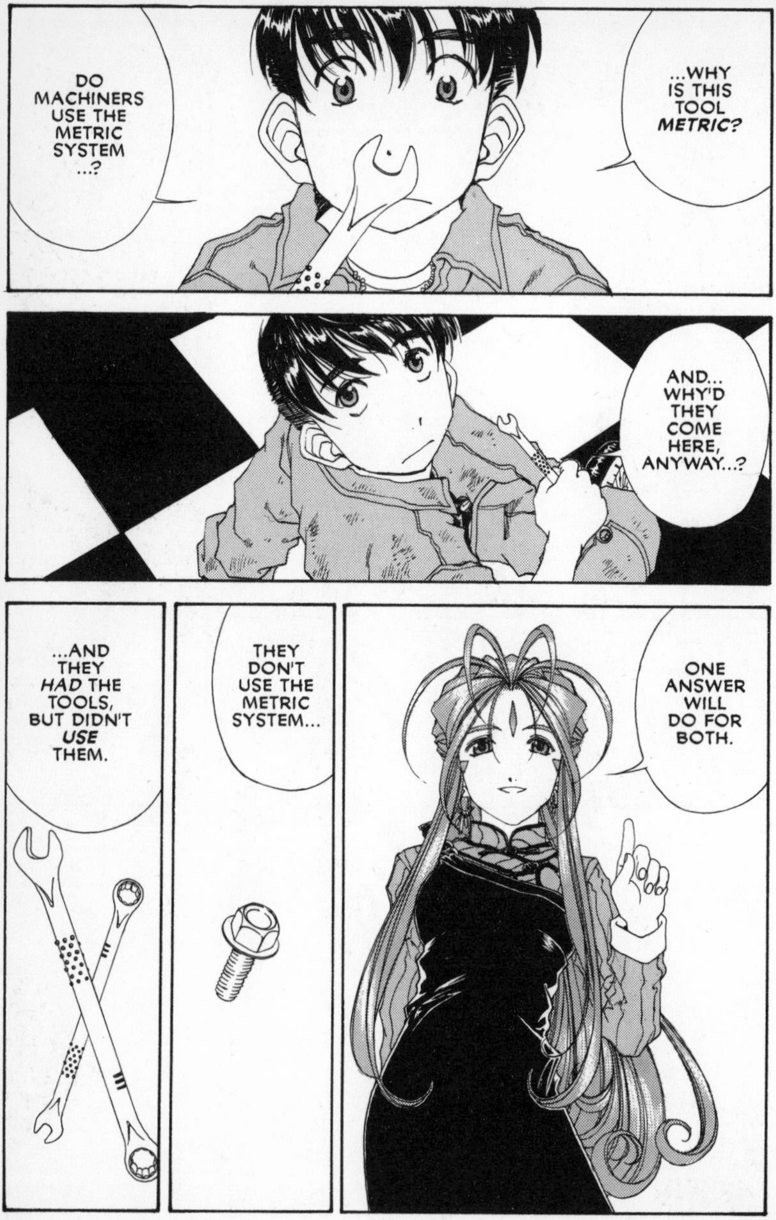
...WHY IS THIS TOOL *METRIC?*
DO MACHINERS USE THE METRIC SYSTEM ...?
AND... WHY'D THEY COME HERE, ANYWAY...?
ONE ANSWER WILL DO FOR BOTH.
THEY DON'T USE THE METRIC SYSTEM...
...AND THEY *HAD* THE TOOLS, BUT DIDN'T *USE* THEM.

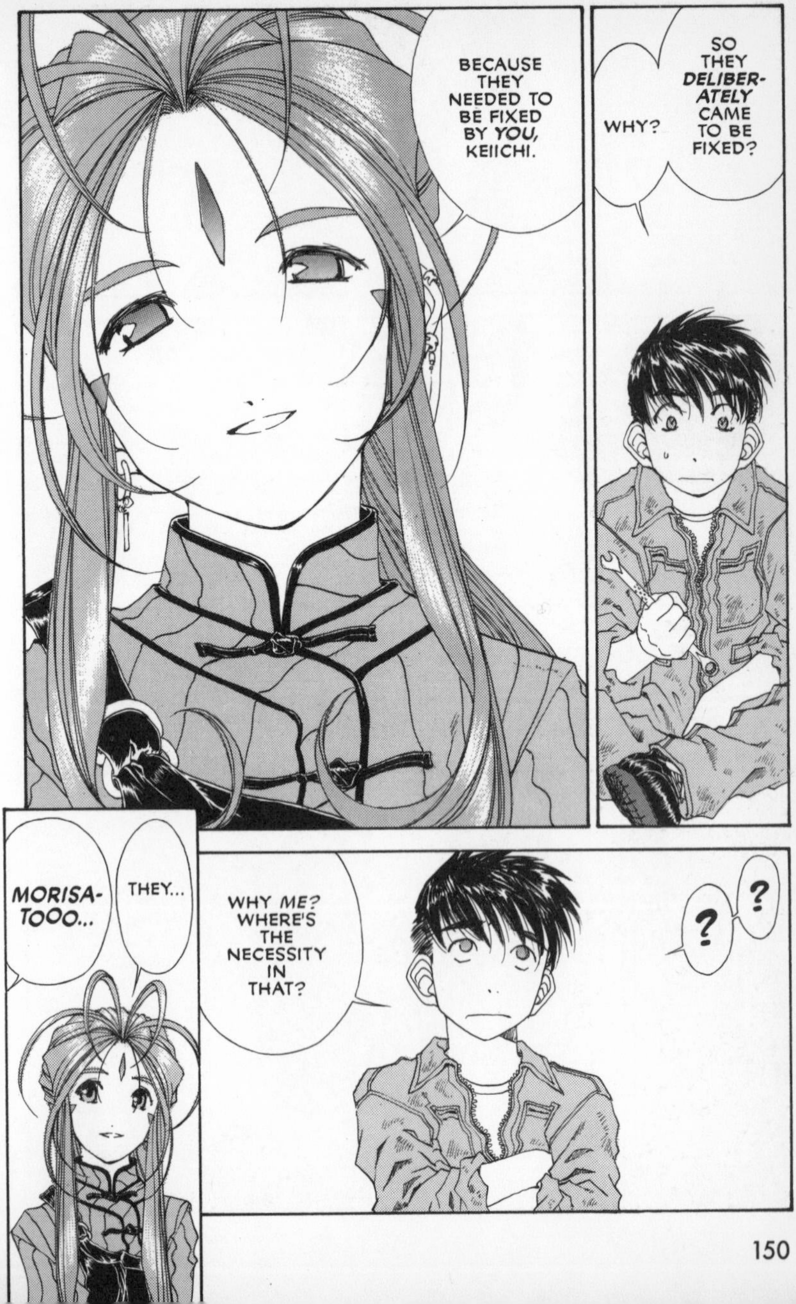
SO THEY *DELIBERATELY* CAME TO BE FIXED?
WHY?
BECAUSE THEY NEEDED TO BE FIXED BY *YOU*, KEIICHI.
?
?
WHY *ME?* WHERE'S THE NECESSITY IN THAT?
THEY...
MORISA-TOOO...

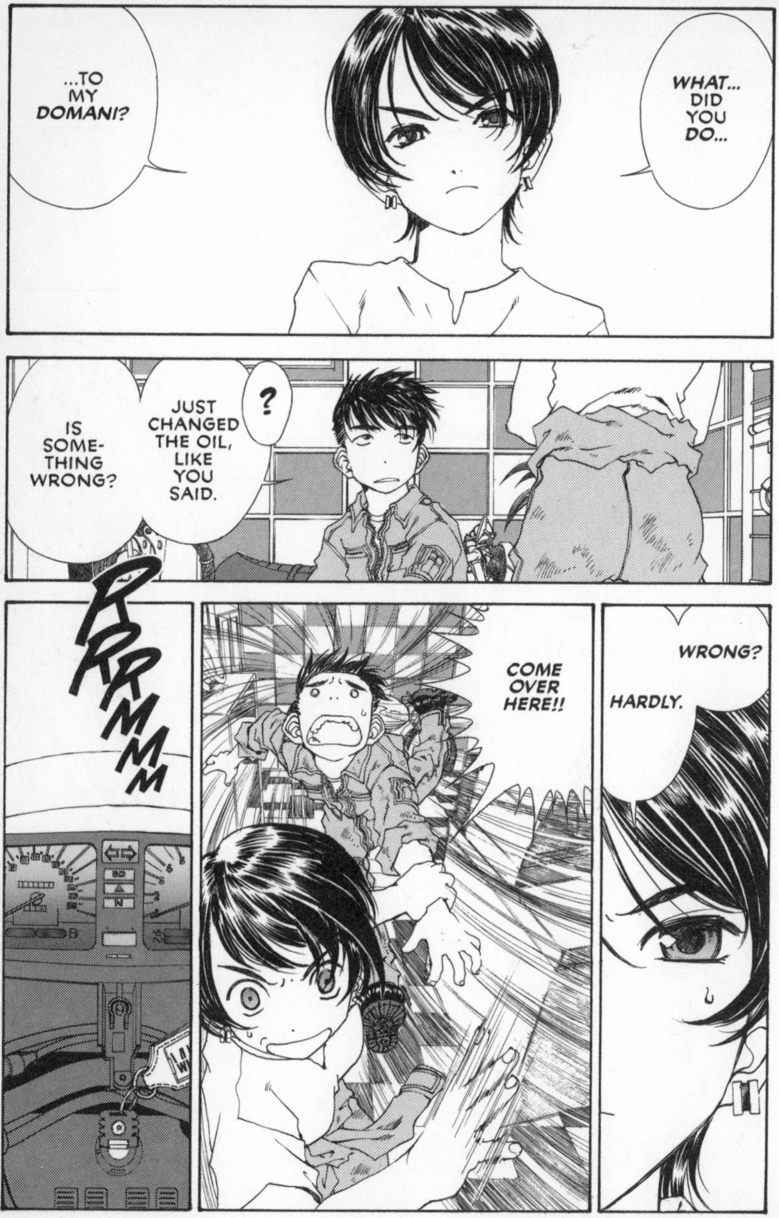
WHAT... DID YOU DO...
...TO MY DOMANI?
?
JUST CHANGED THE OIL, LIKE YOU SAID.
IS SOME-THING WRONG?
WRONG?
HARDLY.
COME OVER HERE!!
RRRMMMM

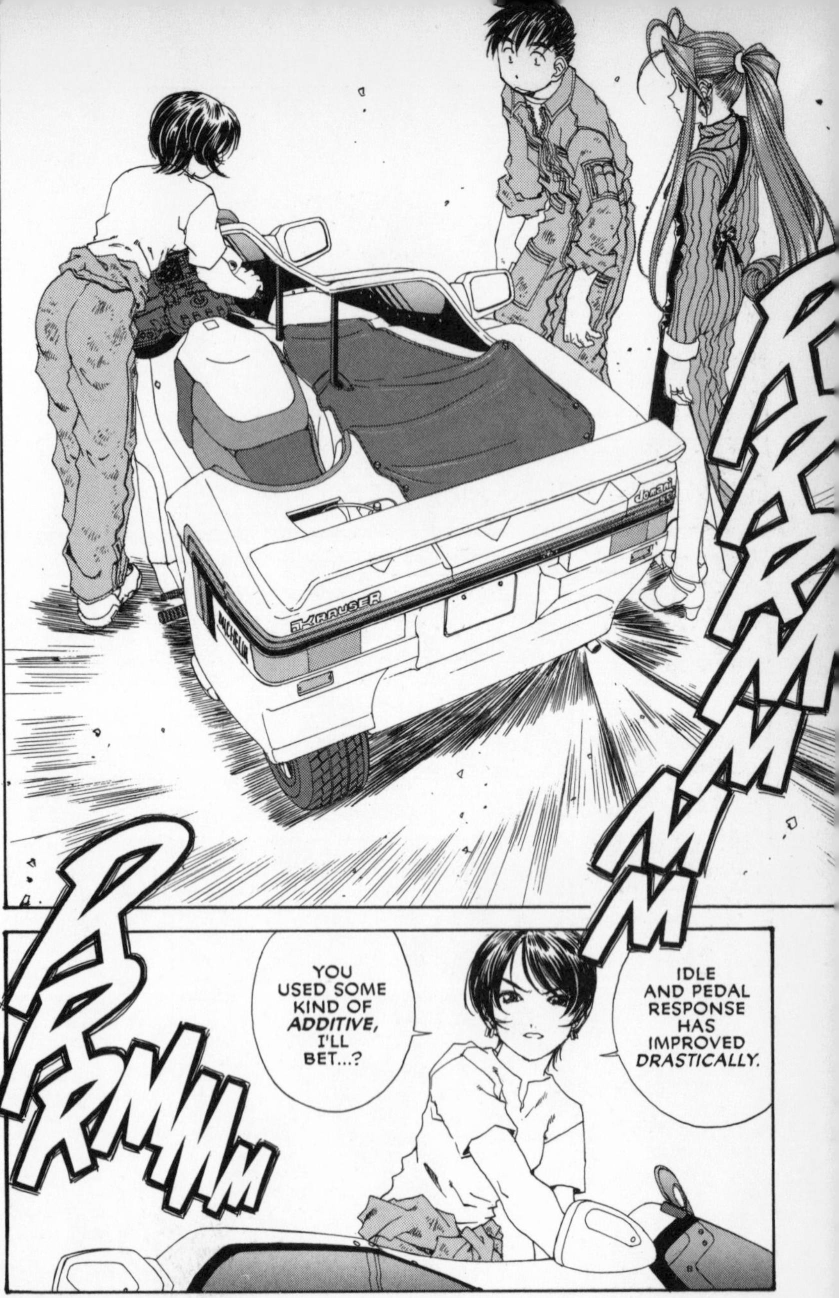
IDLE AND PEDAL RESPONSE HAS IMPROVED *DRASTICALLY*.
YOU USED SOME KIND OF *ADDITIVE*, I'LL BET...?
BRMMMM

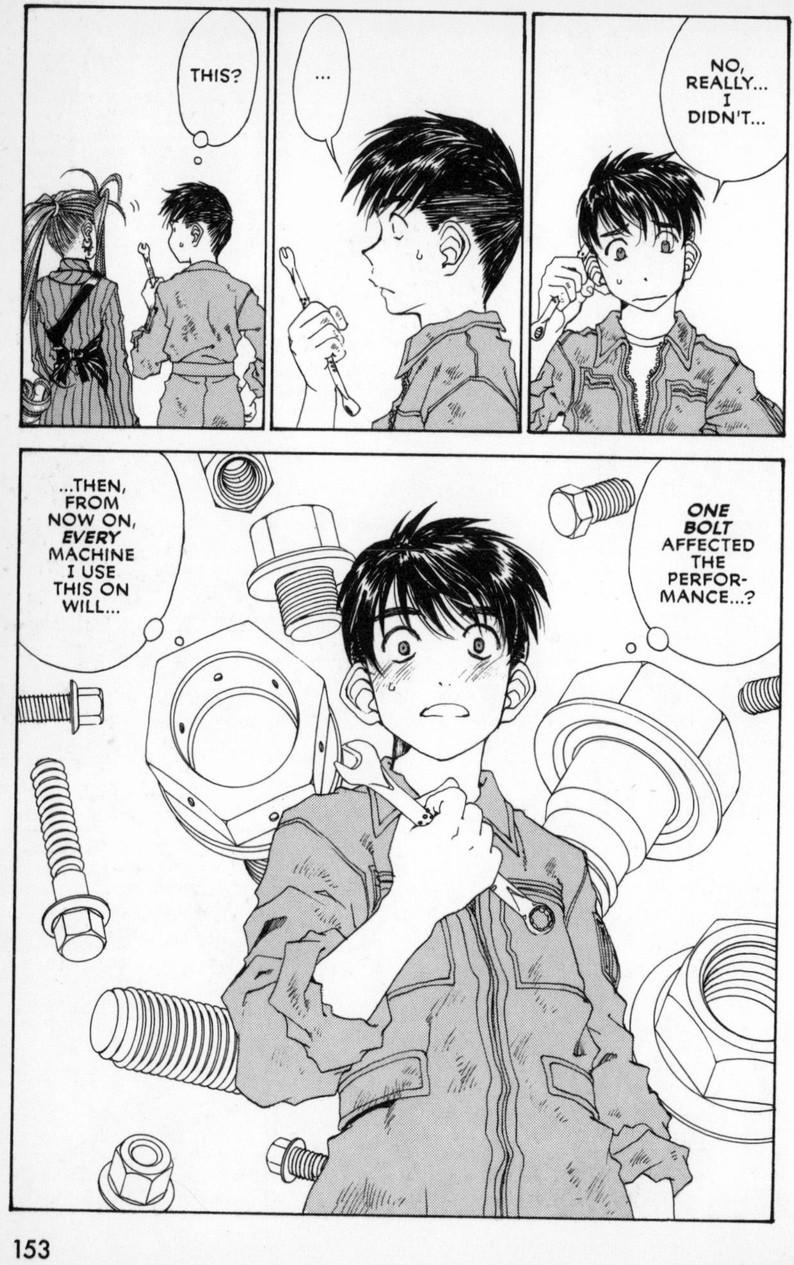
NO, REALLY... I DIDN'T...
...
THIS?
ONE BOLT AFFECTED THE PERFORMANCE...?
...THEN, FROM NOW ON, *EVERY* MACHINE I USE THIS ON WILL...

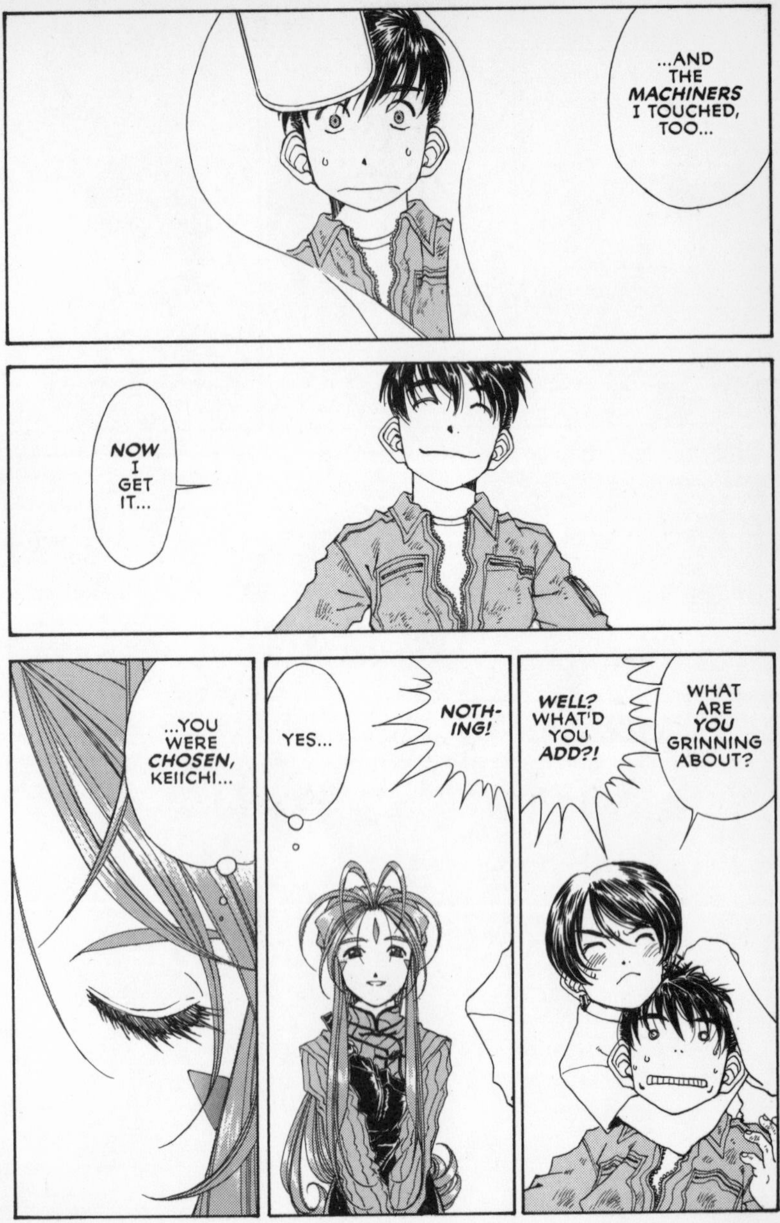
...AND THE MACHINERS I TOUCHED, TOO...
NOW I GET IT...
WHAT ARE YOU GRINNING ABOUT?
WELL? WHAT'D YOU ADD?!
NOTH-ING!
YES...
...YOU WERE CHOSEN, KEIICHI...

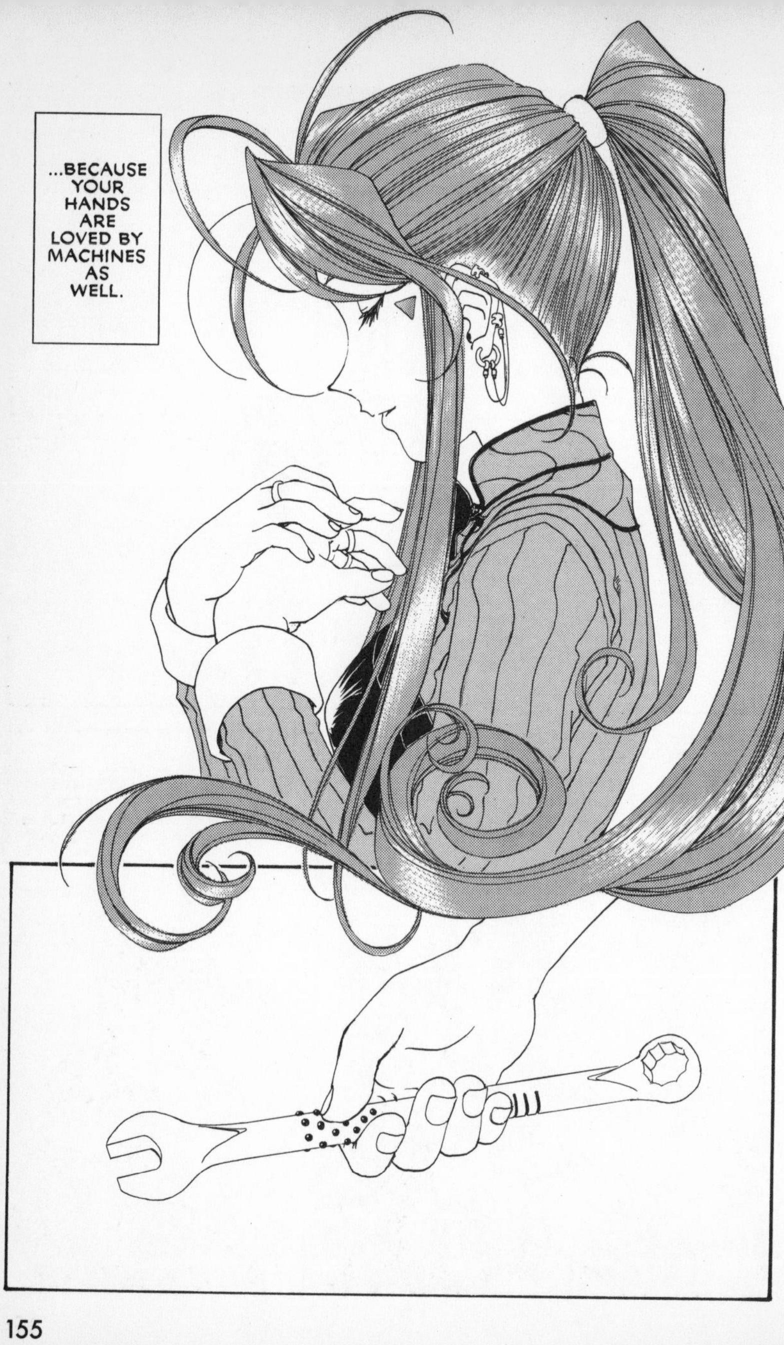
...BECAUSE YOUR HANDS ARE LOVED BY MACHINES AS WELL.

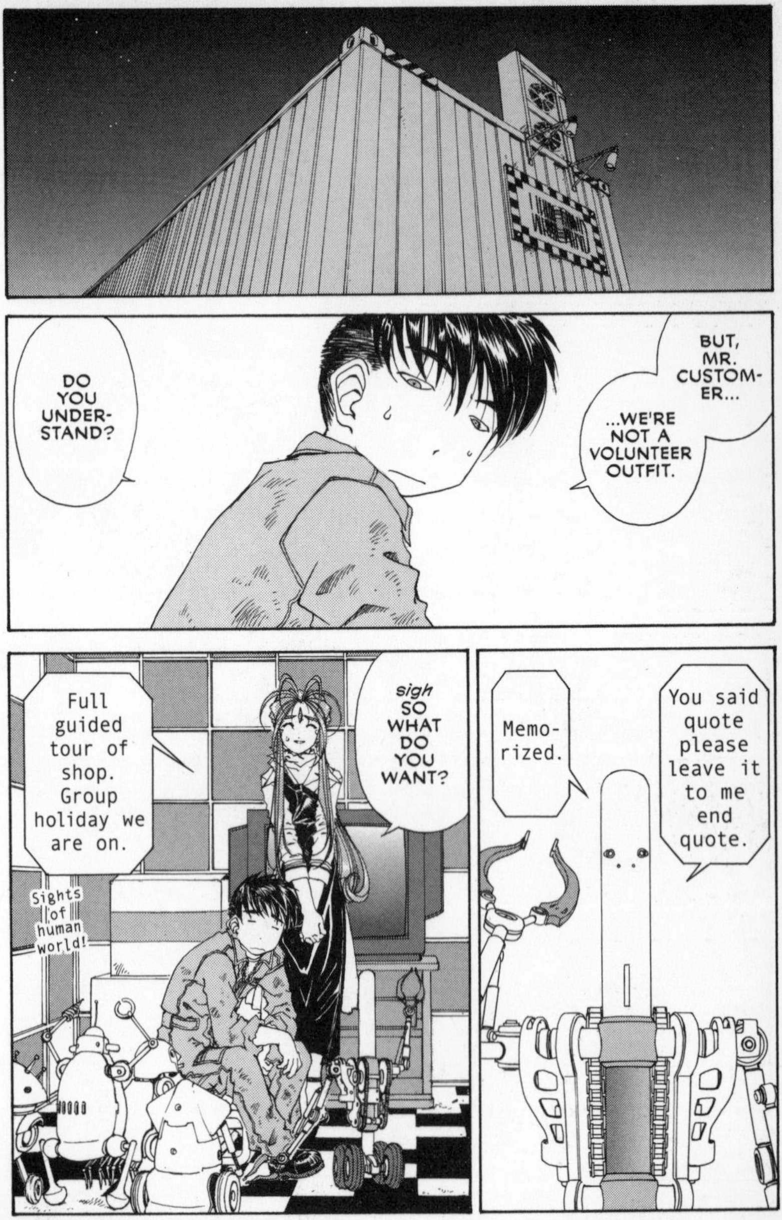

BUT, MR. CUSTOMER...
...WE'RE NOT A VOLUNTEER OUTFIT.
DO YOU UNDERSTAND?
You said quote please leave it to me end quote.
Memorized.
sigh SO WHAT DO YOU WANT?
Full guided tour of shop. Group holiday we are on.
Sights of human world!

ADVENTURES OF THE MINI-GODDESSES SPECIAL: MAGICAL DO-MI-SO KABOOM!

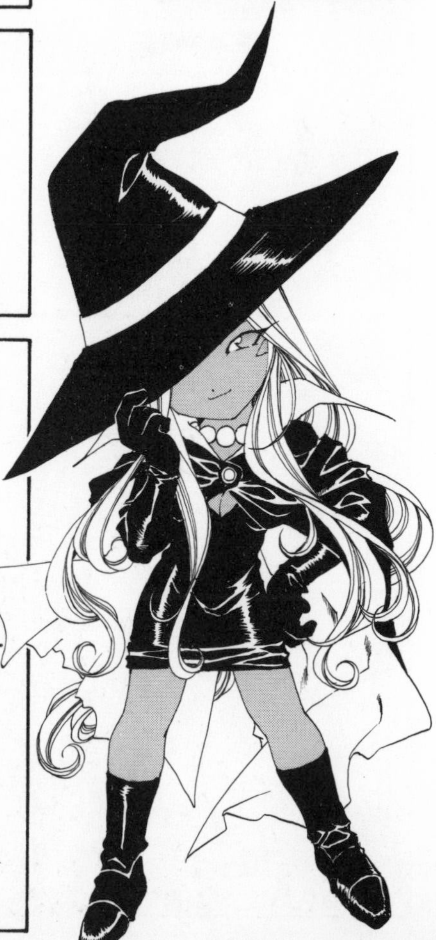

THE KING AND I

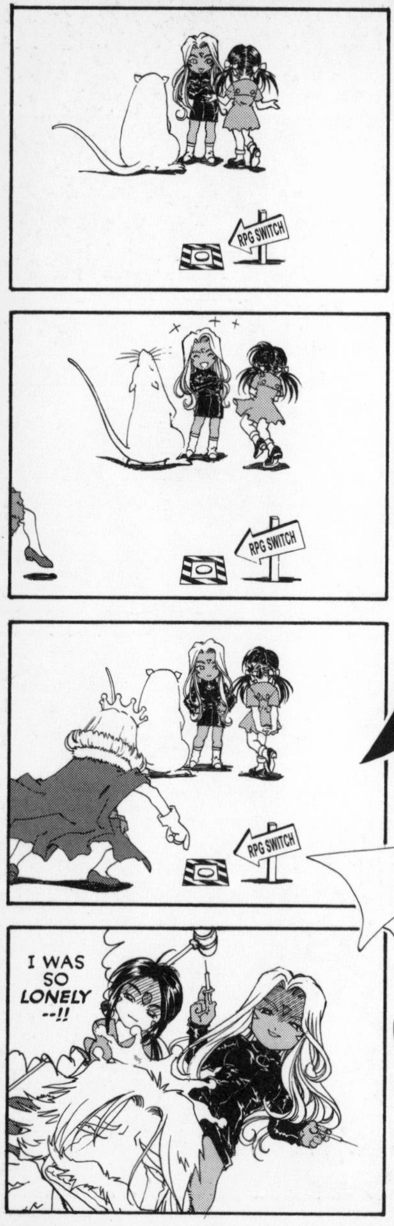
RPG SWITCH
RPG SWITCH
RPG SWITCH
I WAS SO *LONELY* --!!

NO WAY!! I CHECKED FIVE TIMES!!

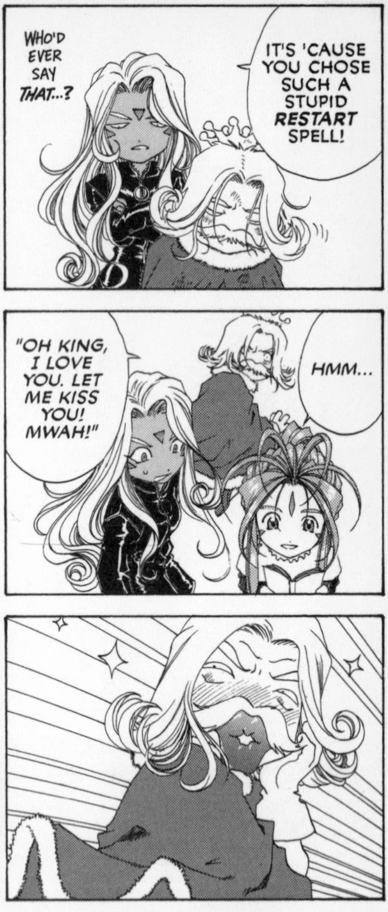
IT'S 'CAUSE YOU CHOSE SUCH A STUPID *RESTART* SPELL!
WHO'D EVER SAY *THAT*...?
HMM...
"OH KING, I LOVE YOU. LET ME KISS YOU! MWAH!"
PER-VERT KING!!
THAT'S *NOT* THE RESTART SPELL...

DOWSING KING

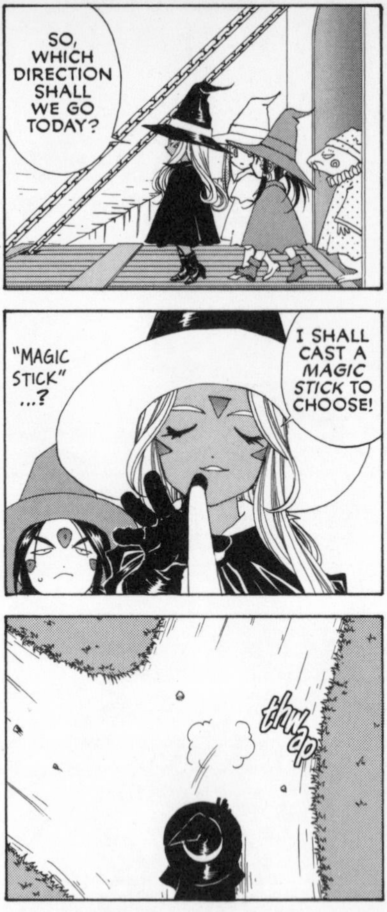
SO, WHICH DIRECTION SHALL WE GO TODAY?
I SHALL CAST A *MAGIC STICK* TO CHOOSE!
"MAGIC STICK" ...?
thwap
NO, YOU WANT *LEFT*, HUH?
LET ME GUESS. YOU'VE SET TRAPS THAT WAY.

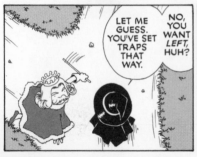

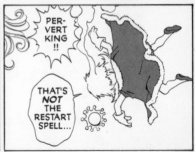

ECHO

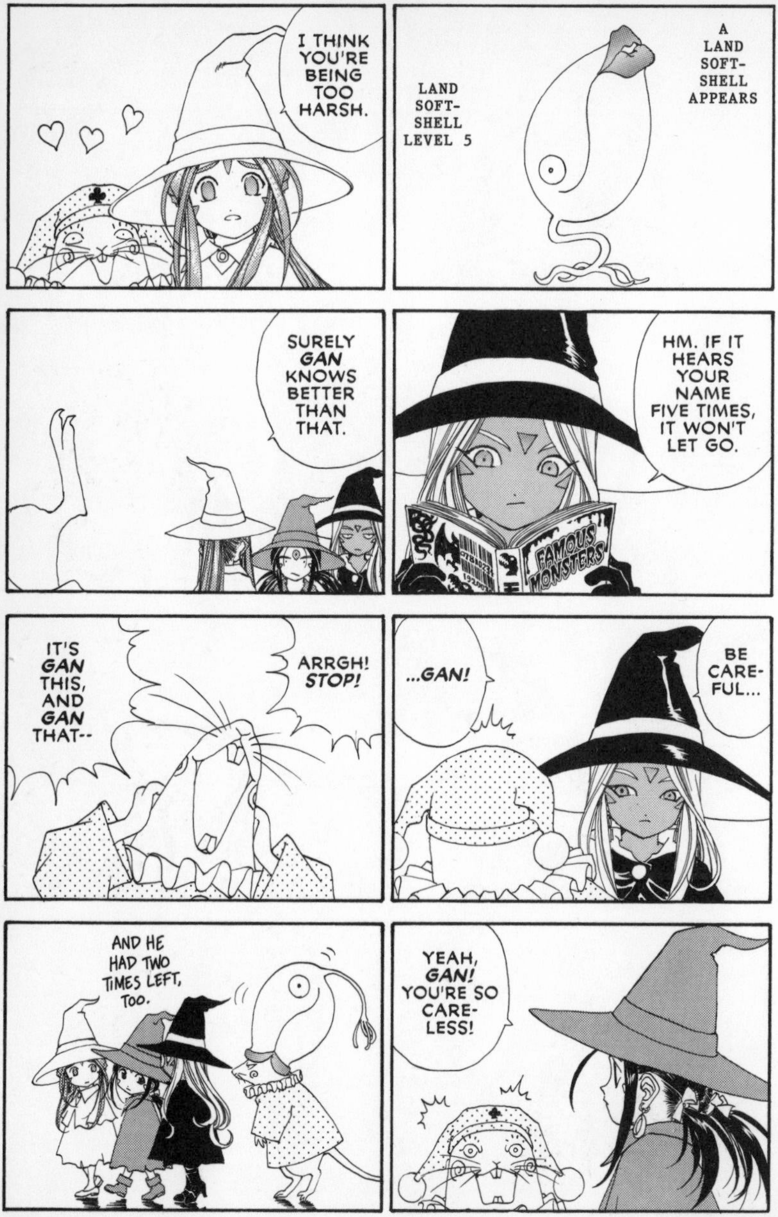
A LAND SOFT-SHELL APPEARS
LAND SOFT-SHELL LEVEL 5
I THINK YOU'RE BEING TOO HARSH.
HM. IF IT HEARS YOUR NAME FIVE TIMES, IT WON'T LET GO.
FAMOUS MONSTERS
SURELY GAN KNOWS BETTER THAN THAT.
BE CAREFUL...
...GAN!
ARRGH! STOP!
IT'S GAN THIS, AND GAN THAT--
YEAH, GAN! YOU'RE SO CARELESS!
AND HE HAD TWO TIMES LEFT, TOO.

I CAN SEE!

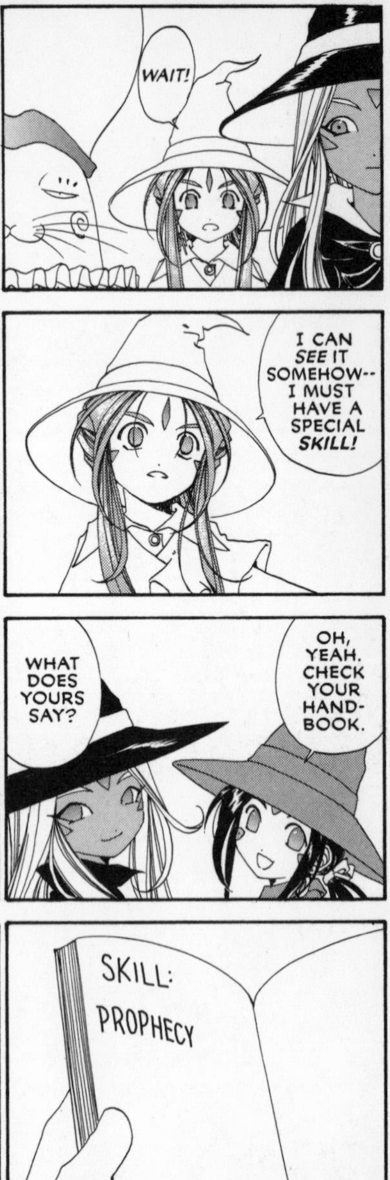
WAIT!
I CAN *SEE* IT SOMEHOW-- I MUST HAVE A SPECIAL *SKILL!*
OH, YEAH. CHECK YOUR HANDBOOK.
WHAT DOES YOURS SAY?
SKILL: PROPHECY

CYCLOTETRAMETHYLENE-TETRANITRAMINE!

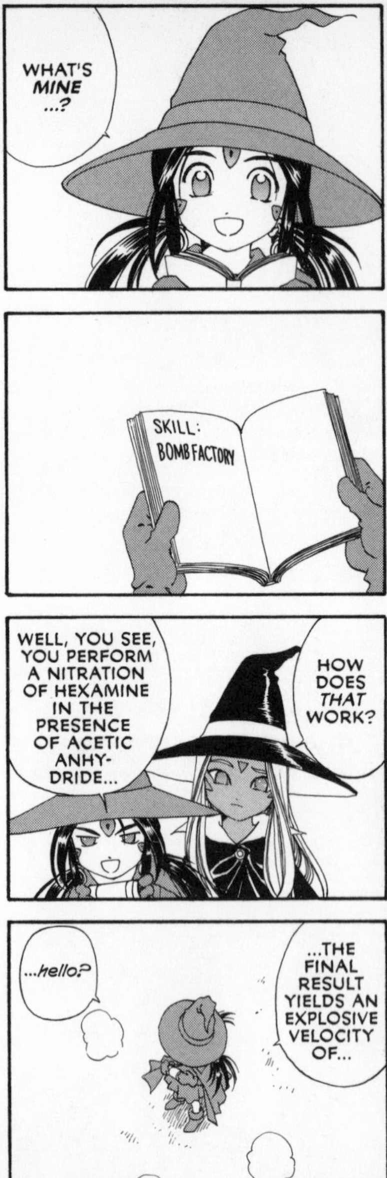
WHAT'S *MINE* ...?
SKILL: BOMB FACTORY
HOW DOES *THAT* WORK?
WELL, YOU SEE, YOU PERFORM A NITRATION OF HEXAMINE IN THE PRESENCE OF ACETIC ANHYDRIDE...
...THE FINAL RESULT YIELDS AN EXPLOSIVE VELOCITY OF...
...hello?

DYNA-GIRL!

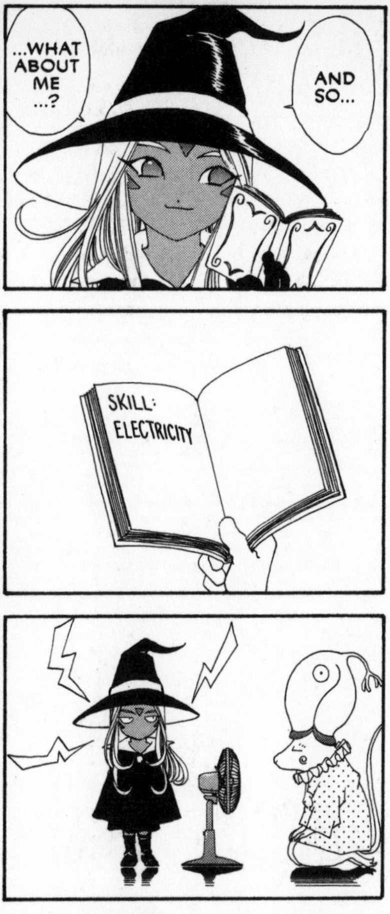
AND SO...
...WHAT ABOUT ME ...?
SKILL: ELECTRICITY

SIMPLY WAITING TO GO OFF

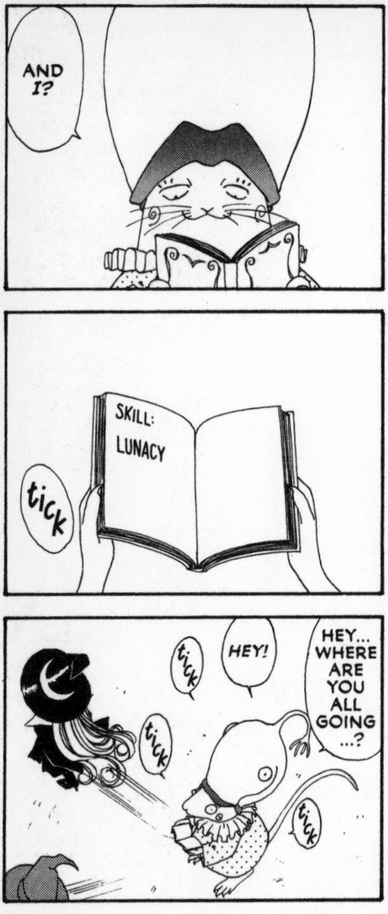
AND I?
SKILL: LUNACY
tick
HEY... WHERE ARE YOU ALL GOING ...?
HEY!
tick
tick
tick
COME BACK! WHAT'S WRONG ?!
tick
tick
DON'T... DON'T MAKE ME GET MAD!
tick
whoosh
whoosh

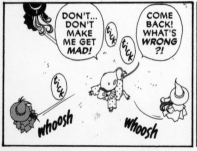

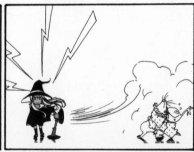

EDITOR
Carl Gustav Horn

DESIGNER
Scott Cook

ART DIRECTOR
Lia Ribacchi

PUBLISHER
Mike Richardson

English-language version
produced by Dark Horse Comics

OH MY GODDESS! Vol. 27
©2007 Kosuke Fujishima. All rights reserved. First published in Japan
in 2003 by Kodansha, Ltd., Tokyo. Publication rights for this English
edition arranged through Kodansha Ltd. This English-language edition
©2007 by Dark Horse Comics, Inc. All other material ©2007 by Dark
Horse Comics, Inc. All rights reserved. No portion of this publication may
be reproduced or transmitted, in any form or by any means, without the
express written permission of the copyright holders. Names, characters,
places, and incidents featured in this publication are either the product of
the author's imagination or are used fictitiously. Any resemblance to actual
persons (living or dead), events, institutions, or locales, without satiric in-
tent, is coincidental. Dark Horse Manga™ is a trademark of Dark Horse
Comics, Inc. All rights reserved.

Published by Dark Horse Manga
A division of Dark Horse Comics, Inc.
10956 SE Main Street
Milwaukie, OR 97222
www.darkhorse.com

To find a comics shop in your area,
call the Comic Shop Locator Service
toll-free at 1-888-266-4226

First edition: September 2007
ISBN-10: 1-59307-788-2
ISBN-13: 978-1-59307-788-4

1 3 5 7 9 10 8 6 4 2

Printed in Canada

ああっ女神さまっ
それぞれの翼

DIRECT FROM JAPAN!!

Belldandy
Approximately 6 1/3" tall

OH MY GODDESS! PVC STATUE

Prototypes shown; final products may vary.

© 藤島康介・講談社/「お助け女神事務所」分室

To find a comic shop or specialty store near you, visit WWW.COMICSHOPLOCATOR.COM
or call 1-888-COMIC-BOOK.
Retailers: to order the merchandise shown in this ad, please contact the sales staff of
Diamond Comic Distributors at 410-560-7100 or newaccounts@diamondcomics.com

CRAFTSMANSHIP

Special Preview of the Upcoming Novel:

OH MY GODDESS!

— F I R S T   E N D —

by Yumi Tohma

We interrupt our regular Letters to the Enchantress—but only for a good reason, to bring you this exclusive preview of the forthcoming novel *Oh My Goddess!—First End*, out in November from Dark Horse! *OMG!—First End* is an officially authorized story from Kodansha's Afternoon Novels line, which, as you might expect, is fiction based on manga associated with *Afternoon* magazine . . . the Japanese home of *Oh My Goddess!*, natch.

Translated by the very talented Camellia Nieh (of DH's *Ghost in the Shell: Stand Alone Complex* novels), *First End* is written by none other than Yumi Tohma, who has played the Japanese voice of Urd in every version of the *Oh My Goddess!* anime since 1993. Another *OMG!* veteran artist contributing to the *First End* novel is its illustrator, Hidenori Matsubara, the longtime character designer of the anime.

What will Ms. Tohma's unique perspective reval about the characters we know so well? Why is the story called *First End*? Well, we hope you'll look forward to reading the entire *Oh My Goddess!—First End* novel when it hits your store in November, and don't forget to keep sending your letters and fan art to Letters to the Enchantress, by post to 10956 SE Main Street, Milwaukie, Oregon 97222, or via e-mail: omg@darkhorse.com!

Illustration by Hidenori Matsubara *Oh My Goddess!—First End* ©2007 Yumi Tohma/Kosuke Fujishima. All rights reserved. First published in Japan in 2006 by Kodansha, Ltd., Tokyo. Publication rights for this English edition arranged through Kodansha Ltd. This English-language edition ©2007 by Dark Horse Comics, Inc.

"Uh-oh . . ."

Keiichi let out a soft exclamation and stopped what he was doing.

In a corner of the temple grounds, he'd been running the cell motor of his sidecar-equipped BMW for more than three hours. Louder and softer, louder and softer . . . its rumble had been irregular but continuous. Now, the motor stopped, gave off a few muffled pops, and was quiet.

Keiichi straightened up slightly—he'd been crouching for hours, completely absorbed in his work.

"Oops."

He let out a long sigh.

The sun shone brightly in the big blue sky, interrupted now and again by cool breezes from the east. The fan-shaped golden leaves of the ginkgo trees danced in the wind.

"I shouldn't have pushed it . . ."

He stood up slowly and began to walk with a heavy stride. The dried leaves scattered on the ground crunched underfoot.

It was a mild, sunny afternoon at Tarikihongan Temple. After glancing around the grounds, Keiichi gave the sliding door to the main building a strong shove, sending it rattling open.

Sunlight streamed into the dark interior.

Once inside the front entryway, Keiichi sighed deeply, as if to belie the vigor with which he had pushed open the door.

"Now I've done it," he lamented aloud.

Reaching back, Keiichi quietly pulled the door shut and sank listlessly onto the stoop that led up into the building. Carelessly, he wiped the sweat from his brow with his sleeve, which was rolled up to the elbow, and gazed down at his still-clenched right fist.

"Out of the way, Keiichi!"

Startled, Keiichi jumped to his feet and did an about-face.

"O-Oh! Skuld!"

Where had she come from? Skuld stood with a shopping basket in hand and a sunny expression that contrasted with Keiichi's flustered one.

"Don't just sit there in the middle of the front entryway. If you're taking a break, at least come inside."

He certainly couldn't argue with that.

"Oh, uh, sorry . . . Are you going shopping?"

"Yep! The new issue of *Dobon* comes out today!"

Dobon was the manga magazine that Skuld read faithfully every month. She could always be counted on to be in a good mood the day it hit the shelves.

"Th-that's great!" That accounted for her cheeriness. As discreetly as possible, Keiichi used his left hand to cover the object he was gripping, hiding it behind his back.

"Well," he offered pleasantly, trying to match Skuld's bright smile, "take care, then!" He began to beat a swift retreat, but unfortunately, human beings are cursed with the tendency to be most obvious when they're trying hardest to hide something.

Not surprisingly, Skuld noticed.

"Just a minute, Keiichi . . . You're hiding something, aren't you!"

"!!"

Bull's-eye. Keiichi froze.

"First you act all panicked and flustered, then you turn all cool and casual . . . something's going on!"

Skuld extended her hand. Unfortunately, her first *Reveal Hidden Object* spell failed. Despite his despondency, Keiichi's reflexes remained intact.

"Rats!"

She attempted the spell a second time, then a third. But each time, her hand only waved impotently in the air.

"Argh!" Skuld glowered at the floor. Her rosy mood had evaporated completely, and ominous angry clouds were beginning to gather.

" . . . id, aren't you . . ."

"Huh?" Keiichi couldn't make out whatever it was Skuld was muttering. But it was plain from her trembling shoulders and clenched fists that her irritation was quickly evolving into rage.

"S-S-Skuld?" Keiichi stammered fearfully. Skuld's anger voltage continued its steady climb.

"You're treating me . . . like a kid . . . aren't you!"

"Wha. . .?"

This time, her words were clear but the message caught him off-guard.

"You're blowing me off because you think I'm just a kid, aren't you?!"

"Huh? No . . . I never . . ."

The unforeseen accusation and unprovoked surge of fury baffled Keiichi. But with the needle of her anger gauge hovering in its red zone, Skuld was in no state to listen to reason.

Slowly, she raised her head. "Fine! If that's how you're going to be . . . I'm telling!"

"What?"

"I'm telling Belldandy on you!"

"What's Belldandy got to do with this?" For some reason, the sudden mention of Skuld's big sister seemed not so much surprising to Keiichi as completely absurd.

But when Skuld was set on getting her way, reason and coherence went out the window. This time, her power play was to use Keiichi's beloved Belldandy as leverage to make Keiichi cave.

"Belldandyyyy . . . Belldandyyy . . . Keiichi's hi—" Skuld began to shout toward the back rooms, her voice triumphant. This was beginning to get out of hand.

"Okay, okay! It's really not that big a deal!"

Reluctantly, Keiichi slowly brought his right hand out from behind his back.

"That's better!" A pleased smile spread across Skuld's face, both from the satisfaction of having won and the excitement of uncovering what she was after.

"I'm afraid you're going to be disappointed," Keiichi found himself muttering when he saw the curiosity glittering in Skuld's eyes.

" . . . A screwdriver?"

Skuld frowned at the uninteresting tool in Keiichi's hand. It was clear from her reaction that this wasn't what she'd expected.

Keiichi sighed. Just as he'd thought.

"I tried to tell you . . ."

"Then why wouldn't you just show it to me? You looked so gloomy—I thought it was something important!" Her interest completely evaporated, Skuld retrieved the shopping basket she'd flung to the ground.

Keiichi's expression clouded slightly at her sudden indifference.

"It *is* important. To me, anyway . . . As it happens, this screwdriver is kind of special . . . I've always done my best to take excellent care of it. But just now, I was using it, and I twisted it just a little bit too hard . . ."

"Oh?"

Skuld took the specialty Phillips screwdriver from Keiichi and examined it closely. A tiny corner was missing from the precision-formed plus-shape at its tip.

"It looks to me like it should still work."

The flaw was so small it was hardly noticeable without careful scrutiny. But a Phillips screwdriver's torque was a function of its head fitting perfectly into the grooves of the screw. Even the tiniest chip would change the tool's feel significantly, hampering its effectiveness at performing delicate tasks.

"If it really bothers you, I'll get you a new one while I'm out. A number 3, right? Until I get back, you can borrow one of mine," Skuld offered breezily.

Keiichi snatched the screwdriver back. "No, Skuld . . ."

"Why not? It's hard to use now, right?"

"That's not the point . . ."

As Keiichi gazed lovingly at his screwdriver, Skuld registered disappointment. Here she'd gone out of her way to be nice, and Keiichi was turning her down?

"Then what *is* the point?"

"It's just that . . ." Keiichi bit his lip. "Remember when I told you that scratches are part of a person's history? That goes for everything we use, including tools. Even when they get chipped, or worse, broken . . . when you've used something for a long time, through good times and bad, that makes that something one of a kind. It makes it irreplaceable. That's how I feel, anyway. . ."

Skuld listened attentively to what Keiichi had to say, but in the end she remained unconvinced.

"Yeah, but . . . it's a tool. Usability is everything, right?" She swung her shopping basket and hopped into her shoes. "Sheesh, what a waste of time! I'm off to buy *Dobon* now!" Where was her rage now? Skuld bounded off into the afternoon sun, her good cheer restored.

"I suppose that makes sense, too . . ." Keiichi smiled wryly from inside the building as he watched Skuld disappear into the distance.

"But I still prefer this old thing," he concluded, grinning.

He squeezed the Phillips screwdriver.

CHAPTER I
Utakata–Ephemera

Dancing gently in the breeze, the large white magnolia flowers looked almost like handkerchiefs tied to the tree's limbs. Amid the blooms, sparrows flew busily hither and thither. Twittering happily, they flitted from branch to branch as if playing hide-and-seek.

Just then, a single sparrow fluttered to the ground, abandoing its companions frolicking among the blossoms. In bouncy little hops, it advanced toward the figure that stood near the front entrance to the main building.

Vreeeeeeee.

A lens focused on the approaching sparrow, capturing the small, round black eyes peeking out from its cap of white and brown feathers.

Banpei RX smiled in spite of himself. Well—to be accurate, the "anti-demon tactical strike robot" built by Skuld to protect the goddesses and Keiichi day and night didn't have the capacity to actually smile. But if he did, Banpei would have been smiling right now.

He was capable of love, of offering aid . . . and even of making mistakes. Endowed with an abundance of both compassion and pathos, Banpei was more tenderhearted than a human being.

The sparrow drew fearlessly closer to Banpei RX, as if it could somehow read the security robot's true nature. Then it leapt into the air, coming to rest on the black conical straw hat on Banpei's head.

Immediately, the rest of the flock, having observed their companion from above, swarmed down toward Banpei. Perching on the robot's hat and arms, the sparrows amused themselves, fluttering and alighting, fluttering and alighting.

Bathed in the gentle rays of the still-dawning sun, it was a peaceful morning like any other at Tarikihongan Temple.

*　　*　　*

In a hot skillet, a pat of butter sputtered and melted, readying the pan to receive the frothy, beaten eggs. Sizzling appetizingly, the eggs cooked quickly.

Belldandy sang a lilting melody as she stirred the eggs with her cooking chopsticks, her long, chestnut-colored ponytail swaying to the tune of her song. A rosy glow flushed her pale, creamy complexion.

When they were scrambled but still moist, Belldandy transferred the fluffy eggs to a plate. Then she added the bacon she'd fried in a separate pan. There—breakfast was ready.

Belldandy smiled, satisfied with her work.

"What should I be doing?"

In the living room, an agitated Keiichi was beginning to regret having sat down at the low table so early.

"Reading the paper? No, that doesn't seem right . . . Watching TV? No, that's not right either . . ."

Belldandy's singing was faintly audible through the sliding paper doors that separated the living room from the kitchen. This was part of her normal breakfast-making routine.

On the other hand . . . the sight that had met Keiichi's eyes that morning made it clear that this was not going to be an ordinary breakfast.

The low table was adorned with a lace tablecloth. Keiichi's normal chopsticks and chopsticks-rest were absent, supplanted by a carefully placed set of sparkling silverware.

"Why am I so nervous?"

Keiichi's pulse thumped loudly in his ears. He couldn't help feeling somewhat ashamed that he was so intimidated by this situation.

"This is pretty pathetic." He gave a wry little laugh and took deep breaths, doing his best to calm down.

The goddess' gentle voice greeted him cheerfully. "Keiichi, your breakfast is ready!"

The paper door slid open, and the living room was transformed by a delicious smell and Belldandy's dazzling smile. For a moment, Keiichi found himself leaning forward in eager anticipation.

"Pardon me," Belldandy excused herself demurely as she entered the room with her well-laden tray.

"Er, of course!"

This was definitely no ordinary breakfast. Flustered, Keiichi sat up as straight as possible.

In a long beige dress and white lacy apron, Belldandy almost looked like a maid-servant. Keiichi was unable to look directly at her as she kneeled beside him and served him with deft, graceful movements.

First, a glass of fresh, antioxidant-rich tomato juice. A bowl of yogurt garnished with chopped strawberries and apples in the upper left corner, and a steaming cup of creamy corn soup in the upper right. A basket of fragrant, piping hot rolls on the left, and finally, the main dish—bacon and scrambled eggs—between the knife and fork.

"Wow!" Keiichi let out a sigh of wonder at the dazzling spread. But immediately, he realized his dilemma. "Um, I don't really know the proper etiquette for this kind of thing . . ."

From the waist up, the use of silverware suggested that Western table manners were in order. But from the waist down, sitting cross-legged at a low table added a definite Japanese element, making Keiichi wonder if perhaps such decorum was unnecessary. Despite this awkwardness, Keiichi racked his brains, trying to remember the correct rules for dining with a knife and fork.

"Keiichi, the most important thing is that you enjoy your meal. I'll be happiest if you just forget about proper etiquette and eat however you like."

Finally, Keiichi's tense expression softened. "Thanks, Belldandy—that's a big relief!"

He set his knife down and transferred the fork to his right hand.

"This looks delicious!"

With a look of pure joy, Keiichi started in on his scrambled eggs. Next, he applied a pat of margarine to a fresh-baked roll. The warm bread quickly melted the margarine, and Keiichi opened his mouth wide and sank his teeth into its softness. A delicious fragrance wafted up into his nostrils.

"I know you've said that rice fills you up better than bread . . . but the photo of a hotel-style breakfast in my magazine looked so lovely, I had to try it," Belldandy explained. "What do you think?"

She pulled a magazine out from under the low table, opening it to the bookmarked article about a vacation resort on some distant shore. Pictures of the cuisine at the hotel restaurant were presented next to the photos of luxurious suite rooms.

A stem of delicate Chinese Lantern Lilies arched gracefully in a small vase. The silver was buffed to a high shine, and the glasses were of sparkling Bohemian crystal. The places were set with Meissen porcelain dishes as if it were no big thing.

Though the tableware in front of him paled in comparison to that of the magazine, to Keiichi, nothing could top a meal that Belldandy had cooked specially for him.

"This is fantastic. No hotel has a better breakfast than this!" Grinning from ear to ear, he stuffed a piece of bacon into his mouth.

Belldandy's lavender eyes danced at the sight of Keiichi's enjoyment. Nothing made her happier than watching him take pleasure in her cooking. His sincere words filled her with inexpressible warmth.

"That was a real feast."

Not the most delicate eater, Keiichi polished off his breakfast in nothing flat and let out a sigh of contentment. The fact that not a single drop of food remained testified to his satisfaction.

"I'll put on some tea." Belldandy began to clear the table, her lacy apron fluttering. Just then, the telephone in the hallway began to ring.

"Who could that be at this hour?" Keiichi frowned. It was unusual for the phone to ring so early in the morning.

"I'll get it." Halfway to the kitchen, Belldandy changed direction and moved toward the hall.

As she stepped out of the living room, the chill in the air told her that spring's arrival was yet to come.

The sound of the telephone grew louder as she made her way down the corridor. But despite its insistent ringing, Belldandy was unhurried as she picked up the receiver.

"Morisato residence," she said.

"Belldandy! It's me, Skuld!"

The voice on the other end conveyed an urgency even greater than the ringing phone.

*　　　*　　　*

It had all begun two days ago.

Then, too, the phone had rung . . . at first, Skuld had ignored it, pretending not to hear. But she was the only one home, and eventually she reluctantly picked up the receiver.

"Yeah?" she said unenthusiastically. It violated her principles, but she was willing to use the I'm-just-a-kid act if it meant dodging a telemarketer.

"Oh, *très bien*! I'm so glad someone's home"

"Peorth?"

Like Belldandy, Peorth was a Goddess First Class Type 2 Unlimited. Her extensive skills were put to use in managing the Yggdrasil system. For that reason, unless something major was happening, they didn't hear from her often.

" . . . er, what's going on?" Skuld asked hesitantly.

"Yggdrasil's in a state of emergency!"

Exactly as Skuld had feared. Of course things had to go wrong when her big sisters weren't home! She felt a wave of gloom at the unfortunate timing.

But up in Heaven, that was the furthest concern from Peorth's mind. Her explanation issued forth like a stormy tirade.

Setting aside the technical and mathematical details, the basic gist of it was that for several days, there had been a sudden epidemic of bugs in Heaven.

Skuld sat down and hugged her knees, listening to Peorth go on and on. After about twenty minutes, Peorth finally paused and Skuld managed to cut in, "but this is nothing new, right? Bugs are always popping up in Yggdrasil—so if you just launch a debugging program . . ."

"*Évidement*. We did that quite some time ago," Peorth interrupted, as if to rebuke Skuld for stating the obvious. The rising pitch of her voice betrayed her irritation. She let out a sigh. "But this is something different. Otherwise, I wouldn't be calling, *n'est pas?*"

"Something different?" Skuld stopped playing with the telephone cord and gripped the receiver with both hands. "Then the debugging program . . ."

"*Complètement inutile*. We executed the program and tried to run a delete, but to absolutely no avail. In fact, things are worse than ever."

Apparently, the problem was beginning to affect Yggdrasil's main system, a completely unprecedented situation. Skuld leapt to her feet. If things were this bad, she had to send her sisters to help as quickly as possible.

"Got it. I'll tell Belldandy and Urd right aw—"

"Never mind that. I want *you* to come."

"Huh? Me?" For a moment, this unexpected request caused Skuld's thoughts to completely freeze. Pointing toward herself and speaking slowly, she tried to confirm what Peorth had just said. "You want . . . me?"

"Yes. You."

The answer hadn't changed.

"Yeah, but . . . if it's a problem with the system, maybe Urd . . ."

Even though Skuld and Urd were both Goddesses Second Class, Skuld's qualifications were a far cry from Urd's Limited Administrator License. Besides, to be completely honest, Skuld wasn't at all eager to return to the celestial sphere overcome by chaos. Quickly, she began to make excuses, but Peorth remained adamant.

"Getting rid of these bugs is the number one priority right now. Who better to round them up than you, Skuld! Return at once!"

"Eep!"

*   *   *

On Earth, two days had passed since then, while in the celestial realm it had probably only been a few hours. But to Skuld, it felt like a thousand years since she'd received her sudden orders to return home.

"Belldandy, listen to me . . . I don't know what to do! I . . . I'm still a long ways away from being able to come home . . . even with my brilliant talents, we're just barely able to keep things from getting any worse . . . no matter how many times I re-calculate, the numbers keep changing! I just can't keep up!"

A flood of tearful lamentations poured out of Skuld. The fact that Belldandy listened to everything with such compassion only increased the deluge.

Once she'd had a good cry, Skuld seemed to feel somewhat better, but now her wailing turned to disgruntlement over being left to handle this job all alone. For a time, Skuld's tirade of complaints flooded forth without pause.

It was then that Belldandy noticed that Urd had sidled up to the phone and was listening in on Skuld's diatribe.

"Urd . . ." Belldandy murmured.

"*Shh.*"

"But why am *I* the one who had to come out here? Systems administration is *Urd's* field. Shouldn't *she* be the one taking care of this?"

Skuld just happened to shift gears in her grousing with deadly timing, unaware that Urd was now at the other end of the line.

"So you know what, Belldandy? I was thinking . . . maybe you could tell Urd that she should come up here and help me restore the system."

It was an excellent proposal. The problem was, she was submitting it to the wrong party.

"She'll listen to you, Belldandy. 'Course, Urd lacks *my* prodigious talents, but a helping hand never hurts . . ."

"Oh, really? I think I'll pass!"

On the other end of the line, Skuld froze. Figuratively speaking, her temperature dropped to -273.15° C—the temperature at which even a rose is reduced to particles.

" . . . U-U-Urd!!"

It was only then that Skuld realized just how deep she'd dug herself. At what point exactly had Urd picked up the phone? But the damage was already done.

"I'm sure we have nothing to worry about if we leave everything to your prodigious talents!"

Poor Skuld was unable to even move.

"Why, this should be a piece of cake for you! A walk in the park! I'm sure that if I were there, I'd only get in your way!"

Skuld was completely incapable of countering Urd's sarcasm-loaded attack.

"Give my regards to Peorth!"

Skuld's mouth was too dry to squeeze out a response.

"And have a nice day!"

Gently, Urd hung up the phone. Only the endless refrain of the impassive dial tone echoed in Skuld's ear.

*　　　*　　　*

"*Ah-ha-ha-ha-ha-ha!* That was *too* perfect!"

Meanwhile, back at the Morisato residence, Urd doubled over with uncontrollable laughter, tears welling up in her eyes.

"Urd . . . are you sure about this?" Belldandy asked her convulsing older sister in a worried tone. But Urd was completely unconcerned.

"Oh, come on, everything's fine! You really are a worrywart, you know that? Look, if things were really that bad, Peorth would contact me directly."

It was true—even though she was a Goddess Second Class, Urd's powers were tremendous. And it wasn't for nothing that she held an Administrator Limited License—when it came to Yggdrasil's system, even Belldandy couldn't hold a candle to her.

"I suppose so, but . . ." Still somewhat concerned, Belldandy stared at the phone. Just then, she felt a tap on her shoulder.

"Belldandy, do you really have time for this right now?" Urd asked.

Oh! Urd's prompting brought Belldandy back to the present. She had to pack Keiichi's lunch before he left . . . besides, he hadn't even finished his breakfast yet!

"Oh, dear! I was going to make Keiichi's tea . . ."

Urd watched, yawning, as Belldandy hurried back to the kitchen, moving much faster than when she'd come for the phone.

"Sheesh! The human world sure is busy, too!"

Urd gazed languidly toward the living room and slowly closed the sliding paper door to her room.

Bereft of the lustrous goddesses that had inhabited it moments earlier, the corridor was restored to its chilly silence.

Just then, a dark form wriggled.

A cloudlike shape came burbling out of the telephone that had moments earlier been connected to the celestial realm. It remained motionless for a time, as if surveying its surroundings, then leapt suddenly down to the hall floor, landing silently on its eight long, spidery legs. It rolled its big, wide eyes vacantly, and its long rabbitty ears twitched incessantly.

A "bug."

This was precisely the enemy against which Skuld was currently waging a one-girl war. In the Yggdrasil system, however, the bugs were mere data errors—but down on Earth they took the form of weird, supernatural creatures. Unfortunately, they also had the inconvenient quality of being invisible not only to the human eye, but to heavenly beings as well.

Nobody knew yet that this bug was here in the human realm.

*   *   *

Kosuke Fujishima's Oh My Goddess!

Can't wait on the Goddesses? Change directions!

Just gotten into the new unflopped editions of *Oh My Goddess!*, and found you can't wait to see what happens next? Have no fear! The first **20 volumes** of *Oh My Goddess!* are available **right now** in Western-style editions! Released between 1994 and 2005, our *OMG!* Western-style volumes feature premium paper, and pages 40% larger than those of the unflopped editions! If you've already got some of the unflopped volumes and want to know which Western-style ones to get to catch up, check out darkhorse.com's "Manga Zone" for a complete breakdown of how the editions compare!

AVAILABLE AT YOUR LOCAL COMICS SHOP OR BOOKSTORE
*To find a comics shop in your area, call 1-888-266-4226

For more information or to order direct:
•On the web: darkhorse.com
•E-mail: mailorder@darkhorse.com
•Phone: 1-800-862-0052 Mon.-Fri. 9 A.M. to 5 P.M. Pacific Time.

Oh My Goddess! © 2000-2005 by Kosuke Fujishima. All rights reserved. These English-language editions © 2005 Dark Horse Comics, Inc. Dark Horse Manga™ is a trademark of Dark Horse Comics, Inc. All rights reserved. (BL 7047)

STOP! This is the back of the book!

This manga collection is translated into English, but arranged in right-to-left reading format to maintain the artwork's visual orientation as originally drawn and published in Japan. If you've never read comics this way before, take a look at the diagram below to give yourself an idea of how to go about it. Basically, you'll be starting in the upper right-hand corner, and will read each word balloon and panel moving right-to-left. It may take a little getting used to, but you should get the hang of it very quickly. Have fun! If this is the millionth manga you've read this way, never mind. ^_^

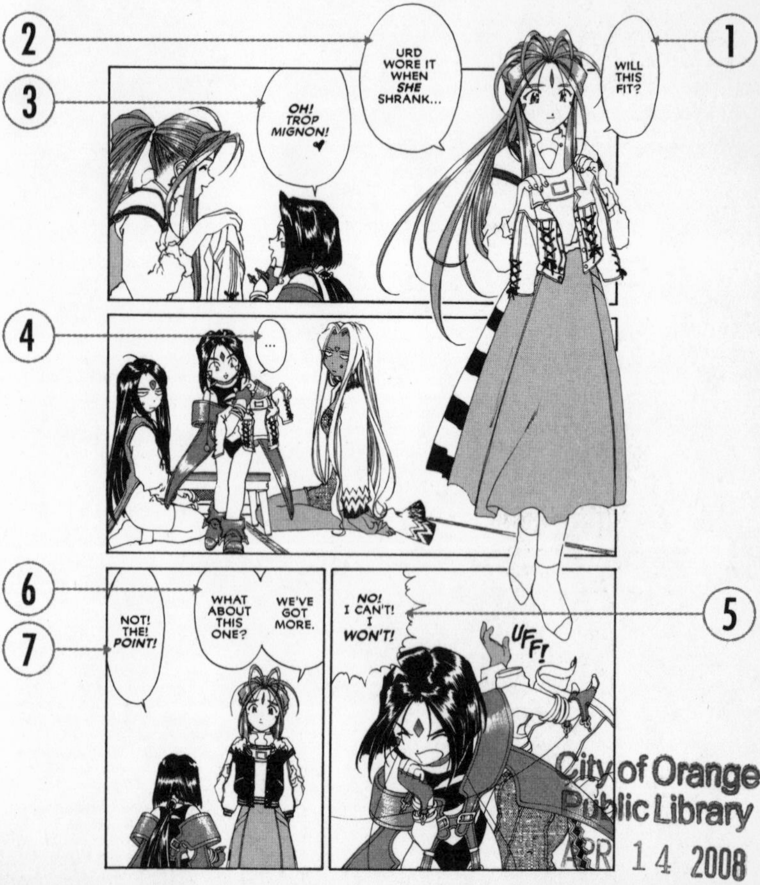
1
WILL THIS FIT?
2
URD WORE IT WHEN SHE SHRANK...
3
OH! TROP MIGNON!
4
...
5
NO! I CAN'T! I WON'T!
UFF!
6
WE'VE GOT MORE.
WHAT ABOUT THIS ONE?
7
NOT! THE! POINT!